Contentious Rituals

RECENT TITLES IN

OXFORD STUDIES IN CULTURE AND POLITICS

Clifford Bob and James M Jasper, General Editors

Plausible Legality
Legal Culture and Political Imperative in the Global War on Terror
Rebecca Sanders

Legacies and Memories in Movements
Justice and Democracy in Southern Europe
Donatella della Porta, Massimiliano Andretta, Tiago Fernandes,
Eduardo Romanos, and Markos Vogiatzoglou

Curated Stories
The Uses and Misuses of Storytelling
Sujatha Fernandes

Taking Root
Human Rights and Public Opinion in the Global South
James Ron, Shannon Golden, David Crow, and Archana Pandya

The Human Right to Dominate
Nicola Perugini and Neve Gordon

Some Men
Feminist Allies and the Movement to End Violence Against Women
Michael A. Messner, Max A. Greenberg, and Tal Peretz

Sex, Politics, and Putin
Political Legitimacy in Russia
Valerie Sperling

Democracy in the Making
How Activist Groups Form
Kathleen M. Blee

Women in War
The Micro-processes of Mobilization in El Salvador
Jocelyn Viterna

Contentious Rituals
Parading the Nation in Northern Ireland
Jonathan S. Blake

Contentious Rituals
Parading the Nation in Northern Ireland

Jonathan S. Blake

OXFORD

UNIVERSITY PRESS

Oxford University Press is a department of the University of Oxford.
It furthers the University's objective of excellence in research, scholarship,
and education by publishing worldwide. Oxford is a registered trade mark of
Oxford University Press in the UK and certain other countries.

Published in the United States of America by Oxford University Press
198 Madison Avenue, New York, NY 10016, United States of America.

Library of Congress Cataloging-in-Publication Data
Names: Blake, Jonathan S., author.
Title: Contentious rituals : parading the nation in Northern Ireland /
by Jonathan S. Blake.
Description: New York, NY : Oxford University Press, [2019]
Identifiers: LCCN 2018027131 (print) | LCCN 2018046274 (ebook) |
ISBN 9780190915599 (updf) | ISBN 9780190915605 (epub) |
ISBN 9780190915582 (hardcover)
Subjects: LCSH: Parades—Northern Ireland—Public opinion. |
Demonstrations—Northern Ireland—Public opinion. |
Nationalism—Northern Ireland. | Northern Ireland—Social conditions.
Classification: LCC GT4046 (ebook) | LCC GT4046 .B53 2019 (print) |
DDC 394/.509416—dc23
LC record available at https://lccn.loc.gov/2018027131

1 3 5 7 9 8 6 4 2

Printed by LSC Communications, United States of America

For Shulie

ACKNOWLEDGMENTS

It is my great pleasure to publicly acknowledge the many people who helped me over the years of researching and writing this book. First among them, I am indebted to the people in Northern Ireland who took part in my research. I thank them for granting me a glimpse into their lives, allowing me to pry and prod into personal thoughts and experiences. I know that many of them will disagree with some of my conclusions, but I hope they still recognize their voices and feel that I have not distorted them in any way.

This book began as a dissertation supervised by Jack Snyder. Jack has helped my thinking on so many topics relevant to this book that it is hard to keep track of his influence. I thank him for all his guidance. I was fortunate to also be advised by Alfred Stepan and Michael Doyle. Al pushed me to think big and make arguments that matter. He took great pride in his students' books—Al would often cite the number of dissertations he advised that were published—and while he isn't here to see it, I'm pleased to add another volume to the substantial Stepanian catalog. And Michael has for years been a vital sounding board as well as a source of calm, wisdom, and moral support. Joining them for my dissertation defense were Timothy Frye and James Jasper. Tim ensured that I was careful with my argument and the book that follows is more measured due to his judicious advice. Finally, Jim, through his writing, his detailed comments on my arguments and prose, and many conversations at Midtown Szechuan and Keralan restaurants, has shaped my ideas and writing significantly. More than anyone else, he steered me from being a dissertation writer to something resembling an author, and nearly every page of this book bears his imprint.

In Northern Ireland, a number of generous scholars provided much-needed counsel on my research: John Barry, Jonny Byrne, Paula Devine, Gladys Ganiel, John Garry, Neil Jarman, Dave Magee, Kieran McEvoy, Dirk Schubotz, Peter Shirlow, and Ben Walker. But this project simply would not have happened without the guidance and support of Dominic Bryan—which fortuitously began on my very first flight to Belfast, when we happened to be on the same plane. Within hours of landing, Dom had given me a tour of the city from the airport bus and handed me a list of names and phone numbers to begin my research. Mark Hammond kindly lent me a bicycle for three of my trips to Belfast—including once before he even met me! Jon Evershed was always game to attend a parade and trade notes afterward over pints of beer. I must recognize the hard work of my survey enumerators, especially Rachel, Brenda, Tracey, Allison, and Julie. Finally, the good folks at Common Grounds Cafe and especially Black Bear Cafe let me work for hours on end and never once complained that I turned their shops into my office on a near-daily basis.

A number of friends and colleagues read drafts of this book or parts of it. Kate Cronin-Furman, Shulie Eisen, Jim Jasper, Jack Snyder, and Steven White provided insightful feedback on the entire manuscript, as well as parts of it more than once. I am immensely grateful to them for their suggestions and encouragement. The two anonymous reviewers for Oxford University Press also greatly improved the shape of the book. I thank them for understanding my vision and proposing ways to better fulfill it. The same is true for James Cook, who, along with Emily Mackenzie and Jim Jasper, diligently shepherded me and my manuscript through the daunting world of first-book publishing.

For their thoughtful comments and valuable criticism on various chapters or proto-chapters, I thank Hadas Aron, John Barry, Ralph Chipman, Arnold Eisen, Jonathan Evershed, Lee Ann Fujii, Jeff Goodwin, Ron Hassner, John Krinsky, Michele Margolis, Aidan McGarry, Tonya Putnam, Stephanie Schwartz, Robert Shapiro, Nicholas Rush Smith, Jonathan Tonge, David Weinberg, Lauren Young, and Adam Ziegfeld. A number of those just listed are affiliated with the Politics and Protest Workshop at CUNY Graduate Center, a weekly meeting that improved this book in numerous direct and indirect ways. I received additional feedback from audiences at Columbia University, Queen's University Belfast, the University of Pennsylvania, Villanova University, and the annual meetings of the American Political Science Association, Association for the Study of Nationalities, International Studies Association, and Midwest Political Science Association. The book also reflects conversations I've had over the years (many of them sustained and happily ongoing) about culture, conflict, mobilization, fieldwork, social science, Northern Ireland, and much more with all the aforementioned as well as Séverine Autesserre, Courtney Bender, Erica Borghard, David Buckley, Simon Collard-Wexler, Nils Gilman, Lucy Goodhart, Jordan Kyle, Isabela Mares, Yotam Margalit, Jeremy Menchik, Sara Bjerg Moller, Bob Scott, Michael Smith, Lee Smithey, Elizabeth Sperber, Alissa Stollwerk, and Dorian Warren. I hope that anyone I've overlooked will forgive me and know my gratitude.

My fieldwork in Northern Ireland was generously supported by a Doctoral Dissertation Improvement Grant from the National Science Foundation

(SES-1263772); the Endeavor Foundation (formerly the Christian Johnson Endeavor Foundation); the Department of Political Science at Columbia University; the Earth Institute's Advanced Consortium on Cooperation, Conflict, and Complexity at Columbia; and the American Political Science Association's British Politics Group. Before I settled on Northern Ireland, Columbia's Center for the Study of Democracy, Toleration, and Religion funded exploratory field research in Jerusalem. Additional support for writing and revising this manuscript came from the Columbia Global Policy Initiative and the Chumir Foundation for Ethics in Leadership, whose chairman, Joel Bell, I want to thank in particular. I remain grateful to them all.

My in-laws, Adriane Leveen and Arnie Eisen, were extraordinarily supportive in the course of my research and writing. I was quite lucky to marry into a family where scholarly writing is the family business. So not only did they feed me, house me, give me a place for holidays, and other in-law-ly roles, but they advised me about book-writing, provided empathic encouragement, and clarified questions I had about Durkheim and Weber.

I would not be where I am, or for that matter who I am, today without the love and support of my family. My parents, Mitch and Judy Blake, have always encouraged me to explore. They nurtured my curiosity and served as models for how to observe the world around me and strive to improve it. I am beyond thankful for all they have given and continue to give to me. The same is true of my grandparents, whose constant championing I have been lucky to receive. Finally, I want to thank my brothers, Aaron and Josh, for working on early designs for the book cover. Aaron also graciously offered a blurb for the back of the book; alas "too long" didn't align with the marketing strategy.

Above all else, I thank Shulie, my wife and best friend. For the years this book lived with me, it lived with her too. She listened to me drone on and on about parades, and even attended more than her fair share. She debated word choice and sentence structure with me, pushed me to clarify my thinking and writing, and edited the whole damn thing. She cheered me on when things went right and cheered me up when things went wrong. And over the past year, especially, she sacrificed many nights and weekends to let me complete this project. Suffice it to say, without her support, I would not have finished this book—though this is the least of the reasons for my love.

CONTENTS

Contentious Rituals

Introduction

O n a summer's afternoon, a crowd is packed along the Lower Newtownards Road in East Belfast, clutching cans of beer, bottles of Buckfast Tonic Wine, and Union Jacks. Some of the assembled have even tied the flag around their shoulders like a cape. Young boys, seated on the curb, bang on toy drums. Men and women, young and old, suck on cigarettes. Food trucks grill cheap hamburgers and deep-fry potatoes and battered fish. Makeshift vendors sell hats, T-shirts, and other souvenirs, all bedecked with the icons of Ulster Protestants: the British flag, the Red Hand, King Billy—William III, the Prince of Orange—riding a white horse into battle. People mill about expectantly. It is a scene I have witnessed many times before: in Belfast's north, west, south, and center; in Derry/Londonderry; in Portadown; in Bangor; in tiny Markethill, a village deep in County Armagh. It is the marching season and we have come to watch a parade.

Even before we see it, we hear it: blasts of flutes, cracks of snare drums, thwacks of bass drums. Once the parade appears, the noise is thunderous and the view is just as loud. Up front is a marching band's color party, bearing flags (British, Northern Irish, Scottish, Orange Order, 1912 Ulster Volunteer Force, Royal Irish Rifles, and more) with military precision. Then comes the drum corps, with side drums slung over their right shoulders to rest on their left hips. Behind struts the bass drummer, wildly slamming the large drum affixed to his chest. Next are the rows and rows of "fluters," instruments raised high. The bandsmen, in matching uniforms, move in unison, playing old favorites like "The Sash My Father Wore" and "No Pope of Rome." The former speaks proudly of family, tradition, and the need to defend "Our unity, religion, laws, and freedom"—with the sword if necessary. The latter dreams of a world with "No nuns and no priests" and "No Rosary beads," where "flute bands play 'The Sash' every day." The crowd cheers and sings along to both.

Following closely behind is the Orange Order lodge, a Protestant fraternal organization dedicated to God, Ulster, and the Crown. Leading the group are two brethren holding aloft a banner that presents the lodge's name and a rich array of iconography: depictions of pivotal moments in Irish Protestant history, biblical scenes, or portraits of past monarchs and unionist heroes. The lodge members pace behind their banner, dressed in dark suits topped by an orange collarette draped around their necks. Behind the lodge marches another band, and then another lodge, and so on for, at times, up to an hour or more. Protestants in Northern Ireland perform over twenty-five hundred such parades each year: Protestant paraders marking Protestant history with Protestant symbols, marching past Protestant spectators singing along to Protestant tunes. Everything is Protestant—except the protesters.

For Northern Ireland's Catholics, loyalist parades are not celebrations but affronts that vividly call to mind centuries of discrimination and repression by the Protestant state and decades of terror by Protestant paramilitaries.[1] When such a pageant is due to pass near their communities, homes, or churches, many Catholics mobilize opposition: applying political pressure to reroute it, sitting in the streets with locked arms to physically block it, or praying the Rosary. When their efforts fail and the parade is permitted, Catholics protest from the sidewalks, bearing placards and sometimes shouting obscenities at the marchers.

Preventing violence in these tense situations requires the muscle of local activists and the state. On a regular basis, the police position themselves in the unenviable space between parade and protest. Some operations allow for soft caps; others require helmets, shields, and fire-retardant full-body armor. On occasion, fighting erupts and bricks crisscross skies darkened by the smoke of shattered Molotov cocktails. Violence like this was common during the Troubles, the thirty-year civil war in Northern Ireland that killed thirty-seven hundred people, but is far less prevalent today. The communal violence that has lingered on since the 1998 peace agreement has often revolved around disputes over parades. This is nothing new: violent sectarian clashes have accompanied loyalist parades in the north of Ireland since their origins in the eighteenth century.

* * *

Loyalist parades are the premier communal ritual of Northern Ireland's Protestants. Like all nationalist rituals, they display the nation: gathering national emblems and bodies in a single space, and thereby making visible

---

1. Following the scholarly literature, I use "loyalist parade" as a general term to include loyal order parades and band parades. See Neil Jarman, *Material Conflicts: Parades and Visual Displays in Northern Ireland* (Oxford: Berg, 1997); and Dominic Bryan, *Orange Parades: The Politics of Ritual, Tradition, and Control* (London: Pluto, 2000).

the "imagined community." The flutes, drums, banners, and flags bring the abstract idea of the nation to life, helping each member feel the "deep, horizontal comradeship" of nationalism.[2] As a result, rituals of the nation play a prominent role in the culture and politics of modern life. Across varied forms—parade, rally, wreath laying, anthem singing, flag raising, state funeral—nationalist rituals are ways for a community to display itself and honor itself; mourn collective tragedies and celebrate collective triumphs; declare its present and imagine its future. They are opportunities for "societies [to] worship themselves brazenly and openly."[3]

Societal self-worship, however, is as much an act of exclusion as an act of inclusion. Representing the nation necessarily illustrates who is *not* a member. Consequently, nationalist rituals can become hotly contested. The history of nationalism is one of rival claims over territory, people, and power, and in the absence of politico-cultural homogeneity, any portrayal of the nation and its ambitions is a potential object of dispute. Loyalist parades in Northern Ireland, therefore, are not only national rituals but *contentious rituals*—repeated, symbolic actions that make contested claims and that are actively challenged by others in society. The Protestant past, present, and future envisioned by loyalist parades conflict with the memories, experiences, and aspirations of local Catholics. At particular times and in particular places, loyalist parades trigger a cycle of angry protest and counter-protest, further distancing Catholic from Protestant. These disputes harm the political peace process and undermine grassroots peace-building on a regular basis.

This feature places the loyalist parades that I shall examine in this book in the company of other divisive symbolic performances found throughout the contemporary world: provocative Hindu processions through Muslim neighborhoods in India that have precipitated many deadly riots, especially since the rise of Hindu nationalism in the 1980s; Confederate flag-flying in the American South, which is seen as an expression of Southern pride by many whites and a symbol of terror by many African Americans; pilgrimages by Japanese leaders to Shinto shrines honoring war criminals from World War II that infuriate the people and governments of China, Taiwan, and the Koreas; prayer in the disputed holy places of Israel and Palestine, such as the Temple Mount/Haram al-Sharif in Jerusalem and the Tomb of the Patriarchs/Ibrahimi Mosque in Hebron, which are seen by many on either side as exclusively theirs; commemorative ceremonies marking dark moments in South Africa's racial history, like the Day of the Vow, when white Afrikaners celebrate a battle that killed thousands of Zulus. While the

2. Benedict Anderson, *Imagined Communities: Reflections on the Origin and Spread of Nationalism*, rev. ed. (London: Verso, 1991), p. 7.
3. Ernest Gellner, *Nations and Nationalism* (Ithaca: Cornell University Press, 1983), p. 56.

enactment of most contentious rituals does not produce violence or protest most of the time, it can still exacerbate group tensions, intensify an "us versus them" mentality, and make conflicts more difficult to resolve.

National rituals, whether contentious or not, are typically thought of and studied as elite phenomena. A rich body of scholarship demonstrates the political power of national rituals for activists, movements, states, and rulers.[4] This intuition is undoubtedly valid—it is elites who typically erect monuments, compose national anthems, and proclaim national holidays. But it is, at best, a partial account. The full story must also include how and why ordinary people visit monuments, sing national anthems, and celebrate national holidays— or not. Many national rites require mass participation that, in democracies, at least, is voluntary. And, as Eric Hobsbawm reminds us, "The assumptions, hopes, needs, longings and interests of ordinary people . . . are not necessarily national and still less nationalist."[5] We cannot, therefore, assume that ordinary participants share the motivations and desires of national elites.

What is more, nationalist rituals produce social and political outcomes that benefit or damage the nation as a whole, such as increased solidarity or the intimidation of a rival group. Yet the costs—time, dues, fees, potential physical harm—fall on the participants alone. Since the benefits do not discriminate between participants and nonparticipants there is no clear or direct incentive for individuals to take part. The public gains and private costs result in a dilemma of collective action, where no rational actor would voluntarily contribute.[6]

Peel away the colorful costumes, lively music, boisterous crowds, and other elements of elaborate spectacle, and contentious rituals, at their most basic, are acts of collective claim-making. In divided societies, the claims they make are both emotive and significant: we are dominant, you are subordinate; this is our territory, you do not belong; we can act with impunity, your desires do not matter to us. These bellicose performances drive wedges between groups, fan the flames of suspicion and hostility, and occasionally spark violence. This book asks why people choose to take part.

RITUAL COLLECTIVE ACTION

A central claim of the book is that to answer this question, we must approach contentious rituals like loyalist parades not just as contentious politics but as

4. For example, David I. Kertzer, *Rituals, Politics, and Power* (New Haven: Yale University Press, 1988).

5. E. J. Hobsbawm, *Nations and Nationalism since 1780: Programme, Myth, Reality* (New York: Cambridge University Press, 1990), p. 10.

6. See Mancur Olson, *The Logic of Collective Action: Public Goods and the Theory of Groups* (Cambridge, MA: Harvard University Press, 1965).

rituals—"symbolic behavior that is socially standardized and repetitive."[7] Though describing an act as "ritual" is often a way to ignore it or downplay its importance ("it's merely symbolic," "she's just going through the motions"),[8] I will argue that the ritual character of these contentious events is a key to their explanation. The argument developed in this book is rooted in theory and evidence from the study of participation in contentious politics as well as two fundamental insights from the multidisciplinary study of ritual. Namely, scholars of ritual—in religious studies, sociology, and anthropology—have consistently found for over a century that rituals affect the people who take part in them and that a ritual's meaning is almost always ambiguous.

The effects of ritual on participants are wide-ranging and profound, including the transformation of a person's social role and identity, cognitive influences on one's understanding of society and the wider world, and immediate as well as sustained emotional reactions.[9] The net result is that ritual participation is often both pleasurable and meaningful. Crowds and colors, symbols and solidarities, motions and emotions come together in public ritual, creating intense moments and lasting moods that we desire. When all goes right, Durkheim teaches, we reach "a state of exaltation."[10]

These varied effects provide what social scientists identify as "process-oriented" benefits, gains that are "intrinsic to the process of participation itself."[11] Intrinsic benefits complement the extrinsic, outcome-oriented reasons generally thought to motivate human action, such as accomplishing an external objective or receiving direct material compensation. When process-oriented motivations are strong, participation need not be incentivized (solely) by expectations of benefits derived from attaining a certain outcome or consuming a selective material reward. Rather, the benefits that are internal and inherent to the process of acting collectively can motivate

7. Kertzer, *Rituals, Politics, and Power*, p. 9. The most comprehensive analyses of the concept are Catherine Bell, *Ritual Theory, Ritual Practice* (New York: Oxford University Press, 1992); and Catherine Bell, *Ritual: Perspectives and Dimensions*, rev. ed. (New York: Oxford University Press, 2009).

8. Jonathan Z. Smith, *To Take Place: Toward Theory in Ritual* (Chicago: University of Chicago Press, 1987), p. 102, attributes the denigration of ritual in Western scholarship to Protestant-influenced understandings of thought and action—what he calls the "Protestant insistence on the 'emptiness' of ritual."

9. See, for example, Mircea Eliade, *The Sacred and the Profane: The Nature of Religion*, trans. Willard R. Trask (New York: Harcourt, 1959); Arnold van Gennep, *The Rites of Passage*, trans. Monika B. Vizedom and Gabrielle L. Caffee (Chicago: University of Chicago Press, 1960); Victor Turner, *The Ritual Process: Structure and Anti-Structure* (Ithaca: Cornell University Press, 1969); Émile Durkheim, *The Elementary Forms of Religious Life*, trans. Karen E. Fields (New York: Free Press, 1995); and Mary Douglas, *Purity and Danger: An Analysis of the Concepts of Pollution and Taboo* (London: Routledge, 1996).

10. Durkheim, *The Elementary Forms of Religious Life*, p. 220.

11. Jon Elster, *The Cement of Society: A Study of Social Order* (New York: Cambridge University Press, 1989), pp. 44–46; and Elisabeth Jean Wood, *Insurgent Collective Action and Civil War in El Salvador* (New York: Cambridge University Press, 2003), p. 240.

action on their own. Conversely, when process-oriented motivations are weak, participation may be motivated by the prospect of extrinsic outcomes or material incentives.

Human actions sit on a continuum between purely intrinsic, process-oriented behavior and purely extrinsic, outcome-oriented behavior. Most of our lives are spent somewhere between the two extremes. Rituals, according to the scholarly consensus, provide particularly rich opportunities for process-oriented benefits, which suggests that motivations for participation lean toward the intrinsic. This insight explains how participants in contentious rituals overcome the problem of collective action.

Students of ritual have also found that rituals speak in multiple voices.[12] Since some actors hear one voice while others hear another, the very meaning of the ritual is ambiguous. As a result, participants need not interpret their action in the same way that organizers, rivals, outside observers, or even other participants do. Contentious rituals, in the eyes of opponents and outsiders, are often seen as really about demonstrating power or deliberately intimidating or insulting others. But, due to ritual's symbolic ambiguity, participants may understand it to mean something completely different. While the belief that a contentious ritual is aggressive or provocative may deter many people from taking part, ritual's multivocality and polysemy mean that potential participants do not necessarily see it that way at all. Even if opposition to the contentious ritual is well known, this does not need to affect the meanings held by participants or their intentions in acting.

CONTENTIOUS RITUALS

The arguments and findings presented in this book are specific to loyalist parading, but they speak to a broader class of political action: contentious rituals. "Contentious ritual" is my term for a ritual that is contested because of the political claims it is seen to make.[13] The concept calls attention to a type of public action that is cultural through and through, and, just as

---

12. See, for example, Victor W. Turner, *The Forest of Symbols: Aspects of Ndembu Ritual* (Ithaca: Cornell University Press, 1967); and Anthony P. Cohen, *The Symbolic Construction of Community* (London: Routledge, 1985).

13. I say that contentious rituals are *seen* to make political claims (rather than simply making political claims) because I agree that "demonstrations do not speak for themselves, they are performances which must be...seen and interpreted." Ron Eyerman, "Performing Opposition Or, How Social Movements Move," in *Social Performance: Symbolic Action, Cultural Pragmatics, and Ritual,* ed. Jeffrey C. Alexander, Bernhard Giesen, and Jason L. Mast (New York: Cambridge University Press, 2006), p. 197. Note that not all political rituals are contentious rituals. Political rituals, such as hegemonic state rituals, that are not widely contested are not considered contentious.

thoroughly, political. This double-irreducibility is central to understanding contentious rituals because it is a source of their appeal and power.[14]

Mass, public rituals are politically valuable for several reasons. They can legitimate the status quo (or challenges to it), construct and maintain an identity, build solidarity, define a political reality, generate strong emotions, gather a crowd, represent a group, create common knowledge, sustain activists' commitment, and make political claims.[15] All the while, rituals are seen by many on both sides of an argument, or outside of it altogether, as legitimate, culturally important forms of action, which makes them difficult for states to regulate or opponents to criticize.[16] After all, what right-minded person can find fault with an age-old, harmless tradition?

This benefit of the doubt, rooted in the fusion of culture and politics found in contentious rituals, provides an "ambiguous space" where, Charles Tilly

14. See Ziad W. Munson, "When a Funeral Isn't Just a Funeral: The Layered Meaning of Everyday Action," in *Everyday Religion: Observing Modern Religious Lives*, ed. Nancy T. Ammerman (New York: Oxford University Press: 2007), p. 126.

15. The scholarship on rituals and politics is voluminous. See, for instance, Steven Lukes, "Political Ritual and Social Integration," *Sociology* 9, no. 2 (May 1975): 289–308; Robert E. Goodin, "Rites of Rulers," *British Journal of Sociology* 29, no. 3 (September 1978): 281–299; Clifford Geertz, *Negara: The Theatre State in 19th Century Bali* (Princeton: Princeton University Press, 1980); Eric Hobsbawm and Terence Ranger, eds., *The Invention of Tradition* (Cambridge: Cambridge University Press, 1983); Lynn Hunt, *Politics, Culture and Class in the French Revolution* (Berkeley: University of California Press, 1986); Kertzer, *Ritual, Politics, and Power*; Mona Ozouf, *Festivals and the French Revolution*, trans. Alan Sheridan (Cambridge, MA: Harvard University Press, 1988); Paul Connerton, *How Societies Remember* (New York: Cambridge University Press, 1989); Mabel Berezin, *Making the Fascist Self: The Political Culture of Interwar Italy* (Ithaca: Cornell University Press, 1997); Wayne Ashley, "The Stations of the Cross: Christ, Politics, and Processions on New York City's Lower East Side," in *Gods of the City: Religion and the American Urban Landscape*, ed. Robert A. Orsi (Bloomington: Indiana University Press, 1999), pp. 341–366; Amitai Etzioni, "Toward a Theory of Public Ritual," *Sociological Theory* 18, no. 1 (March 2000): 44–59; Michael Suk-Young Chwe, *Rational Ritual: Culture, Coordination, and Common Knowledge* (Princeton: Princeton University Press, 2001); Steven Pfaff and Guobin Yang, "Double-Edged Rituals and the Symbolic Resources of Collective Action: Political Commemorations and the Mobilization of Protest in 1989," *Theory and Society* 30, no. 4 (August 2001): 539–589; Amitai Etzioni and Jared Bloom, eds., *We Are What We Celebrate: Understanding Holidays and Rituals* (New York: NYU Press, 2004); Shaul Kelner, "Ritualized Protest and Redemptive Politics: Cultural Consequences of the American Mobilization to Free Soviet Jewry," *Jewish Social Studies* 14, no. 3 (Spring/Summer 2008): 1–37; Alfred Stepan, "Rituals of Respect: Sufis and Secularists in Senegal in Comparative Perspective," *Comparative Politics* 44, no. 4 (July 2012): 379–401; Rachel Tsang and Eric Taylor Woods, eds., *The Cultural Politics of Nationalism and Nation-Building: Ritual and Performance in the Forging of Nations* (London: Routledge, 2014); and Ahsan I. Butt, "Street Power: Friday Prayers, Islamist Protests, and Islamization in Pakistan," *Politics and Religion* 9, no. 1 (March 2016): 1–28.

16. Charles Tilly, *The Contentious French* (Cambridge, MA: Harvard University Press, 1986), pp. 117, 313; Pfaff and Yang, "Double-Edged Rituals and the Symbolic Resources of Collective Action"; Charles Tilly, *Contention and Democracy in Europe, 1650–2000* (New York: Cambridge University Press, 2004), p. 31; and Steven I. Wilkinson, *Votes and Violence: Electoral Competition and Ethnic Riots in India* (New York: Cambridge University Press, 2004), pp. 23–24.

suggests, political actors can press their agenda "without taking the risk of a manifestly political gesture."[17] The capacity to shroud politics in culture is clearly advantageous for making oppositional claims in repressive regimes, but it also provides benefits to political actors in positions of power and citizens in open societies. The cultural face of contentious rituals presents useful ambiguity that serves as political cover for performing otherwise unacceptable actions, swatting away condemnation from out-group and in-group opponents alike. It increases the potential breadth of popular support in a way that naked politicking does not by giving audiences flexibility to see what they want in the event.[18] People who might disapprove of swaggering with guns through a minority community to intimidate the residents can be more comfortable with, even excited about, marching with flags and other traditional symbols in the same place and to much the same effect. The use of contentious rituals is especially potent in ethnic politics because ethnic groups have many important symbols and rituals, are attuned to symbolic politics, and care deeply about symbols of status and power.[19] These effects and advantages make rituals attractive to political actors— and troublesome for their political rivals. The result is that they often become central objects of political contestation.[20]

Once a ritual becomes disputed, the effects can be anything but symbolic. The performance of a contentious ritual, and any challenges to it, can carry significant political consequences, including increased polarization and heightened tension. As political scientist Marc Howard Ross argues, "Cultural expressions are not just surface phenomena. They are *reflectors* of groups' worldviews and on-going conflicts…. [They] play a *causal* role in conflict…. [And they] serve as *exacerbaters* or *inhibitors* of conflict."[21] At their most dangerous, contentious rituals can trigger the onset of violent clashes. In fact, they are one of the most frequent precipitants of ethnic riots globally.[22]

17. Charles Tilly, *Popular Contention in Great Britain, 1758–1834* (Cambridge, MA: Harvard University Press, 1998), p. 60; and Tilly, *The Contentious French*, p. 313.

18. Cohen, *The Symbolic Construction of Community*, p. 21; and Kertzer, *Ritual, Power, and Politics*, pp. 69–75.

19. Donald L. Horowitz, *Ethnic Groups in Conflict*, 2nd. ed. (Berkeley: University of California Press, 2000).

20. The modifier "contentious" in contentious ritual thus has a double meaning: the plain meaning of "controversial" or "likely to cause an argument," and the meaning developed by McAdam, Tarrow, and Tilly, where contention means making claims that bear on the rights and interests of others. See Doug McAdam, Sidney Tarrow, and Charles Tilly, *Dynamics of Contention* (New York: Cambridge University Press, 2001), p. 5.

21. Marc Howard Ross, *Cultural Contestation in Ethnic Conflict* (New York: Cambridge University Press, 2007), p. 3. Emphases in the original.

22. Donald L. Horowitz, *The Deadly Ethnic Riot* (Berkeley: University of California Press, 2001), p. 272. For general and comparative studies, see ibid., esp. pp. 272–277; Ross, *Cultural*

In sixteenth-century France, for instance, "almost every type of public religious event has a disturbance associated with it." Disputes over religious worship, processions, and festivals ignited violence. Riots even erupted from baptisms, weddings, and funerals, as Protestants and Catholics came to blows over which rite to use.[23] Centuries later, public celebrations of religious holidays and life cycle ceremonies continue to teeter "on the edge of violence."[24] In Iran, during the Revolution, the rituals of Ramadan and Moharram, burials, and traditional ceremonies held forty days after a death—often at the hands of state forces—took on a political character. The state, feeling threatened by these contentious rituals, sometimes fired on celebrants—resulting in more burials and mourning rites.[25] The same "cycle of funerals, confrontations, and more coffins" emerged in Libya during the anti-regime protests of 2011—and still take place in Syria's civil war—as government forces killed mourners-cum-protesters marching in funeral processions for people killed in previous demonstrations.[26] And in India, an epicenter of bloody contentious rituals, the calendar of communal festivals and religious rites "can at sensitive times actually channel and direct the shape, expression, timing, and spatial location of ethnic violence."[27]

Contentious rituals can also have profound political consequences short of violence. Even when they do not spark skirmishes, cultural practices such as flying flags, celebrating national holidays, erecting monuments, making pilgrimages to sacred sites, ritually slaughtering animals, and visiting cemeteries

Contestation in Ethnic Conflict; and Ron E. Hassner, "Sacred Time and Conflict Initiation," Security Studies 20, no. 4 (November 2011): 491–520.

23. Natalie Zemon Davis, "Rites of Violence: Religious Riot in Sixteenth-Century France," Past and Present 59 (May 1973): 72–75 (quotation is from p. 72); and Barbara B. Diefendorf, Beneath the Cross: Catholics and Huguenots in Sixteenth-Century Paris (New York: Oxford University Press, 1991), pp. 59, 63.

24. Horowitz, The Deadly Ethnic Riot, p. 275.

25. M. M. Salehi, "Radical Islamic Insurgency in the Iranian Revolution of 1978–1979," in Disruptive Religion: The Force of Faith in Social-Movement Activism, ed. Christian Smith (New York: Routledge, 1996), pp. 54–61.

26. David D. Kirkpatrick and Mona El-Naggar, "Qaddafi's Son Warns of Civil War as Libyan Protests Widen," New York Times, February 20, 2011. On Syria, see, for instance, David Batty, "Syrian Troops Open Fire on Mourners at Funerals for Pro-Democracy Protesters," The Guardian, April 23, 2011.

27. Stanley J. Tambiah, Leveling Crowds: Ethnonationalist Conflicts and Collective Violence in South Asia (Berkeley: University of California Press, 1996), p. 240. See also Peter van der Veer, "Riots and Rituals: The Construction of Violence and Public Space in Hindu Nationalism," in Riots and Pogroms, ed. Paul R. Brass (New York: NYU Press, 1996), pp. 154–176; Paul R. Brass, Theft of an Idol: Text and Context in the Representation of Collective Violence (Princeton: Princeton University Press, 1997); Christophe Jaffrelot, "The Politics of Processions and Hindu-Muslim Riots," in Community Conflicts and the State in India, ed. Amrita Basu and Atul Kohli (Delhi: Oxford University Press, 1998), pp. 58–92; Wilkinson, Votes and Violence; and Paul R. Brass, The Production of Hindu-Muslim Violence in Contemporary India (Seattle: University of Washington Press, 2005).

can exacerbate tensions between groups and make conflicts more difficult to resolve. For example, Croatian president Franjo Tudjman objected strongly when his political opponents repatriated the body of their long-dead political hero for reburial inside the country shortly after the Balkan civil wars. In response to this "provocation," he proposed doing the same for one of his own political heroes, the head of the murderous, ultranationalist Ustaše, who had aligned with the Nazis during World War II.[28] In Lebanon at the dawn of the twenty-first century, the public observance of Ashura came to constitute both an act of personal piety and an act of collective protest against the Israeli occupation of the southern part of the country. Hizbullah-affiliated clerics shifted the meaning of the holiday's rituals "from one of mourning, regret, and salvation to a revolutionary lesson that emphasized action against oppression." Connecting the seventh-century martyrdom of Imam Husayn to contemporary politics explained, justified, and gave religious significance to Hizbullah's goals and tactics. It also turned the mass rituals into demonstrations of support for the organization, which has led to confrontations with supporters of other political parties.[29] And to this day even lower Manhattan hosts contentious rituals. On Good Friday each year, undocumented immigrants perform the Stations of the Cross outside the Federal Building on Broadway. When performed inside of a Catholic church, the sacred rite is not contentious. But, by moving it to the doorstep of the US Immigration and Customs Enforcement office, the portrayal of Christ suffering at the hands of his tormenters takes on a new and contested meaning.[30]

Despite their political importance around the world, contentious rituals have largely been overlooked by students of collective action and contentious politics. Scholars tend to focus their research on a narrow range of political activities, so we only see a slice of the existing "repertoire of contention."[31] Contentious cultural practices are often ignored by scholars in favor of other elements of the repertoire, such as protests, petitions, riots, and sit-ins. In particular, scholars have neglected the people who take part in cultural forms of political action, including contentious rituals.[32] Across

28. Katherine Verdery, *The Political Lives of Dead Bodies: Reburial and Postsocialist Change* (New York: Columbia University Press, 1999), p. 14.

29. Lara Deeb, "Living Ashura in Lebanon: Mourning Transformed to Sacrifice," *Comparative Studies of South Asia, Africa and the Middle East* 25, no. 1 (2005): 122–137 (quotation is from p. 131).

30. Alyshia Gálvez, *Guadalupe in New York: Devotion and the Struggle for Citizenship Rights Among Mexican Immigrants* (New York: NYU Press, 2009), pp. 129–139. Also my own observations in 2014.

31. A concept elaborated most fully in Charles Tilly, *Contentious Performances* (New York: Cambridge University Press, 2008).

32. Underscoring the importance of this omission, a recently published study that directly compares participants in ritual protest events and protest events organized in response to political

a range of cultural practices imbued with political meaning and engaged in political claim-making—from Hindu religious processions in India to Ashura observances by Shias in Lebanon to Roman Catholic rites in New York City—we have limited empirical knowledge about who participates, why they participate, or how they view the political versus cultural aspects of their participation.

The thorough study of parading in Northern Ireland enables me to answer these questions for one case of contentious ritual with fine-grained data. Loyalist parades, in fact, are an ideal site to explore the characteristics and dynamics of contentious ritual because they exemplify the deeply political and deeply cultural nature of this type of public action.

Parades are a major political problem and source of disruption in Northern Ireland. Though conflict over parades has diminished since the mid-1990s, when violence and mass unrest flared, particularly around the Drumcree Church parade in Portadown, old disputes linger and new ones have appeared. In the time I researched and wrote this book, St. Patrick's Church in Belfast emerged as a parading flashpoint and Protestants in North Belfast began more than three years of nightly protests against the decision to restrict the final leg of the Twelfth of July parade in 2013. Peaceful protest is one thing, but violence has been a regular feature of parades for far too long, and recent years have seen both Protestant and Catholic crowds resort to physical force.

At the elite level, political leaders have continually kicked the issue down the road, repeatedly resolving to form new official working groups tasked with addressing the problem.[33] When negotiations dedicated to parades (along with two other sensitive issues at the intersection of politics and culture, flags and dealing with the legacies of the Troubles) were finally convened during the second half of 2013, the parties failed to reach an agreement. They tried again in late 2014 and, at the final hour, reached the Stormont House Agreement, which established a new Commission on Flags, Identity, Culture and Tradition, and stated that "powers to take responsibility for parades and related protests should, in principle, be devolved to the [Northern Ireland] Assembly." But complex budget debates stalled implementation, and devolution has yet to happen.[34]

---

or social changes finds that they are different and mobilize for different reasons. See María Inclán and Paul D. Almeida, "Ritual Demonstrations Versus Reactive Protests: Participation Across Mobilizing Contexts in Mexico City," *Latin American Politics and Society* 59, no. 4 (Winter 2017): 47–74.

33. This was the solution to parading problems reached by the St. Andrews Agreement in 2007, Hillsborough Castle Agreement in 2010, and *Together: Building a United Community*, the Office of the First Minister and deputy First Minister's 2013 strategy document.

34. "Stormont House Agreement," December 23, 2014, paras. 15 and 17. In November 2015, the Northern Ireland Executive, the British government, and Irish government agreed on a deal

Disputes over parades regularly test the robustness of the Northern Irish peace agreements, widely considered a model case of negotiated settlement to civil war—one with "a lesson for conflict everywhere," as Tony Blair has put it.[35] Parades remain a key unresolved issue and point to the limitations of the peace process, particularly its mismanagement of the politics of culture. As such, to study parading in Northern Ireland is to study the continuation of conflict after war. In this book, I explore how and why ordinary people choose to contest ethnic relations in the aftermath of ethnic violence and challenge the resilience of peace. This is fundamental to understanding enduring conflict in Northern Ireland and other "post-violence societies."[36] Northern Ireland's precarious peace often seems to be at the mercy of a small number of men in dark suits and orange collarettes, marching up the road to the sound of piercing flutes and booming drums.

STUDYING CONTENTIOUS RITUALS

My theoretical perspective on contentious rituals, supported by my empirical study of loyalist parades in Northern Ireland, challenges three arguments prominent in the study of political conflict today. The *elite manipulation* argument proposes that elites strategically employ contentious rituals to provoke the out-group into overreacting. Such an overreaction, scholars find, can usefully polarize society, promote distrust between communities, create a negative image of the out-group in local or international courts of opinion, or discredit in-group moderates.[37] The incentives of elites are clear,

---

to actually implement the Stormont House Agreement. In tried and true fashion, their solution for parading was to write a new "discussion paper...[that] will outline options." Northern Ireland Executive, "A Fresh Start: The Stormont House Agreement and Implementation Plan," November 17, 2015, p. 34.

35. There is by now a large literature on the "lessons" we can (and cannot) learn from Northern Ireland. For a good overview, see Timothy J. White, ed., *Lessons from the Northern Ireland Peace Process* (Madison: University of Wisconsin Press, 2013). The Blair quotation is from Roger Mac Ginty, "The Liberal Peace at Home and Abroad: Northern Ireland and Liberal Internationalism," *British Journal of Politics and International Relations* 11, no. 4 (November 2009): 690.

36. John D. Brewer, *Peace Processes: A Sociological Approach* (Malden, MA: Polity, 2010), pp. 16–28.

37. See Wilkinson, *Votes and Violence*; and Rogers Brubaker and David D. Laitin, "Ethnic and Nationalist Violence," *Annual Review of Sociology* 24 (1998): 433. This view is part of a general argument on how elites foment ethnic conflict in order to increase their own power. See Rui J. P. de Figueiredo Jr. and Barry R. Weingast, "The Rationality of Fear: Political Opportunism and Ethnic Conflict," in *Civil Wars, Insecurity, and Intervention*, ed. Barbara F. Walter and Jack Snyder (New York: Columbia University Press, 1999), pp. 261–302; Jack Snyder, *From Voting to Violence: Democratization and Nationalist Conflict* (New York: Norton, 2000); and V. P. Gagnon, *The Myth of Ethnic War: Serbia and Croatia in the 1990s* (Ithaca: Cornell University Press, 2004).

but the average participant is ignored in this perspective.[38] As mentioned above, merely pointing to elite interests is an insufficient account for voluntary mass action. We cannot assume that just because a contentious ritual is beneficial for elites, mass participation will simply appear.

More suitable alternatives to my own account are two broad arguments about why individuals participate in politics generally, each rooted in a different view of human motivation. In one view, people act on their ideals, beliefs, and emotions. In the other, people act on their material self-interest.

The *idealist* argument sees contentious rituals as symbolic assertions of in-group status and power—and of out-group humiliation and subordination. Thus, they are mass events where individuals can collectively and publicly articulate their in-group pride and loyalty as well as animosity for the out-group. Since performances express these attitudes, participation should be explained by a person's thoughts and feelings about these groups. In particular, people should be more likely to participate the more they hold positive views of their own group and negative views of other groups.[39] Overall, this approach suggests that participants are different from nonparticipants in their attitudes toward the in-group and out-group.

The *rationalist* approach sees contentious rituals as no different than any other collective action. As a result, according to this perspective, people will only participate in contentious rituals when the expected private rewards outweigh the private costs. The most direct way for this to happen is to provide participants with selective material incentives.[40] Paul Brass, for instance, finds that contentious rituals in India are often enacted by "fire-tenders" and "riot specialists" who profit from the ensuing violence, both by looting and by payments from local leaders.[41] Another way to motivate rational actors is to raise the costs of nonparticipation. Targeting nonparticipants with social sanctions—for example, shunning them or demoting their social status—has been found to incentivize participation in collective political action.[42]

Both arguments share an instrumental view of participation, meaning that they see it as a method for achieving some result that "logically, causally, or

38. For example, in his award-winning *Votes and Violence*, Steven Wilkinson writes that Hindu political parties in India "organize unusually large religious processions" in order to provoke electorally advantageous ethnic riots (p. 24). But he never explains why this "unusually large" crowd turns out.

39. For example, Horowitz, *Ethnic Groups in Conflict*.

40. Olson, *Logic of Collective Action*, p. 51.

41. Brass, *Theft of an Idol*, pp. 9, 16–17, 285.

42. For example, Dennis Chong, *Collective Action and the Civil Rights Movement* (Chicago: University of Chicago Press, 1991).

probabilistically" follows from the action.[43] In the idealist model, participants act in order to attain an external outcome that reflects their deeply held beliefs. They seek to reshape the world to look more like their fixed ideals. In the rationalist model, participants act to maximize their personal welfare. In both arguments, the reasons to act are distinct from the action itself.[44] I show instead that means and ends "are not always neatly separable" because people often approach ritual participation as an end in and of itself.[45] From the point of view of the participants, the profound meanings and joys inherent in the experience of participation in parades and other rituals are themselves reasons to act.

Testing my argument against the existing alternatives requires careful attention to data and method. I collected a wealth of original quantitative and qualitative data during eight months of field research in Northern Ireland. These data have three primary sources.[46] First, I conducted in-depth semi-structured interviews with eighty-one participants and nonparticipants, most of whom were selected using snowball sampling. They included members of each of the loyal orders and numerous marching bands, former paraders and Protestants who have never paraded, Protestants who love to attend parades and Protestants who avoid them, unionist politicians, members of the Protestant clergy, and ex-combatants from the loyalist paramilitaries. The interviews were loosely structured and conversational, and the goal was not only to collect information on the respondents' background, beliefs, and behavior but also their "worlds and how they experience, navigate, and understand them."[47] Second, to gather broader and more systematic data on how paraders differed from otherwise similar non-paraders, I designed and implemented a household survey with 228 randomly selected respondents in nine Protestant neighborhoods in Belfast. The survey asked about a range of characteristics, opinions, and experiences for each respondent, and measured them in a standardized, quantitative way so that participants and nonparticipants could be methodically compared.

---

43. Alan Hamlin and Colin Jennings, "Expressive Political Behaviour: Foundations, Scope and Implications," *British Journal of Political Science* 41, no. 3 (July 2011): 648. See also Max Weber, *Economy and Society: An Outline of Interpretive Sociology*, trans. and ed. Guenther Roth and Claus Wittich (Berkeley: University of California Press, 1978), p. 24.

44. Indeed, to remain coherent, instrumental arguments require an analytic distinction between desired ends (benefits) and the means used to achieve them (costs). See Albert O. Hirschman, *Shifting Involvements: Private Interest and Public Action* (Princeton: Princeton University Press, 1982), pp. 82–91; and James M. Jasper, *The Art of Moral Protest: Culture, Biography, and Creativity in Social Movements* (Chicago: University of Chicago Press, 1997), esp. pp. 23–26, 82–84.

45. Jasper, *The Art of Moral Protest*, p. 26.

46. For details on the data collection, see appendix A.

47. Lee Ann Fujii, *Interviewing in Social Science Research: A Relational Approach* (New York: Routledge, 2018), p. xv.

Third, to understand what parades felt like and how paraders acted while on parade and in other settings, I recorded ethnographic field notes at many parades, protests, public meetings, marching band practices, and other related events. Whether I was observing a parade from the sidewalk or sitting in the back of a community center as a marching band rehearsed a new tune, I looked for observable clues that could support or confound the varying hypotheses proposed by my argument and its alternatives.[48]

In my analysis of these data, I find four primary reasons for parading: expressing collective identity; taking part in tradition; the social and emotional pleasures of participation; and communicating with outside audiences, both Protestant and Catholic. The first three, best characterized as process-oriented reasons, are articulated by participants more often and with more passion. The desire to communicate externally, an outcome-oriented reason to parade, is expressed less frequently and appears less widely held, but is still present. The preponderance of evidence thus suggests that participants are most interested in the performance of parades, the very act of participation, not their outcomes. I further show that despite the widely recognized political claims and consequences of parades, participants understand them not just as nonpolitical, but as anti-political—that they transcend politics and exist outside of it. This view, which I call the paradox of anti-politics, helps explain how participants seem to downplay or ignore the divisive consequences of their parades.

By collecting data from both participants and comparable nonparticipants, my research addresses shortcomings in existing studies of loyalist parades and other "cultural forms of political expression" that only sample participants.[49]

---

48. There are two conspicuous absences in my data. The first are Northern Irish Catholics. Since my purpose is to explain participation in Protestant events, my research was limited to the Protestant community, and Catholic voices are absent throughout the book. If this study proposed to explain the dynamics of parades and protests in Northern Ireland, the omission would be inexcusable. But given my aims, I explore variation within one community rather than between the two. Catholics remain an important part of the story, but their role is largely filtered through the perceptions of Protestants. See the similar discussion in Lee A. Smithey, *Unionists, Loyalists, and Conflict Transformation in Northern Ireland* (New York: Oxford University Press, 2011), p. 53.

The second absence is women, who are entirely missing from the survey and almost entirely missing from the interviews. Women do participate in parades, but the large majority of paraders are male. For the sake of efficient data collection, I sacrificed the data's richness by focusing on men. On the role of women in loyalist parades, see Linda Racioppi and Katherine O'Sullivan See, "Ulstermen and Loyalist Ladies on Parade: Gendering Unionism in Northern Ireland," *International Feminist Journal of Politics* 2, no. 1 (Spring 2000): 1–29; and Katy Radford, "Drum Rolls and Gender Roles in Protestant Marching Bands in Belfast," *British Journal of Ethnomusicology* 10, no. 2 (2001): 37–59.

49. Jarman, *Material Conflicts*; Bryan, *Orange Parades*; Eric P. Kaufmann, *The Orange Order: A Contemporary Northern Irish History* (New York: Oxford University Press, 2007); Gordon Ramsey, *Music, Emotion and Identity in Ulster Marching Bands: Flutes, Drums and Loyal Sons*

These new systematic data allow me to compare participants to similar non-participants to determine what characteristics distinguish them and what characteristics they share. By methodically constructing these comparisons, I overturn several widely held beliefs about parade participants. For instance, prevailing narratives in Northern Ireland—which take an idealist approach—describe loyalist paraders as either "extreme patriots" or "extreme sectarian bigots," depending on one's perspective. Both views are mistaken. Ethnic attitudes, I find, do not distinguish participants from their nonparticipant neighbors. Paraders may hold strong beliefs about Northern Ireland's two ethnic groups, but they are not notably more extreme than others in their communities.

Loyalist parades clearly illustrate some of the puzzling features of contentious rituals that distinguish them from other forms of collective mobilization. The commonly assumed purposes of parades—to offend and intimidate Catholics or to defend Protestantism and the union with Britain, depending on who one asks—are collective outcomes that cannot explain individual participation. Yet, as I will demonstrate, participants do not receive selective material incentives, as important rationalist theories of participation predict. In fact, these theories notwithstanding, people actually pay money to be able to march in parades. And they do so week after week, year after year, without tangible benefit to themselves or the larger community. Not to mention that parades, due to their deliberately ritualized features, veer toward the type of repetitive, "stereotyped performances" that scholars of contentious politics find ineffective as well as boring for participants and audiences alike.[50]

CONFLICT, COLLECTIVE ACTION, AND CULTURE

The study of participation in contentious rituals touches on fundamental questions about ethnic conflict, collective action, and the role of cultural action in politics. First: why do people participate in ethnic conflict? Research on ethnic conflict tends to conflate conflict and violence, even though they are conceptually distinct. When "pursued within the institutionalized

(Bern: Peter Lang, 2011); and James W. McAuley, Jonathan Tonge, and Andrew Mycock, *Loyal to the Core?: Orangeism and Britishness in Northern Ireland* (Dublin: Irish Academic Press, 2011). For studies of other cases, see Verta Taylor, Leila J. Rupp, and Joshua Gamson, "Performing Protest: Drag Shows as Tactical Repertoires of the Gay and Lesbian Movement," *Research in Social Movements, Conflicts, and Change* 25 (2004): 105–137 (quotation is from p. 106); and Verta Taylor, Katrina Kimport, Nella Van Dyke, and Ellen Ann Andersen, "Culture and Mobilization: Tactical Repertoires, Same-Sex Weddings, and the Impact on Gay Activism," *American Sociological Review* 74, no. 6 (December 2009): 865–890.

50. McAdam, Tarrow, and Tilly, *Dynamics of Contention*, p. 138.

channels of the polity," writes political scientist Ashutosh Varshney, ethnic conflict is a "regular feature of pluralistic democracies" that reflects differing interests and preferences among ethnic groups.[51] Even when ethnic disagreements take "the form of strikes and non-violent demonstrations on the streets, it is an expression of conflict to be sure, but it is not a form of ethnic violence." Indeed, he argues, peaceful, institutionalized conflict "can be quite healthy for a polity."[52]

Political conflict along ethnic lines may not always be violent, yet studies of participation in ethnic conflict almost always focus on its violent side. But rioting, rebelling, or committing genocide is not the same as taking part in an act of nonviolent conflict.[53] Contentious rituals and other episodes of conflict may cause offense, raise tensions, or even precipitate instability and violence, but participation does not carry the high risks to the individual of an act of violence, nor violate widely held norms against committing harm to other people or their property.[54] Contentious rituals also do not provide the opportunities for looting or other economic gain that many have found to incentivize violence.[55] Moreover, research on ethnic conflict developed largely in isolation from social movement research, where nonviolent, confrontational collective action is the center of attention. The social movement literature, in turn, primarily studies movements aimed at broadly "progressive" change in politics and society. It often overlooks collective mobilization aiming to preserve the status quo or produce mass displays of ethnic nationalism.

Loyalist parades, to be clear, are not acts of violence, but, on occasion, they do precipitate violence. With this book, I aim to enrich our understanding of the dynamics of ethnic violence by spotlighting violence's immediate triggers. Sparks are often left under-theorized or are simply presumed to appear, but participation in such events cannot just be assumed.[56]

51. Ashutosh Varshney, "Ethnicity and Ethnic Conflict," in *The Oxford Handbook of Comparative Politics*, ed. Carles Boix and Susan Stokes (New York: Oxford University Press, 2007), pp. 279, 278.

52. Ibid., p. 279.

53. See Alexandra Scacco, "Who Riots?: Explaining Individual Participation in Ethnic Violence" (PhD diss., Columbia University, 2010); Macartan Humphrey and Jeremy M. Weinstein, "Who Fights?: The Determinants of Participation in Civil War," *American Journal of Political Science* 52, no. 2 (April 2008): 436–455; Scott Straus, *The Order of Genocide: Race, Power, and War in Rwanda* (Ithaca: Cornell University Press, 2006); and Lee Ann Fujii, *Killing Neighbors: Webs of Violence in Rwanda* (Ithaca: Cornell University Press, 2009).

54. Furthermore, Randall Collins, *Violence: A Micro-Sociological Theory* (Princeton: Princeton University Press, 2008), shows that humans try to avoid violence as much as possible.

55. For example, Edward C. Banfield, *The Unheavenly City Revisited* (Boston: Little, Brown and Company, 1974); and Paul Collier and Anke Hoeffler, "Greed and Grievance in Civil War," *Oxford Economic Papers* 56 (2004): 563–595.

56. Important exceptions include Beth Roy, *Some Trouble with Cows: Making Sense of Social Conflict* (Berkeley: University of California Press, 1994); Brass, *Theft of an Idol*; Horowitz, *The Deadly Ethnic Riot*; and Ross, *Cultural Contestation in Ethnic Conflict*.

So a complete analysis of the dynamics of intergroup violence must include an explanation for the events that ignite it. This book provides a bottom-up account of a major trigger of communal violence in post-conflict Northern Ireland.

One of my main findings, however, is that participants do not always intend the trouble they arouse. It is clear from speaking to them that achieving the harmful outcomes of their behavior is not what motivates them to act. I therefore investigate how consequences that are so predictable are construed as unintended, furthering our understanding of the relationship between cultural action and political action. This act of interpretation involves what I earlier called the paradox of anti-politics: that participants adamantly insist that their parades, which are considered political action by nearly all observers, have nothing to do with politics. This insistence provides an interesting contrast to decades of scholarship that has sought to show that many acts which may appear apolitical are in fact imbued with political meaning and intended as everyday acts of political resistance.[57]

Finally, by studying participation in a contentious ritual, this book increases our general knowledge of rituals and other cultural behaviors. In particular, I explain why people choose to participate in rituals, an issue that is often ignored by ritual scholars. Potential participants' decision to take part (or not take part) is simply taken for granted. For instance, in *The Elementary Forms of Religious Life*—easily the most influential modern account of ritual—Émile Durkheim disregards choice, describing rituals as if they somehow compel participation. "When a native is asked why he follows his rites," he writes, "he replies that ancestors have always done so and that he *must* follow their example." Ritual participation, for the great sociologist, is a moral obligation, an "imperative," and a "duty"—inner forces that leave little room for free will.[58]

But ritual is, above all, human action. Like all non-trivial acts, it is suffused with meaning and entails costs, benefits, and agency. In the words of Catherine Bell, a preeminent scholar in the field, "Ritual is never simply or

---

57. See James C. Scott, *Weapons of the Weak: Everyday Forms of Peasant Resistance* (New Haven: Yale University Press, 1985); and James C. Scott, *Domination and the Arts of Resistance: Hidden Transcripts* (New Haven: Yale University Press, 1990).

58. Durkheim, *Elementary Forms of Religious Life*, p. 192. Emphasis added. See also Jeffrey C. Alexander, "Cultural Pragmatics: Social Performance Between Ritual and Strategy," *Sociological Theory* 22, no. 4 (December 2004): 535; and Pierre Liénard and Pascal Boyer, "Whence Collective Rituals?: A Cultural Selection Model of Ritualized Behavior," *American Anthropologist* 108, no. 4 (December 2006): 816. Of course, this does not mean that all participants are as engaged or want to be there. Randall Collins, *Interaction Ritual Chains* (Princeton: Princeton University Press, 2004), esp. pp. 116, 353–354, distinguishes between central and peripheral participants. Those on the periphery do not experience the energy of the ritual and can end up feeling excluded from the ritual community.

solely a matter of routine, habit, or 'the dead weight of tradition.' "[59] This points to a simple, perhaps obvious, yet often overlooked truth: even when facing a ritual, we confront the choice to participate or not.

OUTLINE OF THE REMAINING CHAPTERS

In the chapters that follow, I explain how and why men and women of various backgrounds choose to take part in contentious, ritual parades in Northern Ireland. Chapter 1 introduces the historical and political contexts of loyalist parading in Northern Ireland, outlining the relationship between parades, power, and sectarian conflict in the north of Ireland from the eighteenth century until today. The central social and political factor during much of that period is that Northern Ireland was and remains a deeply divided society, meaning it is "characterized by cleavages that are not pacified, as well as by the widespread belief that the state is actively taking the side of one of the part in conflict."[60] In such a situation, symbols and events that represent and glorify only one of the local groups is bound to be contentious. I show how this general dynamic operates on the ground in Northern Ireland, establish the political foundation of parades, and explain the specific sources of disputes over them. Finally, I situate the current parading scene, locating the major players and describing recent trends.

Chapter 2 assesses three established approaches to participation in contentious action—idealist, rationalist, and structuralist—and demonstrates, using quantitative survey and qualitative interview data, that parade participation does not closely follow their logics. Contrary to the idealist expectation, paraders' ideas and attitudes about the Protestant in-group and the Catholic out-group are not substantially different from the ideas and attitudes of Protestants who do not parade, with one possible exception. Contrary to the rationalist expectation, paraders do not receive selective material rewards—access to cash, loans, jobs, or the like—to incentivize their contribution. As a matter of fact, many fear that parading may *cost* them at work, where many coworkers and supervisors view parades negatively. Rational choice theories also predict that social pressure might also spur

59. Bell, *Ritual Theory, Ritual Practice*, p. 92. See also pp. 207–208.
60. Lorenzo Bosi and Gianluca De Fazio, "Contextualizing the Troubles: Investigating Deeply Divided Societies through Social Movements Research," in *The Troubles in Northern Ireland and Theories of Social Movements*, ed. Lorenzo Bosi and Gianluca De Fazio (Amsterdam: Amsterdam University Press, 2017), p. 11. See also Niall Ó Dochartaigh, "What Did the Civil Rights Movement Want?: Changing Goals and Underlying Continuities in the Transition from Protest to Violence," p. 49, in the same volume.

participation, and here the data is mixed—this hypothesis is somewhat supported by the survey evidence but not by the interviews. Finally, contrary to the structuralist expectation, pre-existing social networks do not differentiate paraders and non-paraders. Paraders and non-paraders both have friends and family members who parade, and so proximity to mobilizing structures does not explain differential recruitment. Paraders, likewise, do not have more personal time or availability than nonparticipants. They are, however, more likely than non-paraders to have a history of past participation—parading as a child does help explain parading as an adult. Overall, the data show that none of these three prominent theoretical approaches to collective action can convincingly explain why some Protestants parade and some do not.

Chapter 3 explores the four main reasons why people *do* choose to parade: collective identity expression, tradition, the pleasures of participation, and communication with outside audiences. I take a close look at the language people use to describe what walking in a parade is like and what it means to them. I try to reconstruct the experience of taking part, highlighting the importance of elements such as comradeship, memory, recognition, and pride. The major reasons for parading, I argue, include both instrumental and non-instrumental motivations, but the latter are more prominent. In my analysis of the interview and survey data, I find that participants are more interested in the process-oriented benefits intrinsic to the very performance of parades than any external outcomes that result from them. The most consequential outcomes from parades of course relate to conflict across the sectarian divide. But, what I found most remarkable during my time spent with a marching band in West Belfast was the absence of sectarian talk or stated intention of sending antagonistic messages to Catholics. According to the paraders themselves, the external outcomes have very little to do with their motivations to participate.

Building on this puzzling gap between expectations and outcomes, chapter 4 examines perhaps the most significant result of my analysis, the paradox of anti-politics—the contradiction that exists between parading's fundamental political nature and participants' stated understanding of their action. I scrutinize the paradox, showing that from participants' perspective, parades cannot be political because they are cultural, which they see as mutually exclusive categories. But this is not merely an issue of labeling things appropriately. The language of anti-politics is a powerful tool for paraders and their allies. The paradox, I argue, preserves participants' positive self-image and collective identities. It helps them maintain a vision of themselves as good, moral, and unconnected to the accusations of sectarian politics thrown at them. Furthermore, anti-politics is itself a form of political power, since it allows participants to try to shift debates away from criticism and compromise. As sociologist Nina Eliasoph observes, "Deciding what *counts* as political involvement is in itself a powerful political move."[61] It is a move that paraders, buttressed by the ritual elements of parades, try to use to influence political outcomes.

Lastly, the conclusion briefly considers the similar cases of contentious processions in Israel and India. Research on the Israeli and Indian participants reveals that they share many similarities with Northern Irish paraders. In particular, like members of the loyal orders and marching bands, they appear most interested in the experience of processing, rather than the controversial outcomes. Reflecting on these three cases together, I end by offering two counterintuitive ideas about the nature of contentious rituals and their connection to pluralism, political power, and the state. Contentious rituals, while seemingly a weapon of the weak, are in fact the domain of powerful groups because performing them requires the state's sanction and security. And, while seemingly a product of isolation between groups, contentious rituals require intimate knowledge of the other gained from the continuous exchanges of life in a plural society. The contradiction of intimacy, laid bare by contentious rituals, is that its power to sustain inter-communal relationships is also the power to spoil them.

---

61. Nina Eliasoph, *Avoiding Politics: How Americans Produce Apathy in Everyday Life* (New York: Cambridge University Press, 1998), p. 278. Emphasis in the original.

CHAPTER 1

Identity on Parade in
Northern Ireland

Winding its way for thirteen miles through West Belfast is a
system of barriers separating the Protestants of the Shankill
Road from the Catholics of the Falls Road. Hastily erected with
barbed wire in reaction to sectarian street violence and arson in 1969, today
it is a bricolage of sheet metal, metal fencing, cement, and brick that rises
at some points to forty-four feet high. Metal gates spaced along the twenty-
first-century rampart can be opened when necessary, including for the
minutes it takes the Whiterock Temperance Loyal Orange Lodge to march
through at Workman Avenue, under heavy police protection and surveillance,
during their annual parade in late June.

Cutting through streets, abandoned industrial lots, and families' back
gardens, parts of West Belfast's wall have stood for longer than Berlin's did.
And it is not alone. There are ninety-nine physical barriers—euphemistically
called "peace walls" or "peace lines"—between Protestant and Catholic
neighborhoods in Belfast. This represents an increase since the beginning
of the peace process—at least twenty-one of the barriers were built after the
1994 paramilitary ceasefires.[1]

Proliferating peace walls are but one indication that the years since the
signing of the Belfast/Good Friday Agreement ("the Agreement") in April

---

1. Paul Nolan, *Northern Ireland Peace Monitoring Report, Number 3* (Belfast: Community
Relations Council, 2014), pp. 67–70; and Belfast Interface Project, *Belfast Interfaces: Security
Barriers and Defensive Use of Space* (Belfast: Belfast Interface Project, 2012), esp. pp. 13, 39. On
the Whiterock parade, see Dominic Bryan, *Orange Parades: The Politics of Ritual, Tradition, and
Control* (London: Pluto, 2000), pp. 131–132.

1998 have not always been serene.[2] The Agreement marked the formal end of the Troubles—the thirty years of violence between and among republican paramilitaries seeking a united Ireland, loyalist paramilitaries seeking to remain in the United Kingdom, and British security forces that killed over thirty-seven hundred people and injured at least forty thousand[3]—but not the end of the division. Violence has declined dramatically since 1998, yet conflict between the two communities continues.[4]

The persistent divide between the two ethnic communities structures many, if not most, aspects of public and private life in Northern Ireland.[5] Though the groups are by no means monoliths, "it is hard to deny the reality of two readily discernible blocs" separated by multiple reinforcing differences.[6] Joseph Ruane and Jennifer Todd identify religion, ethnicity, and colonialism as the three central dimensions of difference, producing two overlapping identity clusters: Protestant/British/settler and Catholic/Irish/native.[7] Throughout the book, I use "Protestant" (or "Ulster Protestant") and "Catholic" to refer to these two communities and identities. I find them preferable to the popular but cumbersome Protestant/Unionist/Loyalist (PUL) and Catholic/Nationalist/Republican (CNR), which pinch together each groups' political ideologies and identities.[8] Since I am primarily

2. Even the name of the peace agreement is disputed: Protestants tend toward Belfast, Catholics tend toward Good Friday. Following Brendan O'Leary, "The Nature of the Agreement," *Fordham International Law Journal* 22, no. 4 (1998): 1629, I will call it simply the Agreement.

3. Marie Smyth and Jennifer Hamilton, "The Human Costs of the Troubles," in *Researching the Troubles: Social Science Perspectives on the Northern Ireland Conflict*, ed. Owen Hargie and David Dickson (Edinburgh: Mainstream, 2003), p. 19. Almost 2 percent of the population was killed or injured during the Troubles. As Brendan O'Leary and John McGarry, *The Politics of Antagonism: Understanding Northern Ireland* (London: Athlone Press, 1993), p. 12, point out: "If the equivalent ratio of victims to population had been produced in Great Britain in the same period some 100,000 people would have died, and if a similar level of political violence had taken place, the number of fatalities in the USA would have been over 500,000, or about ten times the number of Americans killed in the Vietnam war."

4. Compared to other post-conflict societies, violence in Northern Ireland has been low. See Michael J. Boyle, *Violence after War: Explaining Instability in Post-Conflict States* (Baltimore: Johns Hopkins University Press, 2014), pp. 60–61, 197–199.

5. I follow Horowitz's "inclusive conception of ethnicity" where "groups are defined by ascriptive differences, whether the indicium of group identity is color, appearance, language, religion, some other indicator of common origin, or some combination thereof." Donald L. Horowitz, *Ethnic Groups in Conflict*, 2nd. ed. (Berkeley: University of California Press, 2000), pp. 17–18.

6. Lee A. Smithey, *Unionists, Loyalists, and Conflict Transformation in Northern Ireland* (New York: Oxford University Press, 2011), p. 56.

7. Joseph Ruane and Jennifer Todd, *The Dynamics of Conflict in Northern Ireland: Power, Conflict, and Emancipation* (New York: Cambridge University Press, 1996), p. 11.

8. Unionism refers to the belief, held mainly by Protestants, that Northern Ireland should remain part of the United Kingdom, while nationalism refers to the belief, held mainly by Catholics, that Northern Ireland should unite with the Republic of Ireland. Loyalism is the more hardline version of unionism. It is held mainly by members of the working class, emphasizes

interested in ethnic relations, I use the ascriptive identities alone and reserve the political designations for discussing political parties and ideas. I do not mean the terms to imply religious beliefs or practices, unless otherwise specified.[9]

"Post-conflict" Northern Ireland has been characterized by "peace without reconciliation."[10] The vast majority of students are segregated in Protestant or Catholic schools, with only 6.5 percent attending schools that are formally integrated.[11] Housing segregation remains high and entrenched.[12] Low-level violence and fear are endemic in interface communities, the areas where Protestant and Catholic neighborhoods meet.[13] The result, of course, is the increased number of peace walls.

Unsurprisingly, there is little contact across the walls. In a detailed survey of residents of Belfast interface communities from 2004, Peter Shirlow and Brendan Murtagh find that only about 12 percent work in the other community's area and 78 percent avoid public facilities there. In fact, a majority often travel twice as far as needed to shop in neutral or in-group dominated areas. Half of the respondents would not walk through a neighborhood on the other side of the interface during the day; over 90 percent would not at night. This segregation, driven primarily by fear of the other community, is magnified among young people.[14]

Among working-class Protestants, this reigning sense of fear, along with little opportunity for economic advancement, has led to disenchantment

Protestant culture and identity, and is often associated with support for paramilitary violence (though see James W. McAuley, *Very British Rebels?: The Culture and Politics of Ulster Loyalism* [London: Bloomsbury, 2016], pp. 49, 55). Its nationalist counterpart is republicanism. See Ruane and Todd, *The Dynamics of Conflict in Northern Ireland*, esp. pp. 84–115; John McGarry and Brendan O'Leary, *Explaining Northern Ireland: Broken Images* (Oxford: Basil Blackwell, 1995), esp. pp. 13–61, 92–137; and Smithey, *Unionists, Loyalists, and Conflict Transformation*, pp. 23–24.

9. On the influence of religion on ethnic identities in Northern Ireland, see Claire Mitchell, *Religion, Identity and Politics in Northern Ireland: Boundaries of Belonging and Belief* (Aldershot: Ashgate, 2006).

10. Nolan, *Northern Ireland Peace Monitoring Report, Number 3*, p. 11. For critiques of the "post-conflict" label, see Séverine Autesserre, *The Trouble with the Congo: Local Violence and the Failure of International Peacebuilding* (New York: Cambridge University Press, 2010); and John D. Brewer, *Peace Processes: A Sociological Approach* (Malden, MA: Polity, 2010).

11. Nolan, *Northern Ireland Peace Monitoring Report, Number 3*, p. 120.

12. Brendan Murtagh, *The Politics of Territory: Policy and Segregation in Northern Ireland* (London: Palgrave Macmillan, 2002); Brendan Murtagh, "Ethno-Religious Segregation in Post-Conflict Belfast," *Built Environment* 37, no. 2 (June 2011): 213–225; and Christopher D. Lloyd and Ian Shuttleworth, "Residential Segregation in Northern Ireland in 2001: Assessing the Value of Exploring Spatial Variations," *Environment and Planning A* 44, no. 1 (January 2012): 52–67.

13. Peter Shirlow and Brendan Murtagh, *Belfast: Segregation, Violence, and City* (London: Pluto, 2006); and Laia Balcells, Lesley-Ann Daniels, and Abel Escribà-Folch, "The Determinants of Low-Intensity Intergroup Violence: The Case of Northern Ireland," *Journal of Peace Research* 53, no. 1 (January 2016): 33–48.

14. Shirlow and Murtagh, *Belfast*, pp. 84–95.

with the peace process. The promised economic "peace dividend" never appeared for many people and, in fact, many Protestants perceive that on multiple dimensions, conditions have actually deteriorated since the violence ended. There is a general feeling among Protestants that the peace process has benefited Catholics more than them—a belief that has steadily increased since 1998.[15] Through a zero-sum, sectarian prism, there is truth to this belief. The peace process transformed Northern Ireland from a social, economic, and political system designed to privilege Protestants over Catholics to one premised on equal opportunity.

On top of political, economic, and security reforms to redress anti-Catholic discrimination, Protestants fear losing their demographic advantage. The borders of the province were carved out of northeast Ireland in 1921 in order to create a territory with a large Protestant majority. But the original two-thirds Protestant majority has declined to near parity: 48.4 percent Protestant and 45.1 percent Catholic, according to the 2011 census.[16] Northern Ireland has always been characterized by a "double-minority" situation[17]—Catholics are a minority in Northern Ireland, Protestants are a minority on the island of Ireland—but that is set to change in the coming years.

The shifting demographics matter because the ultimate answer to the sovereignty question—the keystone political issue in the province—lies in the "principle of consent." Under the terms of the Agreement, a united Ireland "is subject to the … consent of a majority of the people of Northern Ireland."[18] Historically, majority rule meant a Protestant veto over unification, though this may change with a coming Catholic majority. Nevertheless, the union with the United Kingdom currently appears firm—in large part because of growing Catholic acceptance of the constitutional status quo. Surveys show that since 2008, more Catholics favor remaining in the United Kingdom than unifying Ireland. This pattern has remained true, at least so far, in post-Brexit referendum surveys.[19] In 2013, the apex of recent

15. Smithey, *Unionists, Loyalists, and Conflict Transformation*, p. 68; and Henry Patterson, "Unionism After Good Friday and St. Andrews," *The Political Quarterly* 83, no. 2 (April–June 2012): 249.

16. Eric Kaufmann, "Demographic Change and Conflict in Northern Ireland: Reconciling Qualitative and Quantitative Evidence," *Ethnopolitics* 10, nos. 3–4 (September–November 2011): 371; and Nolan, *Northern Ireland Peace Monitoring Report, Number 3*, p. 21.

17. John Whyte, *Interpreting Northern Ireland* (Oxford: Clarendon, 1990), pp. 100–101.

18. Agreement Reached in the Multi-Party Negotiations, April 10, 1998, Section 2, "Constitutional Issues," I.ii.

19. In 2016, the UK voted to leave the European Union, which many predict will cascade into Scotland and Northern Ireland voting to leave the UK. The respondents of post-Brexit surveys, however, are less certain. In the 2016 Northern Ireland Life and Times Survey, only 26 percent believe that Brexit has made a united Ireland more likely (32 percent of Catholics, 21 percent of Protestants), while 51 percent believe it has made no difference (48 percent of Catholics,

Catholic unionism, 52 percent of surveyed Catholics wished to remain in the United Kingdom while only 28 percent desired a united Ireland—a sea change from 2001, when only 15 percent wanted to stay in the UK and 59 percent sought unification. And only a slim majority of Catholics now identify as exclusively Irish, while roughly two in five view themselves as having at least some British identity.[20] Perhaps most important to the recent stability is "the enthusiastic administration" of Northern Ireland by Sinn Féin and others who fought a three-decade campaign to demolish it.[21]

Despite this newfound security, many Protestants fear for their future. At present, these anxieties are focused on a perceived "culture war" against Protestantism. Many believe that Protestant culture and their way of life are under threat from politically assertive republicanism. As a recent report summarizes, "The focus of concern is no longer about Northern Ireland being taken out of Britain, but of 'Britishness' being taken out of Northern Ireland."[22] A primary front in this "war" are contested cultural expressions of Protestantism, unionism, and loyalism.[23] Protests against parades and restrictions placed on them are understood as a major way that Catholics are chipping away at Protestant culture. So too are efforts to remove the Union Flag from public buildings. The Protestant reaction crescendoed in December 2012, when the Belfast City Council voted to stop flying the Union Flag on the city hall every day of the year and instead fly it on eighteen designated days—in line with the policy for government buildings in Britain. This move, supported by the nationalist parties and the nonsectarian Alliance Party, was seen by many Protestants as an assault on their rights and values and another example of Catholic concerns being privileged over theirs. The change in flag policy sparked four months of protests, riots, and

57 percent of Protestants). And only 16 percent say that Brexit has made them personally more in favor of uniting Ireland (28 percent of Catholics, 5 percent of Protestants), while 69 percent say it has made no difference in their views (62 percent of Catholics, 77 percent of Protestants). We shall have to wait and see. See ARK, *Northern Ireland Life and Times Survey 2016*, distributed by ARK, www.ark.ac.uk/nilt/2016, accessed December 16, 2017. Variables: UNIRLIKL and UNIRFAV.

20. ARK, *Northern Ireland Life and Times Survey*, distributed by ARK, www.ark.ac.uk/nilt/, accessed December 16, 2017. See variables NIRELAND (1998–2006), NIRELND2 (2007–2010, 2012–2016), and IRBRIT (2007, 2012–2016). Even among the Catholics who in 2013 said they did not wish to remain in the UK, 61 percent would "happily accept" a democratic outcome that never led to a united Ireland (see FUTURE2, 2013).

21. Patterson, "Unionism After Good Friday and St. Andrews," p. 254.

22. Nolan, *Northern Ireland Peace Monitoring Report, Number 3*, p. 12. Also McAuley, *Very British Rebels?* esp. pp. 142–147; and Patterson, "Unionism After Good Friday and St. Andrews," p. 254.

23. Marc Howard Ross, *Cultural Contestation in Ethnic Conflict* (New York: Cambridge University Press, 2007), p. 2, defines contested cultural expressions as "contextually significant activities, objects, and/or symbols that have strong emotional meaning and become focal points of intergroup conflict."

violent attacks by Protestants—including burning down an Alliance Party office, attempts to burn others, and death threats to several Alliance elected officials—which led to a "marked deterioration in community relations."[24]

There is also a historical dimension to the Protestant narrative of margin- alization and loss. Protestants have long seen their position in Ireland as precarious. Since they first arrived in the sixteenth century, Protestants have been a religious minority on an overwhelmingly Catholic island. Sporadic episodes of sectarian violence, such as the massacres of Protestants by Catholic rebels in 1641, confirmed the sense of Catholic threat and pro- moted a siege mentality that has been held by many Protestants up until this day.[25] An independent or autonomous Ireland, Protestants feared, would curtail religious liberties and subject them to persecution. Preventing such an outcome was paramount. The community's security rested on local Protestant political dominance and the union with the United Kingdom. Any gain by Catholics that could threaten either position was, therefore, understood as a threat to the community's survival. As a result, Protestant politics, especially since the nineteenth century, "has been primarily defen- sive and conservative."[26] The general tenor of modern Protestant politics is summarized in oft-repeated slogans such as "no surrender!" "not one inch!" and "Ulster says no!"

PARADES IN NORTHERN IRELAND

Each year Protestant organizations perform over twenty-five hundred parades to display their allegiance to the Protestant faith, the Protestant people of Ulster, and the constitutional union between Northern Ireland and Great Britain. During parades, participants use their bodies, uniforms, flags, banners, and music to demonstrate their culture and their views to the world. The parades are often festive events along routes lined with cheering

24. Paul Nolan, Dominic Bryan, Clare Dwyer, Katy Hayward, Katy Radford, and Peter Shirlow, *The Flag Dispute: Anatomy of a Protest* (Belfast: Queen's University Belfast, 2014), p. 11. See also Kevin Hearty, "The Great Awakening?: The Belfast Flag Protests and Protestant/ Unionist/Loyalist Counter-Memory in Northern Ireland," *Irish Political Studies* 30, no. 2 (2015): 157–177; Donna Halliday and Neil Ferguson, "When Peace Is Not Enough: The Flag Protests, the Politics of Identity and Belonging in East Belfast," *Irish Political Studies* 31, no. 4 (2016): 525–540; and Paul Nolan and Dominic Bryan, *Flags: Towards a New Understanding* (Belfast: Institute of Irish Studies, Queen's University Belfast, 2016).
25. See A. T. Q. Stewart, *The Narrow Ground: Aspects of Ulster, 1609–1969* (London: Faber & Faber, 1977); Arthur Aughey, *Under Siege: Ulster Unionism and the Anglo-Irish Agreement* (Belfast: Blackstaff, 1989); and McAuley, *Very British Rebels?* pp. 158–159. Historians debate the historical validity of the massacres. See Jonathan Bardon, *A History of Ulster* (Belfast: Blackstaff, 1992), pp. 137–139.
26. Smithey, *Unionists, Loyalists, and Conflict Transformation*, p. 60.

fans waving flags and happily singing along to the tunes. Most parades take place in the spring and summer, with the pinnacle of the parading season on the Twelfth of July. On that day, tens of thousands of members of the Orange Order and marching bands parade past throngs of supporters in cities and towns around Northern Ireland to commemorate and celebrate the military victory of the Protestant King William III (of Orange) over the Catholic King James II at the Battle of the Boyne in 1690.

However, in Northern Ireland's divided social landscape, not all citizens view the parades favorably. Many, if not most Catholics—along with some Protestants—see parades as anti-Catholic triumphalism and provocative "carnival[s] of hate."[27] They associate the loyal orders with Protestant domination and the marching bands, particularly self-styled blood and thunder bands, with loyalist paramilitaries. The Twelfth of July, to take the most well-known example, marks a great victory for Protestants, but for Catholics, the battle marked the start of a long era of subjugation to Protestant supremacy. The Twelfth's content and form symbolize the subsequent centuries of Protestant hegemony in Ireland.

Consequently, groups of Catholic residents often protest parades, causing the police to occasionally block the marchers from entering certain streets. Disputes over parades increase communal tension, disrupt the political peace process, and interfere with local peace-building efforts on a regular basis. These disputes occasionally precipitate violence, including serious rioting in recent years. The seemingly endless cycles of parades, protests, and violence embody what Brendan O'Leary and John McGarry call Northern Ireland's "politics of antagonism."[28]

Though very few parades each year are protested—and even fewer turn violent—all of them are intimately political. Every parade makes a claim about the central question of politics: who should rule? Their answer—the United Kingdom—clashes with the aspirations of many Catholics who seek a united Ireland, free from British control. Though the claim is often made obliquely through the use of flags, music, and other symbols, it touches on the debate that has dominated politics in Northern Ireland— and before that, all of Ireland—since the nineteenth century.

Disputes over parades, then, are about more than just parades—and it is this deeper significance that ignites the evident passion. They are "conflicts between groups over competing, and apparently irresolvable, claims that engage the central elements of each group's historical experience and their

27. "A Carnival of Hate," *An Phoblacht/Republican News* (Dublin), July 4, 1996, quoted in Martyn Frampton, *The Long March: The Political Strategy of Sinn Féin, 1981–2007* (London: Palgrave Macmillan, 2000), p. 126.
28. O'Leary and McGarry, *The Politics of Antagonism*.

identity and invoke suspicions and fears of the opponent."[29] In other words, there is more at stake than whether or not a group of men walks down the street. Parades in Northern Ireland are tangled up in long-standing, often violent, debates over identity, territory, power, and the question of who belongs. They are, at heart, about the great "unbargainables" held dear by Protestants and Catholics.[30]

PARADING IN IRELAND FROM THE EIGHTEENTH
CENTURY TO THE PRESENT

Political parading in Ireland originated in the eighteenth century, when Anglican landowners began commemorating the seventeenth-century events that secured their ascendancy. In 1688, King James II, a Catholic, was overthrown in the Glorious Revolution by his daughter, Mary, and her husband, King William III, a Protestant Dutch prince. After seeking refuge in France, James tried to regain the throne, landing first in Ireland where his Jacobite supporters were already fighting Williamites.

William landed in Ireland with a multinational European army in June 1690 and met James by the River Boyne on the east coast of Ireland on July 1, 1690 (in the old Julian calendar, which is July 11 in today's Gregorian calendar). At the Battle of the Boyne, William defeated James, who retreated to France and abandoned his campaign for the throne. William's victory (along with his more decisive victory over remaining Jacobite forces at Aughrim one year later) assured Protestant dominance in Ireland.[31]

For the eighteenth-century Anglican gentry, major beneficiaries of the Williamite triumph, the events of William's victorious campaign needed to be celebrated. They formed commemorative societies that marked these victories with banquets, bonfires, fireworks, and parades throughout the eighteenth century.[32] But commemorations of William III really rose to prominence in the century's last years with the formation of the Orange

29. Ross, *Cultural Contestation in Ethnic Conflict*, p. 25.

30. Richard Rose, *Governing without Consensus: An Irish Perspective* (London: Faber & Faber, 1971), p. 408.

31. Bardon, *History of Ulster*, pp. 161–165. The Battle of Aughrim took place on July 12, 1691 (Old Style). Due in part to the shift to the Gregorian calendar in the eighteenth century, the commemorations of the Boyne and Aughrim fused, which explains why William's victory at the Boyne is celebrated today on July 12. See ibid., p. 165. For the broader European context of the Williamite War, see Steve Pincus, *1688: The First Modern Revolution* (New Haven: Yale University Press, 2009).

32. Jacqueline R. Hill, "National Festivals, the State and 'Protestant Ascendancy' in Ireland, 1790–1829," *Irish Historical Studies* 24, no. 93 (May 1984): 30–51; James Kelly, " 'The Glorious and Immortal Memory': Commemoration and Protestant Identity in Ireland, 1660–1800," *Proceedings of the Royal Irish Academy* 94C, no. 2 (1994): 25–52; Bryan, *Orange Parades*, p. 31;

Order, or Orange Institution, in County Armagh in 1795.[33] Founded by members of a lower-class Protestant militia, the Peep O'Day Boys, after a skirmish with their Catholic rivals, the Defenders, the Order appeared as a Protestant self-defense movement in a period of severe sectarian clashes in Armagh.[34]

The Orange Order sought to appear respectable—unlike the rowdy Peep O'Day Boys—and took great interest in regalia, icons, and symbols. Inspired by the reformist Volunteer movement of the late 1770s and 1780s, the Orange Order quickly adopted the public commemorative parade as its principal form of mobilization and political expression.[35] The Orange Order held its first Boyne commemorative parade in July 1796. Even at this first parade, a sectarian clash erupted. A Mr. McMurdie exchanged "some words" with a local militia member, the two "came to blows," and "Mr. McMurdie received a stab of which he died."[36] Thus began a sustained relationship between parades, sectarian confrontations, and violence.

In their first years of existence, the combustible nature of Orange parades kept the state wary of them. But with the 1798 United Irishmen Rebellion, the first major Irish republican movement, the government and upper classes warmed to the Orange Order, which was increasingly vocally pro-state and whose members contributed to the defeat of the rebels. Its role in helping to subdue the failed uprising marked an early turning point for the Orange Order: the organization grew in scale and scope as its membership, reach, and ambitions expanded from a local focus to a national one.[37] This social and political influence would only increase as the Order entered the nineteenth century.

and James Kelly, "The Emergence of Political Parading, 1660–1800," in *The Irish Parading Tradition: Following the Drum*, ed. T. G. Fraser (London: Palgrave Macmillan, 2000), pp. 9–26.

33. As late as 1789 and 1790, the centenaries of Derry and the Boyne, respectively, were celebrated by Protestants and Catholics alike as victories for liberty, not for Protestantism. Brian Walker, "1641, 1689, 1690 And All That: The Unionist Sense of History," *The Irish Review*, no. 12 (Spring-Summer 1992): 57.

34. Peter Gibbon, *The Origins of Ulster Unionism: The Formation of Popular Protestant Politics and Ideology in Nineteenth-Century Ireland* (Manchester: Manchester University Press, 1975), pp. 22–42; David W. Miller, "The Armagh Troubles, 1784–95," in *Irish Peasants: Violence and Political Unrest, 1780–1914*, ed. Samuel Clark and James S. Donnelly Jr. (Manchester: Manchester University Press, 1983), pp. 155–191; Sean Farrell, *Rituals and Riots: Sectarian Violence and Political Culture in Ulster, 1784–1886* (Lexington: University Press of Kentucky, 2000), pp. 10–46; and Bardon, *History of Ulster*, pp. 223–227.

35. Bryan, *Orange Parades*, pp. 31–33; and Padhraig Higgins, "Bonfires, Illuminations, and Joy: Celebratory Street Politics and the Uses of 'the Nation' During the Volunteer Movement," *Éire-Ireland* 42, nos. 3–4 (Fall/Winter 2007): 173–206.

36. *Belfast News Letter*, July 15, 1796, quoted in Bryan, *Orange Parades*, p. 33; and Neil Jarman, *Material Conflicts: Parades and Visual Displays in Northern Ireland* (Oxford: Berg, 1997), p. 47.

37. Bryan, *Orange Parades*, p. 35. See also J. G. Simms, "Remembering 1690," *Studies: An Irish Quarterly Review* 63, no. 251 (Autumn 1974): 241–242.

The years after the 1800 Acts of Union, which united the Kingdom of Great Britain and the Kingdom of Ireland, were marked by continued sectarian unrest at parades as the relationship between parades and Protestant-Catholic violence grew.[38] The rise in disorderly parades, however, was not linear. Rather, the size, strength, and truculence of the Orange Order as well as the bellicosity of their parades "waxed and waned in direct proportion to the perceived urgency of the Catholic threat."[39] In the first half of the century, this trend was exemplified by the conflicts of the mid-1820s, as Daniel O'Connell's Catholic Association pushed for Catholic emancipation. In response to Catholic political mobilization, the Orange Order paraded more often and more contentiously, and parades increasingly became "riotous assemblies."[40] For example, in 1829, just months after the passage of the emancipation law, Twelfth parades in Ulster were larger and more widespread than ever before. This aggressive parading sparked riots that killed at least forty people.[41] The parades demonstrated Protestant strength and continued resistance to Catholic rights to Catholics, fellow Protestants, and the British Parliament. "The message was clear," argues historian Sean Farrell, "ignorant politicians [in Westminster] might have changed the law on the statute books, but things would not change on the ground in Ulster."[42]

In what was to become a pattern in times of serious unrest, the upper-class leadership withdrew from parades as the rowdiness challenged their interest in an orderly society. The lower-class mass membership, however, continued parading, even after the Orange Order was outlawed from 1825 to 1828 and all parades in Ireland were banned from 1832 to 1844 and again from 1850 to 1872.[43] Despite regular disorder, Orange leaders tried to maintain control over parades to use as a tool to promote cross-class Protestant unity and loyalty to the state. But, with the absence of the landed gentry and rapid membership growth among the rising urban working class,

38. Bryan, *Orange Parades*, pp. 35–36. Interestingly, large segments of Orange Order—later a stalwart of hardline unionism—opposed the Acts of Union. Uniting the two kingdoms meant abolishing the Irish Parliament in Dublin, where many Orange leaders held power. They feared losing influence as the seat of power moved from Dublin to Westminster. See ibid., p. 35; and D. George Boyce, *Nineteenth-Century Ireland: The Search for Stability*, rev. ed. (Dublin: Gill & Macmillan, 2005), p. 35.

39. David Hempton and Myrtle Hull, *Evangelical Protestantism in Ulster Society, 1740–1890* (London: Routledge, 1992), p. 21.

40. Jarman, *Material Conflicts*, p. 53.

41. Farrell, *Rituals and Riots*, pp. 96–99; and S. J. Connolly, "Mass Politics and Sectarian Conflict, 1823–30," in *A New History of Ireland, Volume V, Part 1: Ireland Under the Union, 1801–1870*, ed. W. E. Vaughan (Oxford: Clarendon Press, 1989), p. 106.

42. Farrell, *Rituals and Riots*, p. 108.

43. Bryan, *Orange Parades*, p. 37. For example, despite the prohibition, an estimated one hundred thousand people marched in the Belfast Twelfth in 1870. Jarman, *Material Conflicts*, p. 65; also W.E. Vaughan, "Ireland *c.* 1870," in Vaughan, *Ireland Under the Union*, pp. 736–737.

this proved a struggle.[44] Urban industrialization led to new levels of sectarian conflict, and Belfast parades were marked by significant unrest in 1852, 1853, and 1855, eventually exploding in the massive riots of July to September 1857.[45]

While urban violence raged, parades also became central sites of democratic party politics.[46] Violence, in fact, was in many ways a result of democratization.[47] Throughout the expansion of the franchise in mid-nineteenth-century Ireland, Anglican political elites used parades and the violence that often followed to polarize voters along Protestant-Catholic lines. In the 1860s, newly enfranchised Presbyterians and Methodists were likely to vote along with Catholics for the Liberal Party. This meant that in parliamentary constituencies where Anglicans were a minority of voters, their favored party, the Tories, was bound to lose, unless they could attract Nonconformist voters. "In the many parliamentary seats with a majority of Protestant voters but a sizable Catholic minority," writes Wilkinson, "the Tory response to this electoral challenge was to play the anti-Catholic card in order to encourage Methodists and Presbyterians to identify themselves with the 'Protestant party,' the Tories, rather than what they tried to label as the 'Catholic party,' the Liberals."[48] Tory elites encouraged aggressive parading in order to elicit a violent response from Catholics, which pushed Protestant voters toward their party.

Starting in the 1860s, parades also became an attractive resource for politicians because of the huge crowds they attracted. As parades proliferated and became bigger events, they doubled as political rallies for the politicians that frequented them. They served as public fora for politicians to connect with voters and vice versa. Parades began to be considered

44. Bryan, *Orange Parades*, p. 38.
45. Riots in Belfast were so common and predictable in this era that Gibbon, *Origins of Ulster Unionism*, pp. 68, 86, describes them as "literally endemic" and "integrated into the local social order." See his analysis in pp. 67–86; as well as Frank Wright, *Two Lands on One Soil: Ulster Politics Before Home Rule* (New York: St. Martin's, 1996), pp. 250–254; Farrell, *Rituals and Riots*, pp. 143–150; and Mark Doyle, *Fighting Like the Devil for the Sake of God: Protestants, Catholics and Origins of Violence in Victorian Belfast* (Manchester: Manchester University Press, 2009), pp. 76–106.
46. Gibbon, *Origins of Ulster Unionism*, pp. 94–104.
47. On the general relationship between democracy, democratization, and violence, see Jack Snyder, *From Voting to Violence: Democratization and Nationalist Conflict* (New York: Norton, 2000); Steven I. Wilkinson, *Votes and Violence: Electoral Competition and Ethnic Riots in India* (New York: Cambridge University Press, 2004); Michael Mann, *The Dark Side of Democracy: Explaining Ethnic Cleansing* (New York: Cambridge University Press, 2004); and Paul Staniland, "Violence and Democracy," *Comparative Politics* 47, no. 1 (October 2014): 99–118.
48. Wilkinson, *Votes and Violence*, p. 212. He uses this brief case study of nineteenth-century Britain and Ireland to show that his electoral theory of ethnic violence theory works outside of India (pp. 212–218).

"respectable"[49]—all while still being proscribed by the Party Processions Act of 1850 that was not repealed until 1872. Over this time, the Orange Order's political power grew.[50]

This power was used in full to oppose the 1886 Home Rule Bill supported by Prime Minister William Gladstone's Liberal government.[51] The result of years of campaigning by Irish nationalists, Home Rule, had it been adopted by Parliament, would have established a local legislature in Dublin to govern Irish domestic affairs. The threat posed by the prospect of becoming a permanent political and religious minority under Home Rule affected all Protestants, regardless of class or denomination.[52] In response to this growing nationalist challenge, Protestants coalesced around the newly crystalized unionist ideology and identity. As the stark unionist/nationalist divide in Irish politics and society became entrenched in these years, membership in the Orange Order swelled. Senior unionist politicians now flocked to the organization and regularly appeared at parades, which came to symbolize a united Protestant community committed to unionist politics and opposed to Irish nationalism.[53] By the century's close, support for the Orange Order and parading reached new heights among the landed and industrial elites, whose economic interests were closely tied to the union and its guaranteed access to the British Empire's global markets.[54]

The Orange Order flexed its political muscle again as it mobilized militant opposition to the third Home Rule Bill in 1912.[55] Many Orangemen were among 237,000 unionists who signed Ulster's Solemn League and Covenant, committing themselves to "all means which may be found necessary to defeat the present conspiracy."[56] Though the previous two Home Rule bills had also been met with threats, this time the threat was backed with guns when the unionist leaders and prominent Orangemen Edward Carson and James Craig formed the Ulster Volunteer Force (UVF)

---

49. Bryan, *Orange Parades*, p. 44; and K. Theodore Hoppen, *Elections, Politics, and Society in Ireland, 1832–1885* (Oxford: Clarendon Press, 1984), p. 324.

50. An important aspect of its growing power was its strengthening relationship with the Conservative Party. Hoppen, *Elections, Politics, and Society in Ireland*, pp. 316–328. See also the extensive discussion of this period in Wright, *Two Lands on One Soil*, pp. 284–382.

51. Twenty thousand Orangemen resolved: "we shall not acknowledge that [devolved Irish] government; we will refuse to pay taxes imposed by it and we will resist to the uttermost all attempts to enforce such payments." Quoted in *Ireland, 1870–1914: Coercion and Conciliation*, ed. Donnchadh Ó Corráin and Tomás O'Riordan (Dublin: Four Courts Press, 2011), p. 78.

52. Boyce, *Nineteenth-Century Ireland*, p. 8.

53. Bryan, *Orange Parades*, p. 50.

54. Ibid., p. 51.

55. Paul Bew, *Ideology and the Irish Question: Ulster Unionism and Irish Nationalism, 1912–1916* (Oxford: Clarendon Press, 1994), pp. 45–46.

56. Quoted in Bardon, *History of Ulster*, p. 437.

paramilitary.[57] Members of the Orange Order enlisted en masse.[58] Tensions mounted and the crisis only ended with the outbreak of World War I in 1914.

Irish nationalists took advantage of British preoccupation with the war to push for independence in the failed 1916 Easter Rising and with the establishment of a parliament, the Dáil Eirean, in 1919. Protestants again responded to Catholic mobilization by parading more often and with more vigor. When the Irish Free State finally gained independence in 1922, the six northeastern-most counties of Ulster, where Protestants were a majority, remained part of the United Kingdom as Northern Ireland.[59]

In the new Northern Ireland, unionist rule was hegemonic and the Orange Order was closely tied to the ruling party. As a result, parades became "rituals of state" that "allowed the full expression of a Protestant state."[60] Throughout the half-century of Ulster Unionist Party (UUP) rule (1921–1972), all of Northern Ireland's prime ministers and all but three government ministers were members of the Orange Order.[61] In this era, membership in the Order was sine qua non for advancement in unionist politics as well as a major route to employment and political patronage. Unionist politicians used parades to legitimize their rule, connect with voters, display Protestant power, and call for Protestant unity. Protestant unity across the economic and religious spectra was seen as the bulwark against threats from the domestic Catholic minority and the Catholic southern state. Unionist leaders understood their economic, political, cultural, and religious interests to be protected by membership in the United Kingdom, and thus strove to maintain the political alliance of the Protestant working class and upper classes that secured the union.[62] Thus throughout the history of Northern Ireland, parades have been used to demonstrate as well as encourage unity.

57. Boyce, *Nineteenth-Century Ireland*, p. 252.

58. Bryan, *Orange Parades*, p. 55. The UVF often practiced drilling in Orange halls and it was the Order that "provided a framework for a citizen army totally opposed to Ulster's exclusion from the United Kingdom." A. T. Q. Stewart, *The Ulster Crisis: Resistance to Home Rule, 1912–1914* (London: Faber & Faber, 1967), pp. 71, 69.

59. Bardon, *History of Ulster*, pp. 476–479. The traditional province of Ulster contains nine counties. Northern Ireland is made up of six of them: Antrim, Armagh, Down, Fermanagh, Londonderry, and Tyrone. The other three Ulster counties (Cavan, Donegal, and Monaghan) had significant Protestant minorities, but remained in Ireland.

60. Bryan, *Orange Parades*, pp. 60, 66.

61. Ibid., p. 60.

62. Paul Bew, Peter Gibbon, and Henry Patterson, *Northern Ireland, 1921–1996: Political Forces and Social Classes* (London: Serif, 1996); and Mark McGovern and Peter Shirlow, "Counter-Insurgency, Deindustrialisation and the Political Economy of Ulster Loyalism," in *Who Are "The People?": Unionism, Protestantism and Loyalism in Late Twentieth Century Ireland*, ed. Peter Shirlow and Mark McGovern (London: Pluto, 1997), pp. 176–198.

Whenever Protestant unity looked threatened, unionist leaders used parades to help bolster it. In the early years of Northern Ireland's existence, this threat came from the union appearing secure and relatively peaceful Protestant-Catholic relations. The absence of an immediate danger from perceived Catholic treachery or violence opened the door to labor agitation and class-based political organizing. The ruling UUP feared that working-class Protestants would start to vote on class interests rather than ethnic interests, breaking the cross-class coalition that kept the party in power. The UUP's priority, therefore, was "to keep the Union as the one burning issue."[63] Among their most effective and reliable tools for stoking the flames were parades, which so readily emphasize communal differences and mobilize people along vertical ethnic lines, rather than horizontal class lines.[64]

After World War II, parading entered a period of relative calm. Sectarian conflict was largely dormant and the parades were populated by the middle class, who brought a sense of respectability. Relaxed Catholic-Protestant relations again concerned the UUP leadership, who feared political defection by working-class Protestants.[65] Calls for Protestant unity continued as the powerful unionist government at Stormont ruled Northern Ireland for the benefit of the Protestant majority—to the exclusion of meaningful representation of the Catholic minority.[66] The discriminatory regime came under increasing pressure in the late 1960s as Catholics, inspired by the African American movement, mobilized for civil rights. Once again, Protestants used parades as a form of counter-mobilization: disrupting civil rights marches, provoking sectarian violence, and preventing unionist leaders from making concessions to Catholics protesters.[67] This rise of naked sectarianism and disorder again led the middle and upper classes to abandon parading—a trend that has never reversed.[68]

63. Marc Mulholland, *The Longest War: Northern Ireland's Troubled History* (New York: Oxford University Press, 2002), pp. 28–45 (quotation is from p. 45). Also John F. Harbinson, *The Ulster Unionist Party, 1882–1973: Its Development and Organization* (Belfast: Blackstaff, 1973), p. 166; and Bryan, *Orange Parades*, p. 62.

64. Paraphrasing from Marc Howard Ross, "Psychocultural Interpretations and Dramas: Identity Dynamics in Ethnic Conflict," *Political Psychology* 22, no. 1 (March 2001): 158.

65. Henry Patterson and Eric Kaufmann, *Unionism and Orangeism in Northern Ireland Since 1945: The Decline of the Loyal Family* (Manchester: Manchester University Press, 2007), p. 29; and Henry Patterson, *Ireland Since 1939* (New York: Oxford University Press, 2002), p. 144.

66. John Whyte, "How Much Discrimination Was There Under the Unionist Regime, 1921–68?" in *Contemporary Irish Studies*, ed. Tom Gallagher and James O'Connell (Manchester: Manchester University Press, 1983), pp. 1–36; and Marc Mulholland, "Why Did Unionists Discriminate?" in *From the United Irishmen to Twentieth-Century Unionism: A Festschrift for A.T.Q. Stewart*, ed. Sabine Wichert (Dublin: Four Courts Press, 2004), pp. 187–206.

67. Bryan, *Orange Parades*, pp. 78–87; and Jarman, *Material Conflicts*, pp. 76–79.

68. Bryan, *Orange Parades*, pp. 78, 93. For an analysis of recent trends in the Orange Order's class composition, see Eric P. Kaufmann, *The Orange Order: A Contemporary Northern Irish History* (New York: Oxford University Press, 2007), pp. 269–274.

Through 1968 and 1969, protests, counter-protests, and sectarian tension increased across Northern Ireland. Then, on August 12, 1969, rioting broke out as fifteen thousand members of the Apprentice Boys, with police protection, paraded through Derry.[69] The Battle of the Bogside, as the riot is known, escalated, triggering violence around the country, and is widely considered the start of the Troubles.

Rioting spread throughout the province, and British troops were called in, initially to protect Catholic communities from Protestant violence. But soon Catholics came to see the military as an enemy and vast swaths of urban territory became "no go zones" for the army and police. The Provisional Irish Republican Army (IRA) grew in strength and support among Catholics, as did the Ulster Volunteer Force and Ulster Defence Association (UDA) among working-class Protestants. Violence between republican paramilitaries, loyalist paramilitaries, and the security forces intensified and attacks against civilians increased. In 1972, the most violent year of the Troubles, 470 people were killed and 1,853 bombs were detonated in the province.[70] By then, order in Northern Ireland had collapsed and the British government suspended Stormont, imposing direct rule from Westminster.

The Troubles had three important effects on parading. The introduction of direct rule meant that the Orange Order lost its connections to the levers of powers in Northern Ireland.[71] Parades were no longer a "ritual of state" and instead came to represent Protestant communal defense. An indication of this shift is the rise of blood and thunder marching bands associated with loyalist paramilitaries in working-class neighborhoods.[72] Parades became rowdier and lost any remaining "respectability." Finally, as Catholic families in Protestant-majority neighborhoods were intimidated from their homes, and vice versa, the Troubles created more firmly defined ethnic neighborhoods with recognizable boundaries. Parades thus came to be seen as violations of those boundaries by Catholic residents, and opposition to them increased.[73]

---

69. Richard Bourke, *Peace in Ireland: The War of Ideas* (London: Pimlico, 2003), pp. 99–102; Niall Ó Dochartaigh, *From Civil Rights to Armalites: Derry and the Birth of the Irish Troubles* (Cork: Cork University Press, 1997), pp. 98–133; and Simon Prince and Geoffrey Warner, *Belfast and Derry in Revolt: A New History of the Start of the Troubles* (Dublin: Irish Academic Press, 2012), pp. 179–206. Jarman, *Material Conflicts*, p. 78, argues that though "the cycle of parades in 1968–70 did not cause the Troubles…they proved critical in opening up the fracture zones in Northern Irish life that had been obscured and ignored for so long."

70. Police Service of Northern Ireland, "Police Recorded Security Statistics in Northern Ireland," November 2015, http://www.psni.police.uk/index/updates/updates_statistics/updates_security_situation_statistics.htm, accessed January 7, 2016.

71. Bryan, *Orange Parades*, p. 78.

72. Ibid., p. 92.

73. Ibid., p. 95.

Catholic resistance to parades through their neighborhoods really exploded in the 1990s, as the peace process developed.[74] These protest movements emerged from long-simmering opposition to parades among Catholics, but the confrontations they provoked were also politically and strategically valuable opportunities for both unionist and nationalist political elites. Parading disputes created a stage on which community leaders could demonstrate their strength and legitimacy to constituents. Protestant leaders, writes Feargal Cochrane, used these conflicts "to display their loyalist credentials and gain valuable publicity as stout 'defenders of the Union.'"[75] Sinn Féin, writes Martyn Frampton, used "emotion-laden, street activism" to appear as "the strident voice of the northern nationalist community, standing in the face of apparent Unionist aggression."[76] Political elites on both sides stood to gain support from this friction.[77]

The most well-known parading dispute occurred from 1995 to 2000 over a route in the small city of Portadown, County Armagh. In 1995, in response to vigorous protests by residents, the Orange Order's annual parade to and from Drumcree Church was prohibited from passing through the Catholic neighborhood along the Garvaghy Road. After a tense three-day standoff between tens of thousands of Protestants and security forces, a compromise was struck and the members of the local Orange lodge were permitted to complete their parade. In 1996, the police again sided with the residents of the Garvaghy Road and announced that the parade had to be rerouted elsewhere. But after Protestants across the province responded with protests and violence, the police reversed their decision. The following year, after death threats against Catholics, security forces barricaded the neighborhood to allow the parade through. The Garvaghy Road residents finally succeeded in 1998 and ever since the police have blocked parades from entering the area.[78]

---

74. Neil Jarman and Dominic Bryan, *Parade and Protest: A Discussion of Parading Disputes in Northern Ireland* (Colraine, UK: Centre for the Study of Conflict, University of Ulster, 1996); and Dominic Bryan, "Parade Disputes and the Peace Process," *Peace Review* 13, no. 1 (2001): 43–49.

75. Feargal Cochrane, *Unionist Politics and the Politics of Unionism Since the Anglo-Irish Agreement* (Cork: Cork University Press, 1997), p. 338.

76. Frampton, *The Long March*, p. 126.

77. I explore the attitudes of Protestant elites (elected officials and clergy members) toward parades in Jonathan S. Blake, "Ethnic Elites and Rituals of Provocation: Politicians, Pastors, and Paramilitaries in Northern Ireland," *Terrorism and Political Violence* (Abingdon: Taylor & Francis, forthcoming).

78. See Dominic Bryan, T. G. Fraser, and Seamus Dunn, *Political Rituals: Loyalist Parades in Portadown* (Colraine, UK: Centre for the Study of Conflict, University of Ulster, 1995); and Chris Ryder and Vincent Kearney, *Drumcree: The Orange Order's Last Stand* (London: Methuen, 2001).

LOYALIST PARADING TODAY

Parading remains a major communal activity among Protestants. From April 1, 2016, to March 31, 2017, the most recent available data, there were 4,643 parades in Northern Ireland, 56 percent of which were organized by the Protestant community (2,598 parades). By contrast, only 3 percent were organized by the Catholic community (140 parades).[79] As figure 1.1 demonstrates, the number of Protestant parades, which have long been the vast majority, has steadily increased since the mid-1980s, when systematic counting began.

Estimates of the number of participants are less exact, but it is a significant number of people. There are approximately forty thousand men in the Orange Order, nine thousand men in the Apprentice Boys of Derry (a similar organization), and twenty-nine thousand people in marching bands.[80]

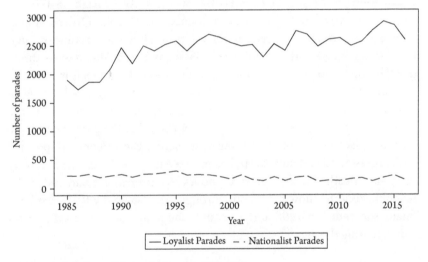

Figure 1.1: Loyalist and Nationalist Parades, 1985–2016
(Sources: Royal Ulster Constabulary and Police Service of Northern Ireland, 1985–2000; Parades Commission, 2001–2016)

79. The remaining 41 percent were classified as "other," which includes "charity, civic, rural and sporting events, as well as church parades." Parades Commission for Northern Ireland, *Annual Report and Financial Statements for the Year Ended 31 March 2017* (Norwich, UK: The Stationary Office, 2017), p. 8.

80. James W. McAuley, Jonathan Tonge, and Andrew Mycock, *Loyal to the Core?: Orangeism and Britishness in Northern Ireland* (Dublin: Irish Academic Press, 2011), p. 1; interview with Apprentice Boys of Derry senior leader, Derry/Londonderry; and Department of Culture, Arts and Leisure, *Marching Bands in Northern Ireland* (Belfast: Department of Culture, Arts and Leisure, 2012), p. 6. RSM McClure Watters, "The Socio-Economic Impact of the Traditional Protestant Parading Sector in Northern Ireland," May 2013, p. 2, estimates there are 34,650 men in the Orange Order, 7,425 men in Apprentice Boys of Derry, and 25,740 band members. Northern Ireland Youth Forum, *Sons of Ulster: Exploring Loyalist Band Members Attitudes Towards Culture, Identity, and Heritage* (Belfast: Northern Ireland Youth Forum, 2013), pp. 4–5,

Due to unknown overlapping membership among the organizations, only a rough calculation of the total number is possible, but I estimate that around 7 to 8 percent of Protestants currently participate in loyalist parades. Among Protestant males, who make up the vast majority of parade participants, about 15 to 17 percent parade.[81]

Compared with other forms of contentious collective action in Northern Ireland, these participation rates are notable. According to a 2005 survey, in the previous two or three years only 2 percent of respondents took part in a strike, 5 percent attended a political meeting, 5 percent took part in a "demonstration, picket or march," and 32 percent signed a petition.[82] These comparisons resonate with Tonge, McAuley, and Mycock's finding that, despite a loss in members in recent decades, the Orange Order alone "still more than quadruples the combined memberships of all Northern Ireland's political parties."[83]

estimates there are 30,000 band members. These figures may include international membership, but the vast majority are in Northern Ireland. Since all members of the Royal Black Institution and Royal Arch Purple are also members of the Orange Order, I do not include their membership figures here.

81. The higher estimates are based on the assumption that 10 percent of participants have overlapping membership in two organizations (74,200 total participants); the lower estimates assume one-third overlap (65,333 total participants). To be specific, I take the sum of the three membership numbers and subtract the overlapping percent of band members and Apprentice Boys to account for multiple memberships. Note that the estimated percentages of Protestant males who parade are upper-bounds because they do not try to subtract the female band members. The survey I conducted, while not nationally representative, finds that 9 percent of participants have been in both loyal orders and bands, but not necessarily at the same time. Among the current participants I interviewed (again, not a representative sample), 32 percent are in more than one parading organization. Bryan, *Orange Parades*, p. 115, estimates that over half of Apprentice Boys members are also in the Orange Order. Given these estimates, between one-tenth and one-third overlap seems like a reasonable assumption. If we assume that fully half of band members and Apprentice Boys are also in the Orange Order (59,000 total participants), participation rates are 7 percent of Protestants and 14 percent of Protestant males.

The population figures, 875,717 Protestants and 424,768 Protestant males, are from the 2011 Northern Ireland Census, "Table DC2115NI: Religion or Religion Brought Up in by Age by Sex," http://www.ninis2.nisra.gov.uk/Download/Census%202011_Excel/2011/DC2117NI.xls, accessed October 29, 2013. Comprehensive, national data on parade participation is unavailable. My survey finds that 12 percent of Protestant men are current parade participants and 31 percent have been at some point of their adult lives. The Northern Ireland General Election Survey, which is representative of the electorate, asks about Orange Order membership, but not about the other loyal orders or marching bands. In 2015, 20 percent of Protestant males in the sample were members of the Orange Order, and in 2017, 13 percent were. Jonathan Tonge, *Northern Ireland General Election Survey, 2015*, distributed by UK Data Service, 2016, doi: 10.5255/UKDA-SN-7523-1; and Jonathan Tonge, *Northern Ireland General Election Survey, 2017*, distributed by UK Data Service, 2017, doi:10.5255/UKDA-SN-8234-1.

82. ARK, *Northern Ireland Life and Times Survey 2005*, distributed by ARK, www.ark.ac.uk/nilt/2005/Democratic_Participation, accessed August 15, 2014.

83. McAuley, Tonge, and Mycock, *Loyal to the Core?* p. 1.

Loyal Orders, Marching Bands, and Cheering Crowds

Broadly, there are two types of parading organizations: the loyal orders and marching bands. The loyal orders are all-male fraternal orders dedicated to the promotion of Protestant culture and the maintenance of Northern Ireland's place in the United Kingdom. They are seen by many Protestants as the embodiment of the community's politics and values. The three main orders are the Orange Order, the Royal Black Institution, and the Apprentice Boys of Derry.[84] The Orange Order is the largest and most prominent loyal order. Though its membership and political power have declined since the mid-twentieth century, it still holds significant influence within unionist politics. A recent survey of members of the Democratic Unionist Party (DUP), Northern Ireland's largest political party, shows that 35 percent are Orangemen. Among DUP elected officials, the proportion increases to 54 percent.[85]

The Orange Order is a hierarchical organization with four levels: Grand Orange Lodge of Ireland, County Lodges, District Lodges, and private lodges.[86] The fourteen hundred private lodges are most important to the lives of members. Each lodge has its own name and number—for example, Pride of Ballymacarrett Loyal Orange Lodge (LOL) 1075 or Ulster Defenders of the Realm LOL 710—and its own bylaws and budget. They also almost all have a banner that they carry on parade, which represents something of importance to the lodge. Popular images include King William III at the Battle of the Boyne, the Crown and Bible, biblical scenes, churches and other places, and portraits of deceased members.[87] When Orangemen parade, they generally parade with their lodge, unless they hold a leadership role at the district, county, or national level and join that group in the parade.

The Royal Black Institution is a higher "degree" of the Orange Order. Although it is an independent organization, one must first be a member of the Orange Order to join. It is seen as more centered on religion than politics. This is reflected in its banners, which focus on scenes and images

84. There are also smaller orders including the Royal Arch Purple, the Independent Orange Order, and the Orange Order's all-female sister organization, the Association of Loyal Orangewomen of Ireland.

85. Jonathan Tonge, Máire Braniff, Thomas Hennessey, James W. McAuley, and Sophie A. Whiting, *The Democratic Unionist Party: From Protest to Power* (Oxford: Oxford University Press, 2014), pp. 139, 149–152.

86. Though Grand Lodge is at the top, it has only limited power over the organization and its members. Bryan, *Orange Parades*, pp. 97, 101–103. The organization as a whole has only a handful of paid employees and functions almost entirely on a volunteer basis.

87. Jarman, *Material Conflicts*, pp. 172–184.

from the Bible.[88] The Apprentice Boys of Derry is a separate organization that is dedicated to commemorating the 1688–1689 siege of Derry by forces loyal to James II.[89] Thus their main parades take place in that city to mark the beginning and end of the siege. But they also hold parades in the rest of the province, including "feeder parades," when they march from a meeting point to the bus that takes them to Derry/Londonderry.[90] The organization's respect for the city of Derry/Londonderry and the reality that the city is majority Catholic has pushed the Apprentice Boys toward a more pragmatic strategy dealing with opposition to their parades than the Orange Order, which tends to take uncompromising stances.

Marching bands are the second type of parading organization. While some of the roughly six hundred bands[91] are quite musically talented, most are not. The majority of bands are known as blood and thunder bands because the bass drummer's hands often bleed after hours of smashing the drum with all his might. Needless to say, blood and thunder bands are noted more for their volume than skill. The general trend in loyalist parading since the 1970s has been the rising prominence of bands, particularly blood and thunder bands.[92] Many people associate bands with the loyalist paramilitaries, and during the Troubles they were often closely linked. The extent of their current ties, however, is debated. Today, although both the loyal orders and bands have a reputation for sectarianism in many quarters, bands are seen as particularly hateful and aggressive. Band members are viewed by many as "thugs" out to offend Catholics by flying loyalist paramilitary flags, carrying banners commemorating paramilitary members, and performing paramilitary and anti-Catholic tunes.[93] Finally, unlike the main loyal orders, some bands have female members, though bands remain a decidedly male affair.

Both loyal orders and bands do more besides parade. Loyal orders hold regular meetings of their members, and bands hold regular practices. They both host social events that are often open to the entire community such as parties, barbecues, and fundraisers for themselves and

---

88. Ibid., pp. 184–187.

89. Bryan, *Orange Parades*, pp. 114–115.

90. The city's official name by royal charter, Londonderry, is preferred by many Protestants. Catholics, and in practice many Protestants too, call it Derry.

91. Department of Culture, Arts and Leisure, *Marching Bands in Northern Ireland*, p. 12.

92. Bryan, *Orange Parades*, p. 145; and McAuley, *Very British Rebels?* p. 112–114.

93. Popular loyalist band tunes include "The Billy Boys," with the lyrics "We're up to our necks in Fenian blood / Surrender or you'll die," and "No Pope of Rome," with the lyrics "Oh give me a home / Where there's no Pope of Rome / Where there's nothing but Protestants stay. … No chapels to sadden my eyes / No nuns and no priests and no Rosary beads / Every day is the Twelfth of July." Available at http://rangerspedia.org/index.php/ No_Pope_Of_Rome, accessed July 7, 2014.

for charities.[94] For both types of organizations, however, parading is their raison d'être.

There are important differences between and among the loyal orders and bands, some of which might affect who joins and why.[95] But they share core features, values, and interests, and sit together on the wider spectrum of "unionist and loyalist contention."[96] It is useful, therefore, to consider these various organizations as a single movement. In this book, I am interested in mobilization in the broader loyalist parading movement rather than a specific organization.[97] As a result, I refer to parade participation as parading with either a loyal order or a band, without distinction.

Yet parades are composed of more than just the marchers. Parades are large, heterogeneous events composed of multiple actors and groups, all of which take part in their own way (including paraders, spectators, protesters, police, journalists, passersby, and visiting researchers).[98] Among Protestants, spectators are the biggest group, though there are not precise counts of the people who line the streets to watch and cheer. Many of the twenty-five hundred parades each year have very few spectators—some can march a long time without seeing a soul. But on the Twelfth, some five hundred thousand people—roughly one-quarter of the entire population of Northern Ireland—go to watch parades in nineteen cities and towns throughout the province.[99] Between marching and spectating, nearly two-thirds of Protestants take part in the Twelfth parades.[100]

94. Ruth Dudley Edwards, *The Faithful Tribe: An Intimate Portrait of the Loyal Institutions* (London: HarperCollins, 2000), focuses on the Orange Order's social role in her sympathetic study.

95. Some scholars have developed typologies to explain differences within the Orange Order itself. Jarman, *Material Conflicts*, p. 117, defines "two poles of 'Orangeism'": "rough" and "respectable," noting however that "both parts are always present." While Kaufmann, *The Orange Order*, esp. pp. 11–15, divides the membership into "rebels" and "traditionalists."

96. Bryan, *Orange Parades*, p. 116; the quotation is from Lorenzo Bosi and Gianluca De Fazio, "Contextualizing the Troubles: Investigating Deeply Divided Societies Through Social Movements Research," in *The Troubles in Northern Ireland and Theories of Social Movements*, ed. Lorenzo Bosi and Gianluca De Fazio (Amsterdam: Amsterdam University Press, 2017), p. 22.

97. For the distinction between a social movement and a social movement organization, see John D. McCarthy and Mayer N. Zald, "Resource Mobilization and Social Movements: A Partial Theory," *American Journal of Sociology* 82, no. 6 (May 1977): 1212–1241.

98. On the many actors involved in public demonstrations, see Olivier Fillieule, "The Independent Psychological Effects of Participation in Demonstrations," *Mobilization* 17, no. 3 (September 2012): 236; and Olivier Fillieule and Danielle Tartakowsky, *Demonstrations*, trans. Phyllis Aronoff and Howard Scott (Halifax: Fernwood, 2013), pp. 16–17. On how social movements construct their audiences, see Kathleen Blee and Amy McDowell, "Social Movement Audiences," *Sociological Forum* 27, no. 1 (March 2012): 1–20.

99. Smithey, *Unionists, Loyalists, and Conflict Transformation*, p. 129; and David Cairns, "The Object of Sectarianism: The Material Reality of Sectarianism in Ulster Loyalism," *Journal of the Royal Anthropological Institute* 6, no. 3 (September 2000): 441.

100. This figure includes a number of marching bands and spectators that travel from Scotland, so it is likely a slight overestimate of the proportion of Northern Irish Protestants.

Spectators are very much part of the event. Beyond applauding (and drinking), they often sing and sometimes dance along to the bands. They even dress in their own symbol-laden uniforms. Many parade spectators wear clothing that is red, white, and blue, often with the Union Jack emblazoned on it; others wear the jerseys of "Protestant" sports teams, such as the Glasgow Rangers, Northern Ireland Football, Ulster Rugby, or Linfield Football Club.[101] The crowd is full of people carrying, waving, or wearing flags, mostly the British flag, but also the Northern Ireland banner, the "historic" UVF flag, or other Protestant symbols.[102] Some spectators even walk alongside the parade for much of its route—often friends and fans following a particular band.

The audience's loud, celebratory behavior helps create the carnivalesque atmosphere of parades. The size of the crowd also amplifies the parades' message. It shows off the number of enthusiastic (perhaps mobilizable) Protestants who support the union. Thus, in some respects, the line between marchers and spectators can begin to blur.[103] Through their active spectating, the audience members demonstrate that participation in a movement can take many forms with varying levels of involvement, commitment, and sacrifice.[104]

Disputed Parades

The annual parading season, which runs from Easter to August, reignites debates over a host of parade-related topics. The most controversial parades

(An informal count of bands in the 2005 Belfast Twelfth by Dominic Bryan shows that approximately twenty-two of seventy-one bands were from Scotland. Data in possession of author.) However, it matches my survey, which finds that 69 percent of respondents either paraded or attended a parade in the previous year.

101. Sports and sports teams in Northern Ireland tend to be associated with one national community or the other. See Alan Bairner, "Still Taking Sides: Sport, Leisure and Identity," in *Northern Ireland After the Troubles: A Society in Transition*, ed. Colin Coulter and Michael Murray (Manchester: Manchester University Press, 2008), pp. 215–231.

102. See also the description of audience clothing and flags in Bryan, *Orange Parades*, pp. 143, 150.

103. Peter Burke, "Co-memorations: Performing the Past," in *Performing the Past: Memory, History, and Identity in Modern Europe*, ed. Karin Tilmans, Frank van Vree, and Jay Winter (Amsterdam: Amsterdam University Press, 2010), p. 116, notes, "The sharpest line is not between performers and spectators but between the immediate spectators, present on stage, and the remote spectators, viewing the marches on television or in the photographs in the next day's newspaper." Also from a performative perspective, see Lee Ann Fujii, "The Puzzle of Extra-Lethal Violence," *Perspectives on Politics* 11, no. 2 (June 2013): 414. Some scholars of ritual even define members of the audience as participants. See Clifford Geertz, "Religion as a Cultural System," in *The Interpretation of Cultures* (New York: Basic Books, 1973), pp. 114–118; Robert Bocock, *Ritual in Industrial Society: A Sociological Analysis of Ritualism in Modern England* (London: George Allen & Unwin, 1974), p. 59; and Mabel Berezin, *Making the Fascist Self: The Political Culture of Interwar Italy* (Ithaca: Cornell University Press, 1997), p. 250.

104. See Gregory L. Wiltfang and Doug McAdam, "The Costs and Risks of Social Activism: A Study of Sanctuary Movement Activism," *Social Forces* 69, no. 4 (June 1991): 987–1010.

are known colloquially as "contentious parades" and are designated as such by the Parades Commission, the independent statutory body charged with regulating parades.[105] Thus the term is used in Northern Ireland to describe the subset of parades that are disputed. Throughout my analysis, however, I use "contentious" to mean claim-making that bears on the rights and interests of others.[106] By this usage, all parades, whether contested or not, are "contentious performances."[107] To avoid confusion, what people in Northern Ireland call a "contentious parade," I will call a "disputed," "contested," "sensitive," or "controversial" parade.

In 2016–2017, the Parades Commission designated 363 parades as disputed (8 percent of the total).[108] Almost all of these were organized by Protestant organizations (93 percent), as figure 1.2 shows, and many of them were organized by two specific groups: the Orange Order in Portadown, who have made a perfunctory effort to complete their march each Sunday since 1998, and the nightly parades in North Belfast to protest the 2013 route prohibition.[109] Though disputed parades are just a fraction of the total, they dominate media coverage, public discussions, and the perceptions of many citizens and international observers. As is common in political conflict, it is the actions of a small minority that set the tone and determine the course of events.

The most common dispute over a specific parade is the route it takes, since some pass by or through Catholic neighborhoods or towns. The paraders insist that marching on their traditional routes is a civil right, but many of the Catholic residents see parading by their homes and churches as triumphalist, hateful, and transgressive. As anthropologist Allen Feldman argues, it "transforms the adjacent community into an involuntary audience

105. The Parades Commission defines contentious parades as "those that are considered as having the potential of raising concerns and community tensions, and which consequently are considered in more detail by the Parades Commission." Parades Commission for Northern Ireland, *Annual Report and Financial Statements for the Year Ended 31 March 2012* (Norwich, UK: The Stationary Office, 2012), p. 9. Starting in the 2014 *Annual Report*, the Parades Commission changed the term to "sensitive parades" (p. 8). On the Parades Commission, see Ciarán O'Kelly and Dominic Bryan, "The Regulation of Public Space in Northern Ireland," *Irish Political Studies* 22, no. 4 (December 2007): 565–584; and Dawn Walsh, "Northern Ireland and the Independent Parades Commission: Delegation and Legitimacy," *Irish Political Studies* 30, no. 1 (2015): 20–40.

106. Doug McAdam, Sidney Tarrow, and Charles Tilly, *Dynamics of Contention* (New York: Cambridge University Press, 2001), p. 5.

107. Charles Tilly, *Contentious Performances* (New York: Cambridge University Press, 2008). Tilly analyzes Irish contention in the eighteenth and nineteenth centuries, including parading, on pp. 163–173.

108. Parades Commission, *Annual Report 2017*, p. 8. The Parades Commission placed restrictions on 94 percent of sensitive parades, such as changing the route or imposing restrictions on timing, music, size, or the number of supporters.

109. These nightly parades took place between July 2013 and September 2016, which explains the large spike on the right side of figure 1.2.

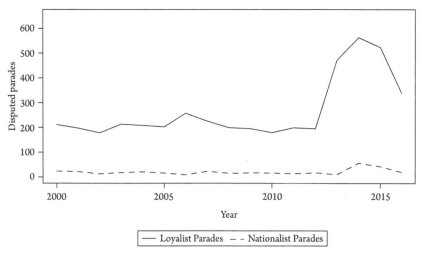

Figure 1.2: Disputed Parades, 2000–2016
(Source: Parades Commission of Northern Ireland)

and an object of defilement through the aggressive display of political symbols and music."[110] The sectarian disagreement is clearly evident in public opinion: while 73 percent of Catholics in a 2015 survey stated that parades should not be allowed in Catholic neighborhoods, only 5 percent of Protestants agreed. Conversely, while 59 percent of Protestants stated that the parades should be allowed to march anywhere they like, only 1 percent of Catholics felt similarly.[111]

Although the dispute over the route of the Drumcree parade in Portadown remains ongoing, the most contested parade during the time of my research was in North Belfast. For years, Catholics from the Ardoyne neighborhood protested and rioted in response to parades on a road adjacent to their community.[112] Against the backdrop of increasingly severe riots following parades in recent years, the failure to reach an agreement

110. Allen Feldman, *Formations of Violence: The Narrative of the Body and Political Terror in Northern Ireland* (Chicago: University of Chicago Press, 1991), p. 29.

111. Jocelyn Evans and Jonathan Tonge, "Religious, Political, and Geographical Determinants of Attitudes to Protestant Parades in Northern Ireland," *Politics and Religion* 10, no. 4 (December 2017): 795.

112. North Belfast was the parliamentary constituency with the second most number of deaths during the Troubles (neighboring West Belfast had the most). But even in North Belfast, Ardoyne stood out as particularly bloody—it was a major center of IRA activity and had one of the highest rates of killings in Northern Ireland. The neighborhood was also the site of one of the other major post-Troubles controversies, the Holy Cross dispute in 2001–2002, over the location of a Catholic girls primary school in the Protestant part of the area. See David McKittrick, Seamus Kelters, Brian Feeney, and Chris Thorton, *Lost Lives: The Stories of the Men, Women and Children Who Died as a Result of the Northern Ireland Troubles* (Edinburgh: Mainstream, 1999), p. 1482; and Ardoyne Commemoration Project, *Ardoyne: The Untold Truth* (Belfast: Beyond the Pale Publications, 2002).

between the Orange Order and Ardoyne residents' groups led the Parades Commission to prohibit part of the route on July 12, 2013. The decision was followed by several nights of rioting by Protestants, the establishment of a full-time protest camp near the interface, and three years of nightly protests by parading right up until a police blockade. The protests ended in September 2016, when an agreement was reached between the local Orange lodges and a local Catholic residents association.[113]

Parades can also become disputed because of the behavior of paraders or supporters. For example, parades on Belfast's lower Ormeau Road became hotly contested in the mid-1990s after several Orangemen and bandsmen mocked the murder of five Catholic civilians by the UDA as they paraded by the site of their massacre.[114] Parades passing St. Patrick's Catholic Church in Belfast became controversial after a band was filmed marching in circles and allegedly playing an anti-Catholic song in front of the church during the 2012 Twelfth parade. The song, "The Famine Song," is the same tune as the Beach Boys' classic "Sloop John B," but with modified lyrics, such as "the famine's over, why don't you go home?"[115] The band, the Young Conway Volunteers, maintained that they were playing the Beach Boys' version, but the Catholic community did not believe it.

The most notable negative consequence of disputed parades is the occurrence of sectarian violence. Although only a small number of parades turn violent, there have been instances of public disorder every year since the Agreement, including significant riots in 2005, 2010, 2011, 2012, 2013, and 2015.[116] Between July 2012 and September 2013, for example, 682 police

113. "Twaddell: Agreement Reached over Long-Running Parade Dispute," *BBC News Online*, September 24, 2016, http://www.bbc.com/news/uk-northern-ireland-37458065.

114. Bryan, *Orange Parades*, p. 134.

115. A Scottish court ruled that the song, associated with Glasgow Rangers Football Club supporters, is racist. For more details on the controversy, see "Q&A: How St Patrick's Became a Flashpoint," *BBC News Online*, August 30, 2012, http://www.bbc.co.uk/news/uk-northern-ireland-19423910, accessed February 21, 2014.

116. There was an annual average of eighteen instances of public disorder reported by the police from 1998 to 2009. Police Service of Northern Ireland, "Parades with Disorder, 1990–2009," spreadsheet in possession of author. For accounts of recent riots, see "80 Officers Injured During Riot," *BBC News Online*, July 13, 2005; "50 Police Officers Injured in Belfast Riots," *The Guardian*, September 12, 2005; Haroon Siddique, "Belfast Riots Continue for Third Night," *The Guardian*, July 14, 2010; Conor Humphries and Ian Graham, "Riots Erupt in Northern Ireland after Protestant Marches," *Reuters*, July 13, 2011; Michael McHugh, "Belfast Riots: 20 PSNI Officers Injured as Violence Erupts in Ardoyne after Orange Parade," *Belfast Telegraph*, July 13, 2012; "Three Arrests after Belfast Parade Trouble," *BBC News Online*, August 26, 2012; Henry McDonald and Ben Quinn, "Police in Belfast Fire Plastic Bullets to Quell Riots," *The Guardian*, July 12, 2013; "Twelfth 2015: Third Night of Rioting in North Belfast—Loyalists 'Trash' Retirement Home, 'Wreck' Own Community," *Belfast Telegraph*, July 16, 2015.

officers were injured at parades and related protests and disorder.[117] The two general dynamics of violence are that Catholics riot against the parade or the police after the parade has passed by with heavy police (and until 2006, military) protection, or Protestant crowds attack the police who have blocked the parade route.

Even without outbreaks of violence, there are serious social and political repercussions to disputed parades. While these disputes might seem like a local affair, the symbolism involved makes them a national political issue that impedes reconciliation between Catholics and Protestants. In the halls of Stormont, parties are continually deadlocked over the issue. On the streets, communal tensions rise during the marching season, with survey evidence showing that fear of the other community increases during that period.[118] Paramilitary groups on both sides exploit the marching season to mobilize new members and demonstrate their continued presence.[119] Further disruptions to normal life are caused by the heavy security at disputed parades. Contested parades often include the presence of police, many in full riot gear, and armored police Land Rovers barricading streets. In the eyes of many residents, parades transform their neighborhoods into temporary battle zones.

CONCLUSION

Parade politics, this chapter has shown, are nothing new. Politics and parading have been intertwined since the Orange Order took its first step in 1796. While at various points and in various places parades have been more controversial and met with more opposition, they have always made contentious claims—on the state and the Catholic population, in particular. Today, they make those claims from the streets of a country with largely stable, but not yet consolidated, ethnic peace. Parades, in fact, are one of the major strains on the peace process. By representing the pride and position of Protestants while denigrating Catholics, parades frequently test the limits of compromise and reconciliation in communities darkened by the shadow of peace walls and in the wood-paneled chambers of Stormont alike.

117. Nolan, *Northern Ireland Peace Monitoring Report, Number 3*, p. 159. See also Henry McDonald, "25% of Northern Ireland Riot Police Hurt in Loyalist Clashes in One Year," *The Guardian*, May 28, 2014.

118. Shirlow and Murtagh, *Belfast*, p. 94.

119. Paul Nolan, *Northern Ireland Peace Monitoring Report, Number 1* (Belfast: Community Relations Council, 2012), pp. 45, 47, 73, 78; and Paul Nolan, *Northern Ireland Peace Monitoring Report, Number 2* (Belfast: Community Relations Council, 2013), pp. 62, 168.

A theme carried through this long history up until the present day is the role of political elites in shaping the character and consequences of parades. As I described, both Protestant and Catholic political elites use parades as instruments of political power, employing them to increase their own popularity and to polarize the electorate into ethnic blocs. This is a compelling account of the politics of parades and is consistent with evidence from other divided societies.[120] Yet it leaves important questions unanswered. In particular, referring only to elite interests cannot answer the "insistent question of why the followers follow."[121] While elite manipulation remains the most prominent theory of contentious rituals, it does not explain mass participation.

What is needed, then, is an explanation that accounts for why ordinary people decide to participate in events with divisive consequences for politics and society, such as the parades described in this chapter. To understand what motivates the average participant, we must turn to the characteristics and views of the participants themselves. The following chapters will do just that.

---

120. For example, Wilkinson, *Votes and Violence*; Paul R. Brass, *Theft of an Idol: Text and Context in the Representation of Collective Violence* (Princeton: Princeton University Press, 1997); and Rogers Brubaker and David D. Laitin, "Ethnic and Nationalist Violence," *Annual Review of Sociology* 24 (1998): 433.

121. Horowitz, *Ethnic Groups in Conflict*, p. 140. Also Stathis N. Kalyvas, "The Ontology of 'Political Violence': Action and Identity in Civil Wars," *Perspectives on Politics* 1, no. 3 (September 2003): 475–494.

CHAPTER 2

For God and Ulster, Self-Interest, or Social Networks?

"Anti-Catholic," declared *An Phoblacht*, Sinn Féin's party organ. The Orange Order, the article continued, is "a racist organisa-tion": "inflammatory, sectarian and divisive."[1]

"The vast majority of members of the loyal institutions are pro-Protestant, not anti-Catholic," rebutted a columnist in the *Belfast Telegraph*. "What the ordinary, decent Orangeman wants is to be allowed to demonstrate his pride in his culture and heritage."[2]

These quotes encapsulate the two dominant views within Northern Ireland on why tens of thousands of Protestants choose to parade. The first, held mainly by Catholics (but also by some Protestant critics of parading), sees paraders as exceptionally sectarian and hateful. The second, held mainly by Protestants, sees paraders as exceptionally proud of and loyal to God and Ulster. The two perspectives, contrary as they are, share an under-lying logic. According to both, people are motivated to parade by their exceptionally strong attitudes and ideas. One says paraders are standout bigots, the other, standout patriots: either way, paraders' beliefs stand out from the crowd.

This is certainly one possible explanation for participation in parades. But this argument—the idealist model, whereby people act on their fully articulated thoughts and ideals—has fallen out of favor with many close

1. Laura Friel, "Twelfth Speeches Expose Orange Order Agenda," *An Phoblacht* (Dublin), July 17, 2008.
2. Ruth Dudley Edwards, "Proud Orangemen Are Pro-Protestant, Not Anti-Catholic," *Belfast Telegraph*, June 15, 2015.

observers of contentious politics and other collective action. Rather than attitudes, scholars of collective participation in recent years have looked to two alternative explanations. One, the rationalist explanation, suggests that people take part in collective action in order to receive direct and specific material rewards. This model locates the roots of collective participation in the incentives and disincentives offered to participants. The second, the structuralist explanation, argues that what matters are the factors that expose people to potential participation opportunities and pull them into the collective action. This model identifies the origins of participation in, above all, a person's social networks, the people who could introduce him or her to an activity.

The three explanations—ideas, incentives, and structures—provide us plausible accounts of participation in loyalist parades. Each narrates a straightforward story of why some Protestants opt to don an orange collarette or raise a flute to their lips while many others do not. According to the idealist model, paraders are more anti-Catholic and/or pro-Protestant than non-paraders. According to the rational choice model, paraders receive selective benefits that nonparticipants do not and/or would have had to pay some price for shirking parade participation. And according to the structural model, paraders had pre-existing social ties to parading that non-paraders do not, and paraders have personal histories and circumstances that do not impede participation.

In the chapters that follow this one, I will suggest that participation is less straightforward than any of these dominant models suppose. In their place, I will propose an alternative model of action that focuses on the intrinsic benefits that are inherent in participating in a meaningful and fun collective ritual with friends and family. But before presenting the evidence for this view of parade participation, I first evaluate the major arguments found in Northern Irish debates on parading and the academic research on contentious politics generally.

To do so rigorously, I introduce novel quantitative and qualitative data on parade participants *and* comparable nonparticipants. Collected over the course of eight months of field research, these original data allow me to isolate similarities and differences between the two groups, something previous research could not do. Existing research on loyalist parades, as well as other "cultural forms of political expression," is based on data from participants; nonparticipants are ignored.[3] We obviously cannot compare one

3. Neil Jarman, *Material Conflicts: Parades and Visual Displays in Northern Ireland* (Oxford: Berg, 1997); Dominic Bryan, *Orange Parades: The Politics of Ritual, Tradition, and Control* (London: Pluto, 2000); Eric P. Kaufmann, *The Orange Order: A Contemporary Northern Irish History* (New York: Oxford University Press, 2007); Gordon Ramsey, *Music, Emotion and*

group to the other when we only have data on one of them. This is a form of selection bias, a methodological shortcoming that can affect the conclusions of a study.[4] By only studying the "positive" cases (people who choose to participate), we do not know whether or how they differ from the "negative" cases (people who do not choose to participate). Consequently, we cannot identify which factors are associated with participation and which are not.

Finding comparable nonparticipants, however, is not always so easy. Even the most systematic, methodologically sophisticated studies of participants in cultural contentious politics, such as Verta Taylor and coauthors' research on same-sex weddings in San Francisco, often cannot do it.[5] I address this problem by taking advantage of Belfast's sectarian housing segregation. Rather than survey only parade participants, I sampled 228 male residents of nine Protestant neighborhoods. Since Protestants tend to live in neighborhoods with other Protestants, data collected from a random selection of people in these neighborhoods yield parade participants as well as Protestant nonparticipants.

Taking a random selection of residents of a particular area increased the likelihood that the sampled participants and nonparticipants are similar in

Identity in Ulster Marching Bands: Flutes, Drums and Loyal Sons (Bern: Peter Lang, 2011); and James W. McAuley, Jonathan Tonge, and Andrew Mycock, *Loyal to the Core?: Orangeism and Britishness in Northern Ireland* (Dublin: Irish Academic Press, 2011). For other cases of contentious cultural action, see Leila J. Rupp and Verta Taylor, *Drag Queens at the 801 Cabaret* (Chicago: University of Chicago Press, 2003); Verta Taylor, Leila J. Rupp, and Joshua Gamson, "Performing Protest: Drag Shows as Tactical Repertoires of the Gay and Lesbian Movement," *Research in Social Movements, Conflicts, and Change* 25 (2004): 105–137 (quotation is from p. 106); Suzanne Staggenborg and Amy Lang, "Culture and Ritual in the Montreal Women's Movement," *Social Movement Studies* 6, no. 2 (September 2007): 177–194; and Verta Taylor, Katrina Kimport, Nella Van Dyke, and Ellen Ann Andersen, "Culture and Mobilization: Tactical Repertoires, Same-Sex Weddings, and the Impact on Gay Activism," *American Sociological Review* 74, no. 6 (December 2009): 865–890. Macro level studies that focus on the event, rather than the individual, also fail to sample comparable negative cases, that is, non-events. See Steven I. Wilkinson, *Votes and Violence: Electoral Competition and Ethnic Riots in India* (New York: Cambridge University Press, 2004), pp. 38–39; though Wilkinson addresses the issue in Steven I. Wilkinson, "Which Group Identities Lead to Most Violence?: Evidence from India," in *Order, Conflict, and Violence,* ed. Stathis N. Kalyvas, Ian Shapiro, and Tarek Masoud (New York: Cambridge University Press, 2008), pp. 271–300.

4. Barbara Geddes, "How the Cases You Choose Affect the Answers You Get: Selection Bias in Comparative Politics," *Political Analysis* 2, no. 1 (1990): 131–150; and Gary King, Robert O. Keohane, and Sidney Verba, *Designing Social Inquiry: Scientific Inference in Qualitative Research* (Princeton: Princeton University Press, 1994), pp. 129–137.

5. Taylor, Kimport, Van Dyke, and Andersen, "Culture and Mobilization." This study is based on "a random survey of all participants in the San Francisco weddings"—a significant improvement on most researchers' reliance on "small and unsystematic samples" (p. 872). But, it still excludes people who remained unmarried because a "sample of nonparticipant gays and lesbians would be virtually impossible to obtain" (p. 873n6). The lack of negative cases means that the study cannot explain why some same-sex couples participated in the weddings while others did not.

many ways. They live in the same neighborhoods, send their children to the same schools, attend the same churches, hold the same types of jobs, and may even know one another. In short, the nonparticipants plausibly could be participants. The data corroborate this assumption: among current non-participants, 71 percent have family members who parade; 89 percent attended parades as children; 64 percent attend parades now; 81 percent consider themselves British; and 84 percent consider themselves unionist. Over one-third of current nonparticipants have even paraded at some earlier point in their lives. Analyzing data from this pool of *potential* paraders allows me to compare men who parade to their (structurally and biographically similar) neighbors who do not.[6]

Using this new, systematic survey data as well as interview data from current participants, former participants, and nonparticipants, I find evidence against all three theoretical models.[7] I show that, contrary to the idealist approach, participants are neither more pro-Protestant nor more anti-Catholic than comparable nonparticipants. Contrary to the rationalist approach, participants do not receive selective material benefits. And contrary to the structural approach, participants do not have more pre-existing social ties to other participants than nonparticipants, nor do they have fewer personal responsibilities constraining their time and attention. Yet I also find evidence for the structural hypothesis that participants were more likely to have paraded as youths than nonparticipants, as well as mixed support for the rationalist hypothesis on the effect of social sanctioning: the quantitative data support it, while the qualitative data do not. The survey, finally, shows that participants are more likely to attend church and come from a working-class background.

THE IDEALIST APPROACH

When presented with an action that glorifies their in-group, to the exclusion and humiliation of an out-group, do a person's beliefs and feelings about these groups affect the likelihood of participation? In other words, do parade participants hold different attitudes toward fellow Protestants or Catholics than nonparticipants do? Many, if not most, people in Northern Ireland think so. Many Protestants believe that people march in parades

6. Note that the neighborhoods were selected purposely, not at random, so the survey is not representative of all Protestants in Belfast or Northern Ireland. But respondents were selected randomly within each neighborhood. For more detail on the survey and sampling, please consult appendix A.

7. All interviewees are identified with a pseudonym.

because they are exceptionally steadfast and loyal members of the community, acting on their strong faith and belief in the union. Many Catholics believe that people join parades because they are exceptionally bigoted Protestant supremacists, acting on their deep hatred for Catholics. Despite clear disagreement about the content of paraders' convictions, many members of both groups believe that participants' convictions are extreme. A close look at patterns in the data, however, reveals that this is not the case.[8]

To test whether Protestants who identify more with their own ethnic group are more likely to participate than Protestants with a lower sense of ethnic identification, I created a survey measure that captures how strongly the respondent identifies with the Protestant community.[9] Using this barometer, I find in table 2.1 that stronger identification is *not* associated with an increased probability of parade participation. Rather, both groups expressed enthusiastic views about membership in the Protestant community. This result remains in alternative measures of identification, including entering each component variable individually or substituting with an indicator for self-description as British (as opposed to Irish, Northern Irish, or Ulster-Scots).[10]

8. The dependent variable in this chapter's quantitative analysis, *Parade Participant*, takes a value of 1 if he is currently a member of a loyal order or marching band and a value of 0 if he is not. Twelve percent of the sample are current parade participants (N=28). A benefit of this outcome variable is that it measures participation in a specific, discrete action, rather than general support for a cause or vague "movement participation." See Doug McAdam, "Recruitment to High-Risk Activism: The Case of Freedom Summer," *American Journal of Sociology* 92, no. 1 (July 1986): 66–67; and Gregory L. Wiltfang and Doug McAdam, "The Costs and Risks of Social Activism: A Study of Sanctuary Movement Activism," *Social Forces* 69, no. 4 (June 1991): 987–1010.

I estimate the determinants of participation using logistic regressions with standard errors clustered by neighborhood and interviewer fixed effects. To account for deleted observations due to missing data I report results obtained using multiple imputations. The results are presented in table 2.1. For the original, non-imputed results, as well as a re-estimation using rare events logit, consult appendix C. The results do not vary much in any of the estimations.

9. *Protestant Identification* is an additive scale of three survey questions, each with five response categories. Respondents were first asked if they strongly agree, agree, neither agree nor disagree, disagree or strongly disagree with the statements "I feel strong ties with other Protestants in Northern Ireland" and "In many respects, I am like most other Protestants in Northern Ireland" (coded from -2 to 2). Then they were asked, "Would you be proud to be called an Ulster Protestant?" on a five-point scale from "not at all" to "very much" (coded 0 to 4). The three responses were summed to produce a scale ranging from -4 to 8. For similar measures, see Bert Klandermans, Jojanneke van der Toorn, and Jacquelien van Stekelenburg, "Embeddedness and Identity: How Immigrants Turn Grievances into Action," *American Sociological Review* 73, no. 6 (December 2008): 992–1012; and Bernd Simon, Michael Loewy, Stefan Stürmer, Ulrike Weber, Peter Freytag, Corinna Habig, Claudia Kampmeier, and Peter Spahlinger, "Collective Identification and Social Movement Participation," *Journal of Personality and Social Psychology* 74, no. 3 (March 1998): 646–658.

10. See appendix C, table C.4. Generalized ordered logit analyses demonstrate that non-attenders do have lower in-group identification than both attenders and paraders (appendix C, table C.6). This suggests that while there is no significant difference in the level of pro-Protestant

Table 2.1. THE DETERMINANTS OF CURRENT PARADE
PARTICIPATION: MULTIPLE IMPUTATION LOGIT ANALYSIS

	Model 1 (Limited model)	Model 2 (Main model)	Model 3 (Disaggregate social pressure)	Model 4 (With income)
Idealist Approach				
Protestant Identification	.19 [.12]	.11 [.15]	.13 [.16]	.13 [.14]
Anti-Catholicism	1.27 [1.14]	2.14 [1.40]	2.53 [1.38]*	2.38 [1.80]
Rationalist Approach				
Social Pressure	.84 [.19]***	.76 [.22]***		.76 [.24]***
Family Expected Participation			.57 [.20]**	
Community Thinks Less of Nonparticipant			.75 [.34]**	
Structural Approach				
Family Marched	.25 [.82]	.13 [.70]	.29 [.61]	.09 [.74]
Close Friends at Age 16	.21 [.32]	.10 [.33]	.01 [.33]	.11 [.34]
Been Asked to March	.63 [.52]	.49 [.55]	.49 [.49]	.46 [.57]
Children under 18		−1.01 [.52]*	−.88 [.50]*	−1.07 [.46]**
Full-Time Job		.96 [.66]	.80 [.55]	.81 [.98]
Age		−.02 [.02]	−.02 [.02]	−.02 [.02]
Marched as Youth		.71 [.33]**	.70 [.28]**	.74 [.35]**
Control Variables				
Education		−.26 [.66]	−.36 [.68]	−.33 [.66]
Church Attendance		.25 [.09]***	.27 [.10]**	.25 [.08]***
Income				.10 [.27]
Constant	−5.71 [.83]***	−5.42 [1.27]***	−5.55 [1.25]***	−5.88 [1.87]**
Number of observations	227	227	227	227

Standard errors clustered at neighborhood level in brackets. Enumerator fixed effects are not reported.
* $p<.10$, ** $p<.05$, *** $p<.01$

Some paraders I interviewed do see themselves as committed Ulster Protestants. For instance, Mikey, after explaining that he is not a religious man, mentioned that "as far as being a Protestant is concerned, I would class myself as being a good Protestant, but not a religious Protestant." "So what makes you a good Protestant then?" I asked. He replied that parading

feelings between parade attenders and participants, there is a difference between those who are at all involved in parading and those who choose to stay away from parades altogether. In other words, people who do not feel much of an attachment to their ethnic in-group avoid parading, but once one crosses some baseline level of attachment, the strength of this feeling does not predict whether one is a spectator or a parader. Spectators and paraders share a strong sense of Protestant identity.

is what makes him a "good Protestant": "I stick up for the Protestant faith. I stick up for Protestantism as my culture. ... I stick up for my Protestant identity and British identity, my loyalist identity. I stick up for my country. ... I would say I'm a good Protestant, but I'm not a practicing Christian." Sammy goes a step further, contrasting his friends from his Orange lodge and marching band who are "great comrades and ... real brothers" to his "Protestant friends that are wishy-washy, that haven't got involved and wouldn't put up with the hassle maybe of being treated badly for being involved with the loyal orders or the bands."

Many other paraders, however, disagree. They see themselves as no more committed to their community than people who do not parade. "You don't have to be in the band or in the Orange or be in one of the other [loyal orders] to be a good Protestant," Lee says. Jamie agrees: "People wouldn't ... think them any less of a Prod, for want of a better way of putting it."

If positive feelings toward the Protestant in-group does not explain participation, what about negative feelings toward the Catholic out-group? Are people who feel more hostility toward Catholics more likely to participate? I measure these negative feelings with a variable, *Anti-Catholicism*, that captures the degree of anti-Catholic views professed by the respondent.[11] As with pro-Protestant feelings, I find that anti-Catholic prejudice is not a significant predictor of participation in most model specifications.[12] The statistical strength of this result, however, is not ironclad. The finding's statistical insignificance may be driven by high uncertainty in the measure and a relatively small sample size in the survey, rather than an actual pattern in the population. The absence of evidence of a relationship between anti-Catholicism and parading is not necessarily evidence that the relationship does not exist.

11. The questions were designed to increase the likelihood that respondents will give their actual beliefs, rather than a socially desirable answer. The first question asked how much the respondent would mind if a close family member married a Roman Catholic. The second asked, "Do you think that sometimes Catholics need to be reminded that they live in the United Kingdom?" The third asked, "How much of the sectarian tension that exists in Northern Ireland today do you think Catholics are responsible for creating?" The fourth: "Do you strongly agree, agree, disagree, or strongly disagree that over the past few years, Catholics have gotten more economically than they deserve?" Each measure was scaled from 0 to 1, with 1 as the most anti-Catholic view, then they were added together and the sum was rescaled from 0 to 1. The first question is asked annually by ARK's *Northern Ireland Life and Times Survey*, distributed by ARK, http://www.ark.ac.uk/nilt/results/comrel.html. The third and fourth questions, as well as the scaling, are adapted from P. J. Henry and David O. Sears, "The Symbolic Racism 2000 Scale," *Political Psychology* 23, no. 2 (June 2002): 253–283.
12. The null finding holds if I recreate the scale without the question on whether Catholics deserve their economic gains, which has substantially more non-responses than the other three questions (appendix C, table C.5).

What is more, anti-Catholic sentiment is or is almost statistically significant in some regression specifications presented in this chapter and appendix C. What does this mean? To further examine what is driving this
near-significance, I disaggregate the variable in the appendix (table C.5,
model 1). Breaking the measure into its four component parts is revealing.
The results show that parading is perhaps about expressing grievances, but
seemingly not about expressing deep-seated hatred. Paraders are not any
more likely than nonparticipants to express concern about a close family
member marrying a Catholic. Nor are they more likely to express the beliefs
that Catholics sometimes need to be reminded that they live in the United
Kingdom or that Catholics are primarily responsible for the sectarian tension in Northern Ireland. But, they *are* more likely to agree that "over the
past few years, Catholics have gotten more economically than they deserve."
All four of these variables capture a dimension of bias against Catholics, but
the former two focus on bias against Catholics as people (that is, not wanting them in one's family and believing that they are inherently traitorous),
while the latter two focus on beliefs about Catholic behavior and the
political economy of post-Agreement Northern Ireland (that is, thinking
they raise the level of sectarian tension and achieved unearned economic
success). The one measure that is statistically significant captures the latter form of bias: a negative perception of Catholic economic outcomes. So
paraders remain undifferentiated from nonparticipants in their expressed
bias directed at Catholics for being Catholic. Rather, they express higher
levels of economic-based grievances against perceived Catholic undeserved
gains.

Another way to interpret this result is that participants are not any more
biased against Catholics as individuals than comparable nonparticipants,
but they may be slightly more biased against the imagined community of
Catholics at an abstract level, a finding consistent with previous research.[13]
In interviews, paraders often went to great lengths to explain that they had
no issues with their Catholic compatriots. Their problem was with Roman
Catholicism and the Catholic Church and/or with republicanism and the

13. McCauley, Tonge, and Mycock, *Loyal to the Core?* p. 166, find that 57 percent of Orange
Order members agree that the Orange Order is "anti-Roman Catholic Church," but only 20 per-
cent agree that it is "anti-Roman Catholic." "Respect for the rights of individual Roman
Catholics," they conclude, "is thus distinguished from rejection of the trappings of their danger-
ous, expansionary church and the evils of 'popery.'" Their full discussion of the subject is on
pp. 164–169. See also Bryan, *Orange Parades*, esp. pp. 108–109; John D. Brewer with
Gareth I. Higgins, *Anti-Catholicism in Northern Ireland, 1600–1998: The Mote and the Beam*
(Houndsmill, UK: Macmillan, 1998), esp. pp. 124–126; and John D. Brewer and Gareth
I. Higgins, "Understanding Anti-Catholicism in Northern Ireland," *Sociology* 33, no. 2 (May
1999): 235–255.

republican movement, both of which they distinguished from "ordinary Catholic[s]," in Jamie's words. First, there is a theological dispute with Catholicism and opposition to the Catholic Church—"because we're Protestant," as Frankie puts it. But this does not translate into hatred for Catholic people, he explains: "You do not offend...Roman Catholics. You do them no harm....You have no problem with them at all. And [it's] the Roman Catholic teachings in the Roman Catholic Church which is the problem."

Then there is the dispute with republicans. Frankie also articulates this distinction: "We have nothing against Roman Catholics, nothing at all. Against extreme republicans? Yeah. But nothing against Roman Catholics." Some paraders, such as Mikey, even tied republicanism and the Catholic Church together:

> I've got absolutely nothing against any Roman Catholic. I've loads of problems against republicans, but to me they're not proper Roman Catholics anyway, because you don't profess to being a murderer or a bomber and then say you're a good Roman Catholic. During the Troubles...whenever IRA men were going out and murdering people, they were going back to the chapels, to the priests, and the priests would absolve them of their sins, so they believed they were okay. Obviously we have a problem with that. But that's not because I'm a Christian Protestant, that's because I just think it's wrong.

While other paraders expressed a religious problem with Catholicism, Mikey's opposition to the Catholic Church stems from its perceived relationship to republican violence. As Dominic Bryan finds, "For many involved in the parades, opposition to the doctrines of the Church of Rome is subsumed under a general distrust of Irish Catholics—the 'other' community....[T]he central reasoning is that Catholics are viewed as Irish nationalists and therefore a threat to Northern Ireland remaining in the United Kingdom."[14]

In all, the "style" of sectarian talk by paraders separates individual Catholics from the Catholic Church, on the one hand, and armed republicanism, on the other.[15] But sometimes the distinction bleeds away. For instance, earlier in my interview with Mikey, before his disclaimer "I've got

---

14. Bryan, *Orange Parades*, pp. 108–109.

15. Eduardo Bonilla-Silva, *Racism Without Racists: Color-Blind Racism and Racial Inequality in Contemporary America*, 3rd ed. (Lanham, MD: Rowman & Littlefield, 2010), p. 53, defines the "style of an ideology" as "its particular *linguistic manners and rhetorical strategies*" (italics in original). His analysis of how white Americans talk about African Americans has parallels in how Protestants talk about Catholics. For example, his discussion of the use of the phrase "Some of my best friends are black" (pp. 57–58) is relevant to the many interviewees who, usually unprompted, told me about their Catholic friends.

absolutely nothing against any Roman Catholic," he connected seemingly all ordinary Catholics to the IRA. "It's all IRA men within Sinn Féin. So our concept of them [Catholics] was that they were always voting for hardline republicans." Increasing his suspicion, he felt that "whenever we met Catholics, every Catholic I spoke to, none of them supported Sinn Féin. So if none of them supported Sinn Féin, how come they were getting so many votes? They will never be honest with you."

These beliefs and sentiments about Catholics, however, are not restricted to paraders: they are fairly widespread among Protestants. For numerous historical, social, political, and theological reasons, John Brewer and Gareth Higgins argue, "Anti-Catholicism is a culturally sanctioned and legitimate resource available to Protestants."[16] More generally, sectarian beliefs are common throughout society. Sectarianism "is *everywhere* in contemporary Northern Ireland."[17] What is perhaps most notable is the frequency of these attitudes among paraders and non-paraders alike.

In sum, the survey reveals that, all else held equal, participants do not express notably extreme ethnic attitudes.[18] Compared to their non-parading neighbors, they do not express a higher degree of in-group identification or out-group prejudice. Note that this does *not* mean that paraders are not stalwart Protestants nor that they are not prejudiced against Catholics.

---

16. Brewer and Higgins, "Understanding Anti-Catholicism in Northern Ireland," p. 253n1.

17. Robbie McVeigh and Bill Rolston, "From Good Friday to Good Relations: Sectarianism, Racism and the Northern Ireland State," *Race & Class* 48, no. 4 (April 2007): 17. Emphasis in original.

18. Both identification with the in-group and hostility toward the out-group are plausibly endogenous to parade participation. It is easy to imagine that membership in a parading organization and marching in parades increases one's attachment to the Protestant community and prejudice toward the Catholic community. However, collecting a valid retrospective measure of these attitudes from before a respondent joined would be near impossible. We would not believe answers to a question like "How did you feel about Catholics thirty years ago, when you were eight years old?" Therefore, we cannot attribute any causality and settle only for correlation. Had I found a positive and significant relationship between in-group and out-group attitudes and participation, we could attribute little to the correlation. This is because the standard model of participation argues that attitudes precede and motivate participation, but we also know that attitudes can be a function of involvement. As a result, distinctive attitudes among participants could be a cause or an effect of their participation. In a cross-sectional study, we have no way of knowing. Finding no difference in attitudes, however, actually provides more confidence that holding particularly strong attitudes did not motivate participation. Unless we assume that people with *less* of an attachment to Protestants and prejudice toward Catholics join parading organizations and then increase those attitudes through their participation, the data show that parade participants' attitudes reflect the communities they come from. (Although it is highly unlikely that people with extremely low ethnic attitudes join, it is not impossible. For example, Ziad W. Munson, *The Making of Pro-Life Activists: How Social Movement Mobilization Works* [Chicago: University of Chicago Press, 2008], p. 189, finds that 23 percent of his sample of pro-life activists were pro-choice prior to mobilization; another 20 percent expressed ambivalent beliefs about abortion.)

My argument is not that participants do not express high levels of Protestant identification or anti-Catholicism, only that they do not express levels that are notably higher than nonparticipants. In short, their attitudes are typical of their neighborhoods.

This result matches a robust finding across a number of studies of social movement mobilization: ideological support for a movement does not explain why some people join while others do not. For example, Bert Klandermans and Dirk Oegema find that 74 percent of Dutch respondents supported the goals of a large peace demonstration, but only 4 percent actually attended.[19] In his study of the 1964 Mississippi Freedom Summer, Doug McAdam concludes that attitudinal and ideological support for civil rights did not distinguish participants from accepted applicants who withdrew before the summer's action. Each group was equally supportive of the project's goals, so ideological sympathy does not explain their different choices.[20] And Ziad Munson shows that people with a wide range of attitudes about abortion become active in the pro-life movement. Even activists who considered themselves pro-life before they were mobilized often held "thin beliefs" about abortion, not the "more robust ideological commitments" that idealist models of action expect to precede activism.[21] Rather, they worked out their beliefs through their participation. As with these movements, the idealist approach does not explain why people participate in loyalist parades.

THE RATIONALIST APPROACH

Rather than looking to a person's attitudes, the rationalist approach looks to the private costs and benefits of participation. From this perspective, even if a person supports the goals of a collective action, she is better off if someone else contributes their time, money, and energy to achieving it. This way, she gains the benefits of the collective outcome without expending any of her own scare resources. To overcome this dilemma, scholars have proposed two main ways to motivate rational participation in collective action: selectively reward participants or selectively punish nonparticipants. Nevertheless, survey and interview evidence show that loyalist parade participants do not receive selective material benefits, and the evidence on social pressure to parade is inconclusive.

19. Klandermans and Oegema, "Potentials, Networks, Motivations, and Barriers," p. 524.

20. McAdam, "Recruitment to High-Risk Activism"; and Doug McAdam, *Freedom Summer* (New York: Oxford University Press, 1988).

21. Munson, *The Making of Pro-Life Activists*, p. 186.

Selective Material Benefits and Parading

Selective material benefits have long been seen as a way to overcome the free rider problem and produce collective action.[22] So, throughout my fieldwork I sought evidence that parade participants received selective material incentives. I found almost none—and the few hints I did find were unsystematic. There is limited evidence that participants could find employment through their parading networks, but for the overwhelming majority of participants, parading is not a material benefit—it is a net financial loss. Only three out of the seventy men who paraded as an adult reported in the survey that it had ever helped him financially.[23] The remaining 96 percent responded that they had never received an economic benefit from parading. Likewise, in open-ended survey responses to "Why did you march last Twelfth?" not one current parader mentioned anything even slightly related to material gain.

The interview data corroborate this absence. Nearly every time I asked a parade participant if there were any personal financial benefits the answer was an emphatic no. Without skipping a beat, many respondents continued by saying that parading actually costs them a lot of money. Time and again, I heard from respondents that they have never benefited economically from their participation, either in the form of direct rewards or from preferential access to employment, contracts, or promotions. This is a big shift from generations past, when membership in the Orange Order was an important path to work and advancement for Protestants in many industries. In some fields, such as unionist politics, membership was a virtual requirement.[24]

Even nonparticipants I interviewed know that parading costs participants far more than it brings in. And among nonparticipants I surveyed, only 11 percent reported that they thought that joining a parading organization

22. Mancur Olson, *The Logic of Collective Action: Public Goods and the Theory of Groups* (Cambridge, MA: Harvard University Press, 1965); Samuel L. Popkin, *The Rational Peasant: The Political Economy of Rural Society in Vietnam* (Berkeley: University of California Press, 1979); and Mark I. Lichbach, *The Rebel's Dilemma* (Ann Arbor: University of Michigan Press, 1995).

23. The question read: "Did being in your Order/band ever help you financially, such as by helping you to get a small loan, job, or promotion?" This question was only asked of men who had ever been parade participants, so it is not included in the regression.

24. Bryan, *Orange Parades*, documents the history of the many economic, social, and political benefits of membership throughout the book. In summary, he writes: "There have been some very practical reasons for being an Orangeman.... [F]rom the mid-nineteenth century onwards, belonging to the Orange Institution clearly had economic and political advantages. It was an institution of economic and political patronage" (p. 109). But, he shows, due to changes in economic and political structures, these advantages began to fade during the Troubles. As McAuley, Tonge, and Mycock, *Loyal to the Core?* p. 162, conclude, "there are no pecuniary or political benefits to modern membership [in the Orange Order]."

benefited people financially. So it is unlikely that expectations of financial gain are a major motive for joining a parading organization.

Though a limited number of participants did mention minor economic benefits available to paraders. In particular, several told me that by joining a wide network, membership can help people find employment.[25] For example, Walter and Chris are bandmates who co-own a small business. Over the years, they have hired three other fellow band members for casual work "a couple of days here and a couple of days there." Walter explains: "if you're in a band and you become unemployed and there are people in your band that are working, they're going to be looking for work for you." But when I then asked if finding a job was a reason why people joined bands, he cut me off: "No, no, no." So though social connections formed through parading may occasionally lead to work opportunities, very few interviewees mentioned it at all, and those that did only discussed opportunities for odd jobs, not sustained employment. My findings echo Bryan's conclusion: "While membership of the Orange Institution can certainly facilitate the organisation of both economic and political influence, I think that it is unlikely that this now forms a significant reason for individuals to join. Being an Orangeman may still have its advantages, but many brethren would certainly feel that it now carries disadvantages with it."[26]

The easiest disadvantages to observe are the direct economic costs of parading. As Billy quips, "The financial benefit is that it actually costs you money! There's absolutely no financial gain in being in the Orange Order or in the band." A 2013 report estimated that the loyal orders and bands spend £15.4 million per year (roughly $23.5 million at the time the report was released) on expenses such as uniforms and regalia, catering, transportation, musical instruments, and capital projects.[27] Loyal order members have to pay dues, membership fees, and other incidental expenses,[28] but it is band members who really pay dearly. Buying new musical instruments and uniforms can costs members hundreds if not thousands of pounds, and these purchases are largely self-financed. Steven described some of his

---

25. See also Bryan, *Orange Parades*, p. 109; Kaufmann, *The Orange Order*, p. 1; and Ray Casserly, "The Fyfe and My Family: Flute Bands in Rathcoole Estate," *Irish Journal of Anthropology* 13, no. 1 (2010): 8–12.

26. Bryan, *Orange Parades*, pp. 110–111.

27. RSM McClure Watters, "The Socio-Economic Impact of the Traditional Protestant Parading Sector in Northern Ireland," May 2013, pp. 5–6. In addition, the report estimates that parading organizations contribute £38.6 million to the economy annually "through provision of facilities, community/volunteer work and fund raising for charities" (p. 3).

28. See also Kaufmann, *The Orange Order*, p. 273; RSM McClure Watters, "The Socio-Economic Impact of the Traditional Protestant Parading Sector," p. 56; and Bryan, *Orange Parades*, p. 99.

band's expenses: £700 for a flute, £600 for a drum, £250 to £400 for a uniform, and £25–30,000 for an upcoming trip for the whole band to the Somme battlefield in France.[29] And for all those expenses, he emphasizes, "We're subsidized by no one…Everything we do we do ourselves." Bands can make some money by selling CDs, DVDs, performing at functions, and hosting fundraising parades, but generally this generates a pittance compared to their expenses, and members have to pay a significant amount out of pocket.[30] Some bands get an occasional grant from the Arts Council of Northern Ireland or other funding agencies (including the Irish government), but it all goes to the organization, not the members.[31]

In addition to the direct costs of membership, parading carries indirect costs as well. In particular, many participants believe that parading could hurt them in finding employment or advancing in their careers.[32] Seventy percent of current paraders in the survey reported that they would not put a parading leadership position on a résumé or job application. Michael, for example, is a manager in an industry that is "predominantly made up of Catholics." As a result, he knows that for the sake of his professional life, he needs to keep the fact that he is an Orangeman quiet. He chose his words carefully as he confided: "I—I know my—I know my position. I know I can't go out and say, 'I'm—Arms up, I'm in the Orange Order here.' I know it might be detrimental to my progression, so I just keep it to myself. You know, I'm not ashamed of it, but I don't—I don't—"

He paused, so I began to ask, "Do you think it could affect your—"

"To answer your question, yes. There is a risk factor in my standing in my organization."

29. See also Lee A. Smithey, *Unionists, Loyalists, and Conflict Transformation in Northern Ireland* (New York: Oxford University Press, 2011), p. 197; Jacqueline Witherow, "Parading Protestantisms and the Flute Bands of Postconflict Northern Ireland," in *The Oxford Handbook of Music and World Christianities*, ed. Jonathan Dueck and Suzel Ana Reily (New York: Oxford University Press, 2016), p. 388; and Michael Hamilton, *Strategic Review of Parading in Northern Ireland: Views of Key Stakeholders* (Belfast: Strategic Review of Parading Body, 2007), p. 14.

30. See Department of Culture, Arts and Leisure, *Marching Bands in Northern Ireland* (Belfast: Department of Culture, Arts and Leisure, 2012), pp. 17–18; Smithey, *Unionists, Loyalists, and Conflict Transformation*, p. 197; RSM McClure Watters, "The Socio-Economic Impact of the Traditional Protestant Parading Sector," pp. 38, 41; and David Cairns, "The Object of Sectarianism: The Material Reality of Sectarianism in Ulster Loyalism," *Journal of the Royal Anthropological Institute* 6, no. 3 (September 2000): 448.

31. See Department of Culture, Arts and Leisure, *Marching Bands in Northern Ireland*, pp. 17–18. Kaufmann, *The Orange Order*, p. 314, remarks: "cultural funding which has flowed from the civil society provisions of the Good Friday Agreement has led to a new culture of grant writing within Orangeism."

32. A recent study by the Orange Order based on interviews with members reaches similar conclusions. Loyal Orange Institution, *Fairness & Fear: An Investigation of the Treatment of Protestants in the Northern Ireland Civil Service* (Belfast: Loyal Orange Institution, 2016). Also Bryan, *Orange Parades*, p. 109.

That said, despite Michael's concerns, he did not feel that he had ever actually been discriminated against. In fact, none of the interviewees mentioned that they had personally faced discrimination. I repeatedly heard general complaints or rumors about people being fired for being a parader, but no one seemed to personally know anyone to whom it had actually happened.

Even those who are less fearful of outright discrimination tend to keep quiet because parading is a potential source of conflict with coworkers. For example, Lee recalled a situation at his office where one colleague—"I assume she's Catholic, I don't really know to be honest"—was complaining about parades delaying traffic throughout the city. A colleague from England then mentioned that Lee was in those parades, leading the first colleague to "shut up" about it. The English man tried to goad the conversation a bit further, but the woman sought to end it. Relating the story to me, Lee reflected that he "wasn't going to get into it in case I offended anybody."

Avoiding this kind of awkward, uncomfortable situation leads participants to keep private. Scott, who plays a flute in a band, goes so far as to lie to his colleagues at his middle-class job when they ask him about weekend plans; he says he is not doing anything or makes something up. The exception that proves the rule is that when his band performed a prestigious concert at a major arts venue, he was willing to talk about it at work. The respectability of performing at a reputable concert hall, rather than in the raucous, liquored streets of a working-class neighborhood, even made him feel comfortable enough to invite colleagues to the show. He seemed proud recounting that several came to see him perform. By contrast, he was clear that he would not invite them to a regular band parade because he would not want them to make assumptions and form the wrong opinions of him.

Both the interviews and survey suggest that the offer of selective material incentives is *not* a cause of parade participation. While this rational, materialist hypothesis is intuitive and others have found evidence of selective incentives at work in a wide-range of collective action, including Orange parades in previous decades, I find that they are unrelated to parading in Northern Ireland today. My survey interviewers thought that even looking for financial benefits was futile. The questionnaire included the open-ended question "What attracted you to the specific lodge/band that you joined first?" Interviewers were to mark any of the fourteen listed items that the respondent mentioned. One of them was "financial/employment," and several times when reviewing the survey with the interviewers during training, they laughed or told me that there was no reason to have it as an option. I would insist that though it might be unlikely, I really wanted to know if anyone mentioned it as a reason. In the end, my interviewers were of course correct: the box was never ticked.

Social Sanctions and Parading

Rather than being enticed with rewards, a rational actor could be motivated to take part if they expect to pay a social cost for not participating.[33] To assess the role of this cost in the survey, I summed the amount of social pressure from two sources: family and community.[34] Family pressure is measured by how much the respondent believes his family expected him to participate.[35] Community pressure is measured by whether the respondent believes that his community thinks less of nonparticipants.[36] I find that the measure of social sanctioning is positively and significantly associated with participation in loyalist parades. Substantively, increasing this variable from its minimum to maximum raises the probability of participating by 10 percent.[37] To explore further, I disaggregate social pressure into its two sources, family and community. The results show that the relationship is substantively and statistically stronger with the measure of community-based social pressure. Men who believe that their community thinks less of nonparticipants are more likely to parade.

The role of social pressure previews a subject I will explore in greater depth in the next chapter: parading is an eminently social activity. If, as I will argue, people participate to attain the process-oriented benefits intrinsic to collective participation in a symbol-laden action with friends and family, it follows that social incentives are more important than material calculations. So it is notable that the quantitative results show that social punishment matters while economic rewards do not. In other words, the pleasures and pains of human relationships are at the center of what motivates participation. The prospect of material gain, conversely, plays little role. Though the social sanctioning hypothesis sprouts from a view of human motivations that is narrowly rational and self-interested, the finding's interpretation need not be constrained to this stance. It can be interpreted just as easily to fit the broader view of motivation that I adopt.

33. Dennis Chong, *Collective Action and the Civil Rights Movement* (Chicago: University of Chicago Press, 1991), esp. pp. 31–72; and Timur Kuran, "Ethnic Norms and Their Transformation Through Reputational Cascades," *Journal of Legal Studies* 27, no. S2 (June 1998): 623–659.

34. *Social Pressure* ranges from 0 indicating no pressure to 6 indicating most pressure.

35. "Do you think that your family expected you to join a loyal order or band? Would you say definitely, somewhat, not really, or definitely not?"

36. "Do people in this community think less of people who choose not to join loyal orders or bands? Would you say definitely, somewhat, not really, or definitely not?"

37. Holding all other variables in Model 2 in table 2.1 at their median value. Calculated using Clarify for Stata 10 on the original data set, without multiple imputations. Standard errors were not clustered in the simulated model.

Nevertheless, the interviews tell a somewhat different story about social sanctioning. Barring several exceptions, my interviewees do not recall experiencing direct or indirect social pressure to participate in parades.[38] One of those exceptions is Samuel. Samuel has never been a member of any parading organization, and has no real interest in parades or parading culture. He is "happy enough once a year, twice a year watch a parade, go to a bonfire, and then I would be happy enough not to mention it for another twelve months." But, he is involved in unionist politics and most of his close friends are members of the loyal orders. His friends tease him about not joining and constantly ask him to join: "I mean, I have been asked I don't know how many times to join the Orange Order, every single week for about the past three years," he said.

"Do you feel pressure?" I asked.

"Yeah, yeah."

"Because they are friends or because—?"

"Yeah. Not because of anything else, just because they are my friends. Yeah, I do, no doubt about it."

One strategy that his friends use is appealing to his identity. When Samuel tells his friends that he simply has no interest in joining the loyal orders, he "instantly get[s] a lecture, 'Well you should have an interest, you know. You call yourself a unionist; you call yourself a member of the unionist community; you'll do anything you can within peaceful means to maintain the union—Well this is one way that we mark our territory.'" And though it is just friendly teasing—a "bit of banter"—it is directed at his self-image and identity as a Protestant and unionist. "If I go on holiday [over the Twelfth of July], Johnny would send me a message, 'Are you going again then, Seamus?'"[39] By calling him by a stereotypically Irish name, Johnny suggests that Samuel's loyalties are in question. Although these comments are delivered and received in jest, they demonstrate that this is usable material for a joke. If there was nothing wrong with skipping town during the Twelfth, calling Samuel "Seamus" would make no sense. But instead the mocking taunt makes complete sense both to Samuel and Johnny. In these ways, Samuel experiences direct pressure from friends to

38. Note that I never heard of or otherwise saw any evidence of physical coercion by parading organizations to recruit members, despite the fact that paramilitaries continue to use force to elicit conformity in Northern Ireland's working-class communities. See, for instance, Heather Hamill, *The Hoods: Crime and Punishment in Belfast* (Princeton: Princeton University Press, 2010).

39. It is fairly common for Catholics and middle-class or liberal Protestants to leave Northern Ireland on vacation over the Twelfth.

parade. And though it gets irritating, he has easily been able to resist participation.

More common in my interviews are reports of the *absence* of direct pressure or social sanctioning. Even between fathers and sons, the relationship where we might anticipate that expectations about carrying on family traditions would compound identity-based pressures, I found little evidence. Many men were asked by their fathers to join their parading organization, but say they felt no pressure from it. Several interviewees recall that it was, in fact, their father *not* asking them or pressuring them to join that inspired their decision. Alexander states:

> What kind of impressed me was I asked my dad, "Should I join?" and he says, "It's your decision, you decide." That encouraged me to join more, because I didn't feel like I was being forced to join, and I wasn't.... And it impressed me more that he didn't try and encourage me. He just said, "I'd like you to join, I'd like you to follow in my footsteps, but clearly it's a decision for you." That made me really want to join.

The fact that his father made it clear that the decision was one that he had to make for himself left a lasting impression on Alexander. Decades later, the memory of this conversation—regardless of accuracy—still resonates.

Indirect social pressure is just as rare. By indirect I mean an emphasis on maintaining a reputation of loyalty to the community and gaining recognition, status, and respect that is generally present in the social atmosphere, but not aimed at a particular individual.[40] Despite several exceptions, the general experience of Protestant men does not seem to include feeling such pressure to parade. Mark, for instance, grew up in a "very staunch Protestant area," the exact place where we would expect young men to feel that they had to join parades. But in his recollection, "There was no real drive that you had to do something [i.e., join a lodge or band]."

Among participants, I did not even find agreement about whether paraders are respected, high-status members of the community.[41] Many interviewees believe that paraders do gain recognition and respect through their actions: the community admires them for the commitment they have made to represent and defend Protestant culture. But many others report that

40. See Chong, *Collective Action and the Civil Rights Movement*; Robb Willer, "Groups Reward Individual Sacrifice: The Status Solution to the Collective Action Problem," *American Sociological Review* 74, no. 1 (February 2009): 23–43; and Gwyneth H. McClendon, "Social Esteem and Participation in Contentious Politics: A Field Experiment at an LGBT Pride Rally," *American Journal of Political Science* 58, no. 2 (April 2014): 279–290.

41. In his survey of band members, Ramsey, *Music, Emotion and Identity*, pp. 257–258, finds that 59 percent believe that playing in a flute band brings respect within their own community and 34 percent believe it brings respect within wider society.

they do not feel that parading brings them any additional respect among their peers and neighbors. Billy claims that Orangemen are "not put on a pedestal against somebody in the community that's not in the Orange." Tom agrees, saying, "there's no particular kudos [for parading]....You're not elevated" by the community. "Like everything," he tells me, "some are [respected], some aren't."

All in all, the clearest instances of social pressure in my interviews were people who felt pressured *not* to parade. The most common examples were parents not wanting their children to participate in, or even associate with, parades. For instance, Rachel, a rare female band member and one of the few women I interviewed, came from a family with a "very strong Christian background," where "sometimes bands are seen as being alcoholic monsters." She still joined a band, but was "a wee bit apprehensive about telling [her] parents" about it. Several others I interviewed, by contrast, had parents prevent them from joining bands when they were younger. Michael's mother had similar concerns as Rachel's parents: "people would associate bands with alcohol." As a result, Michael avidly followed the bands as a youth, but his "mom would never have allowed [him] to join" one. Matt's and Jamie's families were more worried about violence. Matt's mother did not want him to join a band because "there was a lot more trouble... around parades" when he was growing up. Similarly, Jamie recalls that his father "wouldn't let [him] join until [he] was a bit older" because "back then bands were very, very associated with paramilitaries." Even before the Troubles, Rosemary Harris, in her classic ethnography of "Ballybeg," recounts the story of a Mrs. Baxter, who prevented her husband and son from joining the Orange Order, on account of its inter-class social egalitarianism and encouragement of poorer Protestants' bigotry.[42]

A final piece of evidence opposing the role of social pressure in initial mobilization is that parading organizations do not even succeed in maintaining all the members they have. Of the seventy respondents who have paraded as adults, only 40 percent are currently members of a parading organization. Fully 60 percent have withdrawn from parading.[43] This is reflected in the Orange Order's membership figures, which have been declining for decades.[44] What is more, several interviewees explained that

42. Rosemary Harris, *Prejudice and Tolerance in Ulster: A Study of Neighbours and "Strangers" in a Border Community* (Manchester: Manchester University Press, 1972), pp. 100–101.

43. Engaging in contentious politics for a spell, rather than a lifetime, is typical behavior. See Catherine Corrigal-Brown, *Patterns of Protest: Trajectories of Participation in Social Movements* (Stanford: Stanford University Press, 2011).

44. Jarman, *Material Conflicts*, pp. 94–95; Bryan, *Orange Parades*, pp. 111–113; Kaufmann, *The Orange Order*, pp. 267–285; and McAuley, Tonge, and Mycock, *Loyal to the Core?* pp. 126, 185.

men who join without being fully committed are likely to quit anyway, thus invalidating the logic of pressuring people to join.

Regarding the role of social sanctioning, then, the quantitative and qualitative evidence diverge. The statistical analysis suggests that men who report feeling social pressure are more likely to participate. The semi-structured interviews, conversely, suggest that social pressure plays little to no role in motivating participation. Looking at only one source would have provided an incomplete perspective. For the quantitative data, participants could be more likely to believe retrospectively that their family expected them to participate, since they see participation as a good thing. Similarly, they could be more likely to report that their community thinks less of non-participants because it reflects their own thinking and desires. For the qualitative evidence, people recalling the narrative of how they joined a beloved organization that is central to their self-image may downplay the possibility that joining was not entirely self-motivated. I do not believe they are intentionally misrepresenting their history, but rather that the story they tell themselves emphasizes free choice over outside pressure.[45] When explaining positive personal developments, agency is more appealing than structure.

In the end, the data point in different directions and do not provide a satisfying answer—perhaps reflecting varying personal experience, biases in memory, or the lack of an underlying causation. The clearest conclusion we can draw is that social pressure is a far more complex factor than its cousin, selective material benefits. Social sanctions may or may not have an effect; economic incentives certainly do not.

THE STRUCTURAL APPROACH

The "push" of attitudes and incentives, no matter how strong, is unlikely to have much impact without factors that can "pull" a potential participant into a movement. These "pull" factors encompass what scholars call a person's structural location or structural availability. The key intuition of the structural approach is that "it is relatively unimportant if a person is ideologically or psychologically predisposed to participation when they lack the structural location that facilitates participation."[46] Put starkly, a person cannot support or join a movement that he or she has never heard of. Potential participants have to have some degree of exposure to a movement if they

45. See James M. Jasper, *The Art of Moral Protest: Culture, Biography, and Creativity in Social Movements* (Chicago: University of Chicago Press, 1997), p. 82.

46. Doug McAdam and Ronnelle Paulsen, "Specifying the Relationship Between Social Ties and Activism," *American Journal of Sociology* 99, no. 3 (November 1993): 643–644.

are ever to get involved. The likelihood of gaining such exposure depends, above all, on one's social networks. Even the very possibility of social pressure that I just discussed relies on the presence of networks connecting a potential participant to the movement. Like so much of life, participating in contentious collective action often comes down to who you know.

Getting connected to opportunities to participate, however, is often not enough. The structural approach highlights that a person must also be in a position to take advantage of the opportunities presented. The factors that shape one's ability to act are thought of as biographical factors. Biographical variables that influence one's willingness to participate include the lack of other time-consuming commitments and having a prior history of participation. Participation, in the structural view, is the result of an available person being pulled into an opportunity he or she encounters.

Social Networks and Parading

Across a broad range of activities in a broad range of contexts, social ties to other participants have consistently been found to be "one of the strongest predictors of individual participation" in contentious politics.[47] Social ties can serve as conduits for information (why an issue is important, what time to show up for a rally, and so on); relationships in which collective identities are formed, spread, strengthened, and secured; and sites of informal social exchange that develop incentives, such as the social pressure examined above, each of which can play a role in initiating and sustaining

---

47. Alan Schussman and Sarah A. Soule, "Process and Protest: Accounting for Individual Protest Participation," *Social Forces* 84, no. 2 (December 2005): 1086. See, for example, David A. Snow, Louis A. Zurcher Jr., and Sheldon Ekland-Olson, "Social Networks and Social Movements: A Microstructural Approach to Differential Recruitment," *American Sociological Review* 45, no. 5 (October 1980): 787–801; McAdam, "Recruitment to High-Risk Activism"; Bert Klandermans and Dirk Oegema, "Potentials, Networks, Motivations, and Barriers: Steps Towards Participation in Social Movements," *American Sociological Review* 52, no. 4 (August 1987): 519–531; McAdam and Paulsen, "Specifying the Relationship Between Social Ties and Activism"; Roger V. Gould, *Insurgent Identities: Class, Community, and Protest in Paris from 1848 to the Commune* (Chicago: University of Chicago Press, 1995); Sharon Erickson Nepstad and Christian Smith, "Rethinking Recruitment to High-Risk/High-Cost Activism: The Case of the Nicaragua Exchange," *Mobilization* 4, no. 1 (April 1999): 25–40; Florence Passy and Marco Giugni, "Social Networks and Individual Perceptions: Explaining Differential Participation in Social Movements," *Sociological Forum* 16, no. 1 (March 2001): 123–153; and Mario Diani and Doug McAdam, eds., *Social Movements and Networks: Relational Approaches to Collective Action* (New York: Oxford University Press, 2003). For overviews of the large body of research, see James A. Kitts, "Mobilizing in Black Boxes: Social Networks and Participation in Social Movement Organizations," *Mobilization* 5, no. 2 (October 2000): 241–257; and John Krinsky and Nick Crossley, "Social Movements and Social Networks: Introduction," *Social Movement Studies* 13, no. 1 (January 2014): 1–21.

participation.[48] To measure the effects of social ties on parading, I use three variables from the survey: whether or not family members were paraders (*Family Marched*), how many of their close friends at age sixteen were paraders (*Close Friends at Age 16*), and whether or not a respondent has been personally asked to join a parading organization (*Been Asked*).[49] Contrary to prior studies, none of these measures are statistically associated with parade participation, as table 2.1 shows. In other words, having more social ties does not actually increase the probability of parading.

This is a striking finding given existing research, including that on loyalist parading.[50] The discrepancy results from the methodological problem that I discussed earlier: previous studies did not sample nonparticipants, and thus cannot compare the social networks of participants to those of nonparticipants. Consequently, scholars failed to observe that while participants do know many participants prior to joining, nonparticipants know many participants as well. This reflects how deeply embedded parading organizations are in Protestant communities. It is hard *not* to know a member of a loyal order or band. Among men who have never participated in their adult lives, 83 percent have friends and/or family members who parade and 22 percent have been asked to parade. These figures are even higher when restricted to working-class neighborhoods, where parading organizations are stronger (91 percent and 28 percent, respectively).

Yet this methodological issue does not explain why the result is inconsistent with many well-designed studies of participation in other forms of contentious politics. The divergent finding reflects the fact that key characteristics of parading organizations and the social environment in which they recruit new members differ from those of other movements.

48. Kitts, "Mobilizing in Black Boxes."

49. *Family Marched* takes the value of 0 if no family marched, 1 if either the father or other family members marched, and 2 if both the father and other family members marched. *Close Friends at Age 16* is retrospective since current friends are clearly endogenous to parade participation. It ranges from 0 for none or almost none to 4 for all or almost all of the respondent's friends at age sixteen paraded. *Been Asked* takes the value of 0 if he has not been asked and 1 if he has. On the importance of being asked to mobilize, see Snow, Zurcher, and Ekland-Olson, "Social Networks and Social Movements," p. 795; Sidney Verba, Kay Lehman Schlozman, and Henry E. Brady, *Voice and Equality: Civic Voluntarism in American Politics* (Cambridge, MA: Harvard University Press, 1995); Schussman and Soule, "Process and Protest"; and Stefaan Walgrave and Ruud Wouters, "The Missing Link in the Diffusion of Protest: Asking Others," *American Journal of Sociology* 119, no. 6 (May 2014): 1670–1709.

50. James W. McAuley and Jonathan Tonge, " 'For God and for the Crown': Contemporary Political and Social Attitudes among Orange Order Members in Northern Ireland," *Political Psychology* 28, no. 1 (February 2007): 37; McAuley, Tonge, and Mycock, *Loyal to the Core?* pp. 65–68; and Northern Ireland Youth Forum, *Sons of Ulster: Exploring Loyalist Band Members Attitudes Towards Culture, Identity and Heritage* (Belfast: Northern Ireland Youth Forum, 2013), p. 14.

Crucially, they differ from what social movement theory was developed to explain, namely the protest movements that emerged and flourished in the United States and Western Europe from the 1950s through the 1970s: the civil rights movement, women's movement, student movement, antiwar movement, and others in the new-left family.[51] Because scholars have been so focused on these and others like them, certain assumptions about the role of social networks have been baked into social movement theory. Among these assumptions are that most people are *not* connected to the movement; that movements and their issues are *not* well known or supported among the general population; and that movements operate in an unfriendly, often hostile, environment. Under such conditions, it is logical that networks matter for recruitment.[52]

Loyalist parading, by contrast, does not face these conditions. Parading organizations are deeply embedded in the communities in which they recruit. They have been around for a long time, their cause is widely supported, their symbols and repertoire of action are well known, and their events are very popular and well attended. Major parades are a fixed and familiar part of the community's calendar. And almost everyone in the pool of potential recruits was socialized into the movement's culture and tactics from a very early age. Parades and their music, banners, flags, and uniforms have been a part of their lives from before they can remember. They waved Union Flags while watching parades from a stroller, enjoyed Orange picnics and parties with their family and friends, and grew up hearing stories of the lodge or the band from their fathers, grandfathers, uncles, and cousins.[53]

Parades, moreover, can be hard to avoid even if you try. Parading organizations are near-ubiquitous features of public space in Northern Ireland. On average there are almost seven parades each day of the year. But in actuality, they are concentrated during several months and in certain neighborhoods and towns, meaning that in many Protestant areas during the marching season, parades are practically inescapable. Even if not planning

---

51. Doug McAdam, Robert J. Sampson, Simon Weffer, and Heather MacIndoe, " 'There Will Be Fighting in the Streets': The Distorting Lens of Social Movement Theory," *Mobilization* 10, no. 1 (February 2005): 1–18.

52. For studies of the conditions under which networks matter for recruitment, see Florence Passy, "Social Networks Matter. But How?" in Diani and McAdam, *Social Movements and Networks*, pp. 21–48; and Florence Passy and Gian-Andrea Monsch, "Do Social Networks Really Matter in Contentious Politics?" *Social Movement Studies* 13, no. 1 (January 2014): 22–47.

53. Put another way, parading organizations have created their own networks. Their networks are endogenous, rather than the independent, preexisting "mobilizing structures" envisioned by structural theorists. See Jeff Goodwin and James M. Jasper, "Caught in a Winding, Snarling Vine: The Structural Bias of Political Process Theory," *Sociological Forum* 14, no. 1 (March 1999): 41–42, 45–46.

to attend, you are likely to see parades, hear parades (the thunderous sound of marching bands can be heard far off the route), or get stuck in traffic because a parade is passing by. No one in Protestant society, or really in Northern Ireland as a whole, lacks an awareness of parading or parading organizations. Parades make themselves known.

Given parading's longevity, social embeddedness, visibility, and popularity, we would not expect social ties to matter in the same way as they did during, say, the Mississippi Freedom Summer. "Protest comes in diverse forms," Florence Passy and Gian-Andrea Monsch rightly observe, "and networks do not have a uniform, or universal, influence on participants in contentious politics."[54] Accordingly, theories generated to explain patterns of participation in emerging movements will overlook key features of long-established movements like loyalist parading. It remains true that people with no ties to parading are unlikely to join, but the presence of ties does not increase the likelihood of participation: there are many, many nonparticipants who also have structural connections to parading. In fact, if social ties did operate as the structural approach expects them to, there would be far more paraders filling Northern Ireland's streets. As McAdam reflects in an insider's critique of the structural approach, "We are left with the unfortunate impression that individuals who are structurally proximate to a movement are virtually compelled to get involved by virtue of knowing others who are already active."[55] That is, structural proximity is too often understood as a deterministic, quasi-sufficient condition for mobilization. Deep and wide ties, at least in the case of loyalist parading, do not lead to bloc recruitment, the wholesale mobilization of a social network into a movement.[56] They lead instead to a large community of Protestants with strong ties to paraders and parading who nonetheless choose to cheer from the sidewalk or stay home altogether.

The statistical results, however, do not mean that social networks are irrelevant to parading, and it is important not to overstate the finding. Although the presence of social ties to participants does not increase one's likelihood of participation, those who do choose to join generally still do so through their social connections. Pre-existing social ties, then, remain a crucial pathway to mobilization. We can see this in both the quantitative and qualitative data. Among men who have ever paraded, 77 percent cited social ties as what attracted them to the specific parading organization that

54. Passy and Monsch, "Do Social Networks Really Matter in Contentious Politics?" p. 43.

55. Doug McAdam, *Political Process and the Development of Black Insurgency, 1930–1970*, 2nd ed. (Chicago: University of Chicago Press, 1999), p. xii.

56. On bloc recruitment, see Aldon D. Morris, *The Origins of the Civil Rights Movement* (New York: Free Press, 1984); and McAdam, *Political Process and the Development of Black Insurgency*.

they joined (59 percent said friends, 17 percent said their father, and 20 percent mentioned other family members; they could list more than one attraction). It is, therefore, unsurprising that 93 percent of them already knew a few (37 percent) or many (55 percent) members in the group at the time of joining.[57] Men who joined with no reported pre-existing social ties were exceedingly rare, a finding that is consistent with much of the previous literature.[58]

The interviews corroborate these trends. Jamie is typical when he relates that he chose to join the band that he did because he "wanted to be in a band that was more home. And the [band] has quite a few of my family: one, two, three, four family members in it, cousins and stuff like that. And then all the other guys in it, there's quite a few I used to go to school with." The band is the only band from the neighborhood that he grew up in, and even though he now lives in a different part of Belfast, Jamie says that joining this band was a "no-brainer."

Social ties, despite not affecting the likelihood of initial mobilization, clearly still matter greatly for those who are mobilized. This becomes especially apparent when we focus on the role of family. Paraders commonly mentioned family ties as a major motive for joining. Indeed, many participants explained their own decision to parade by stating simply: it is a "family tradition." As if to prove it, a number of participants placed themselves in a lineage that traces back several generations of marchers. Billy, for instance, proudly states, "My grandfather was an Orangeman, my father was an Orangeman, and I'm an Orangeman." And though he has no sons, "Hopefully, my grandchildren will be Orangemen. Hopefully they'll follow in the tradition. That's just the way we were brought up. Just tradition after tradition." Likewise, the Orange Order's publication, the *Orange Standard*, frequently features photographs of multi-generation Orange families. "The importance of family bonds to Orangeism cannot be overstated," McCauley, Tonge, and Mycock conclude.[59] This "narrative of continuity" is an important part of individual participants'

57. See also McAuley, Tonge, and Mycock, *Loyal to the Core?* pp. 65–68. Their survey finds a similar result: 83 percent of Orangemen joined "through direct associations with family or friends" (p. 65).

58. But see James M. Jasper and Jane D. Poulsen, "Recruiting Strangers and Friends: Moral Shocks and Social Networks in Animal Rights and Anti-Nuclear Protests," *Social Problems* 42, no. 4 (November 1995): 493–512; and Bert Klandermans, Jacquelien van Stekelenburg, Marie-Louise Damen, Dunya van Troost, and Anouk van Leeuwen, "Mobilization Without Organization: The Case of Unaffiliated Demonstrators," *European Sociological Review* 30, no. 6 (December 2014): 702–716.

59. McAuley, Tonge, and Mycock, *Loyal to the Core?* pp. 66, 65.

personal stories and how they understand their own motivation to parade.[60]

The most lauded family tie in loyalist parading is between father and son. In "The Sash," the most popular Orange tune, passing the parading tradition from father to son is celebrated in the chorus: "My father wore it as a youth in bygone days of yore, / And on the Twelfth I love to wear the sash my father wore." Whenever the song is played, which is usually many times in each parade, the assembled spectators gleefully sing (or shout) along to the line "the sash my father wore!" Parading can be a way to literally follow in one's father's footsteps, and many sons do. But many sons do not. In the survey, eighty-six respondents had a father who marched (38 percent of the sample). Of them, 50 percent have themselves marched and 50 percent have not. Lee and his three brothers exemplify this pattern: he and one brother chose to join the Orange Order with their father, while his other two brothers did not. One of the two who did not join will occasionally go to watch a parade, but otherwise does not care; the final brother, he told me, could not be bothered to leave his Xbox.

Thus, even men with strong social ties to paraders often do not participate. In fact, as noted earlier, the majority of nonparticipants have friends and family that march. Gary's story illustrates one possible path away from parading, despite having the right social networks. Gary grew up in working-class Protestant East Belfast, where Orangeism and band culture were the way of life. His own family was "up to their neck and beyond in the Orange," as he recalls. His father was the past Master of his lodge; his uncle was an Orange chaplain. And it rubbed off on him: "As a kid, the two biggest days in the year for me were Christmas and the Twelfth. . . . It was a big, big part of my year. I mean, my birthday was just before it, and I looked forward to the Twelfth more than I ever looked forward to my birthday. Massive, absolutely massive in my young life." Then two things changed: he was admitted to a grammar school and had an evangelical conversion. Suddenly, his social world was flipped upside down. His new friends and peers at "church and school were not part of that Orange culture. They were part of a middle-class culture," where parading was less popular, even less acceptable. Consequently, he never joined the Orange Order or a band, as we (and he) might have expected.

Social networks can thus push people away from parades as much as they pull people toward them. We live in complex social worlds with many

60. Lorenzo Bosi and Donatella Della Porta, "Micro-Mobilization into Armed Groups: Ideological, Instrumental and Solidaristic Paths," *Qualitative Sociology* 35, no. 4 (December 2012): 380.

connections to all sorts of people and organizations—a situation that can present "conflicting behavioral pressures."[61] So even those who have many ties to parade participants likely also have ties to nonparticipants. And there is no ex ante reason to believe that one set of social connections should matter more than another; or that pressure from some friends and family to participate should outweigh pressure from other friends and family to not participate.

Another common barrier to participation is simply never being asked to parade. Just knowing paraders can often be insufficient to spur mobilization; sometimes it requires an explicit, personal invitation. Robert, for instance, was a big supporter of parades—"I would have went out to every parade"—but had never taken the next step himself to actually parade. Then "some of the men said to me, 'Boy, it's about time you joined.' And I joined." The importance of being asked is the "quasi consensus" among scholars of collective action.[62] In their influential study of protests in the United States, Alan Schussman and Sarah Soule find that being asked to participate is such an important factor that they propose a two-stage model of mobilization: a person is first asked to participate or not and then she decides whether or not to do it.[63] In loyalist parading, participants are more likely to have been asked to march than nonparticipants (54 percent versus 22 percent), but among men who have been asked to march, only 51 percent actually did.

Contrary to the findings of many prominent and diverse studies, I find that social ties are not a correlate of mobilization. The three quantitative measures of ties are statistically insignificant in the regression analysis, and interview data show that people with connections to participants choose both to participate and to not participate. Yet the evidence also suggests that social ties remain an important part of the story, and a major pathway through which people choose to participate. When people do participate it is generally because of family or friends, and their connections influence which specific organizations they join. Furthermore, when participants decide to move to a new band or lodge (whether because their old one disbanded, they had personal disagreements with other members, they are looking for something new, etc.), they tend to move to one where they have friends or family. Social networks, in short, seem critical to drawing people into parading, but they hardly guarantee it.

61. McAdam and Paulsen, "Specifying the Relationship Between Social Ties and Activism," p. 641.

62. Walgrave and Wouters, "The Missing Link in the Diffusion of Protest," p. 1675.

63. Schussman and Soule, "Process and Protest."

Biography and Parading

Even if a potential participant is willing and connected to a movement, they are unlikely to get involved if they lack the time or capacity. The probability of participation thus increases with "biographical availability," or "the absence of personal constraints that may increase the costs and risks of movement participation, such as full-time employment, marriage and family responsibilities."[64] The straightforward hypothesis is that people are more likely to participate in contentious politics at points in their lives when they have fewer competing claims to their time, such as families or careers. The logic is clear, though research on the effect of biographical availability is inconclusive, with studies pointing in opposite directions.[65] In my survey, three variables measure biographical availability: whether or not a respondent has *Children under 18*, whether or not a respondent has a *Full-Time Job*, and the respondent's *Age*. If biographical availability influences the likelihood of participation, we would expect that younger men without young children or a full-time job are more likely to parade. However, these variables deliver mixed results. I find that men with young children are less likely to be participants, but men with full-time jobs are more likely. And though the young are generally thought to be more available, I find that age is not significantly associated with the likelihood of participation.

A second feature of a person's biography speaks less to their present availability than to their past structural location: prior participation. The argument is that people with a history of past activism should be more likely to participate than people without such a history.[66] In the case of loyalist parading, people have the opportunity to begin participating as children. Boys can join the Junior Orange Order (up to age sixteen) or marching bands, and some march in their first parade even before they can formally become a member, usually carrying the strings tied to the banner of their father's lodge. As Tom recalls, "From an early age I started to parade, carrying the strings for a while. You walked a bit of the way—you were too young—until gradually you walked in the Twelfth day the whole way."

---

64. McAdam, "Recruitment to High-Risk Activism," p. 70.

65. McAdam, "Recruitment to High-Risk Activism"; McAdam, *Freedom Summer*; Wiltfang and McAdam, "The Costs and Risks of Social Activism"; Nepstad and Smith, "Rethinking Recruitment to High-Risk/High-Cost Activism"; Passy and Giugni, "Social Networks and Individual Perceptions"; Schussman and Soule, "Process and Protest"; and Kraig Beyerlein and John Hipp, "A Two-Stage Model for a Two-Stage Process: How Biographical Availability Matters for Social Movement Mobilization," *Mobilization* 11, no. 3 (October 2006): 299–320.

66. See Doug McAdam, "The Biographical Consequences of Activism," *American Sociological Review* 54, no. 5 (October 1989): 752; Doug McAdam, "The Biographical Impact of Activism," in *How Social Movements Matter*, ed. Marco Giugni, Doug McAdam, and Charles Tilly (Minneapolis: University of Minnesota Press, 1999), pp. 121–122; and Corrigal-Brown, *Patterns of Protest*.

I measure past participation with the ordinal variable *Marched as Youth*.[67] Consistent with previous research, I find that prior participation increases the likelihood of current participation. Although not all paraders started early in life and many youth paraders did not continue into adulthood, there is a clear pathway from parading as a boy (which was often the result of having a father parade) to parading later in life. Billy's story represents one common trajectory:

> When I was a child, my father and my grandfather were in the Orange. I can remember going along and carrying the string on the Twelfth of July, probably wasn't very old— five, six, seven, eight years old. Carried the string and went—enjoyed the music, enjoyed the bands. I enjoyed the atmosphere and the feeling that the Twelfth gave. Your dad got a pot of chips, got the ice cream or whatever.... Whenever I was over in the Orange Hall, you'd have got crisps and lemonade. Maybe the Orange would have given me fifty old pennies for carrying the string or something. It's just a tradition since I was there. It was always like, Oh, I can't wait until I'm sixteen, until I can join the Orange. I can't wait until I'm sixteen to join the Orange.

So when he turned sixteen, he did. "I couldn't wait to join," he reiterated.

A personal history of parading, unlike biographical availability, does help to explain participation. Current paraders are more likely than non-paraders to have participated in childhood. Despite this finding, however, the structural approach to participation does not fare well. Social networks, which are the approach's star variable, do not predict parade participation. This is the case, I argue, because of the long-established role of parading organizations in the communities from which they draw new members.[68] Loyalist parading's contribution to structuralism in social movement theory is to highlight the variety of social environments and network effects that exist among "understudied" forms of contention.[69]

EDUCATION, RELIGIOSITY, AND INCOME

The models in table 2.1 include three control variables without theoretically motivated hypotheses. I do not find any meaningful relationship between a respondent's level of *Education* and participation. The coefficient

---

67. *Marched as Youth* takes a value of 0 if the respondent never marched in a parade before he turned sixteen, a value of 1 if he marched as a young boy but not as a formal member of a parading organization, and a value of 2 if he marched as a member of a junior loyal order or band.

68. The high rate of youth participation among current paraders is itself a reflection of the enduring position of the loyal orders and bands in Protestant communities.

69. Passy and Monsch, "Do Social Networks Really Matter in Contentious Politics?" p. 24.

is negative, as expected, but it is not significant.[70] *Church Attendance,* a proxy for religiosity, is positively related to participation: paraders attend church more frequently than non-paraders.[71] *Income,* finally, is not significantly related to parade participation. However, the role of socioeconomic status is likely more complex than this one statistical finding indicates. First, the statistical analysis controls for neighborhood, meaning that the result shows that participants are no wealthier or poorer than non-participating neighbors. It does not mean that they are equal to the sample as a whole.[72] This is important because recent research highlights the important role of class in parading. In contrast to much of the twentieth century, when parading organizations drew heavily from middle- and working-class communities, parading today is primarily a working-class phenomenon.[73] My survey substantiates this conclusion. For instance, 16 percent of residents of working-class neighborhoods are paraders, compared to only 4 percent of middle-class residents. And only 10 percent of the surveyed paraders reside in middle-class areas. Finally, education, which is strongly related to class, is, as previously mentioned, negatively associated with the propensity to participate, although not significantly so.

These results reveal two important characteristics where paraders differ from otherwise similar nonparticipants. Compared to their neighbors, paraders are more likely to attend church, and compared to the overall sample, they are more likely to be working class. Along with the findings presented earlier in this chapter we can begin to outline a rough sketch of parade participants: church-going, working-class Protestants who began parading in their youth. They had many social ties to paraders, which helped pull them into their loyal order or band, but not noticeably more ties than many other Protestants who do not parade. They are not paid or otherwise incentivized for their involvement, although some may have felt social pressure, and their attitudes toward Protestants and Catholics are not that different from those of their non-parading neighbors.

70. *Education* takes 0 for no qualifications, 1 for qualifications less than degree level, and 2 for degree level.

71. *Church Attendance* ranges from 0 for never attending church to 6 for attending more than once a week. Note that technically, church attendance is required of Orangemen, though not of band members. McAuley, Tonge, and Mycock, *Loyal to the Core?* p. 160, also find high church attendance among Orangemen (60 percent attend weekly). For their discussion of the religiosity of Orange Order members, see pp. 158–162.

72. Note also that only 65 percent of respondents answered the income question, so much of the data are imputed.

73. Kaufmann, *The Orange Order;* Bryan, *Orange Parades;* Ramsey, *Music, Emotion and Identity;* McAuley, Tonge, and Mycock, *Loyal to the Core?* esp. p. 58; and Gordon Ramsey, "Band Practice: Class, Taste and Identity in Ulster Loyalist Flute Bands," *Ethnomusicology Ireland* 1 (February 2011): 1–20.

CONCLUSION

The image of paraders formed in this analysis does not adhere to any of the profiles proposed by the three prevailing explanations. Participants do not unequivocally follow a logic of extreme sectarianism, precise cost-benefit analysis, or structural availability. Thus the prominent arguments found in the Northern Irish opinion pages and academic journals alike do not explain participation in Northern Ireland's foremost contentious ritual. One important reason is that these theories do not account for the parades' ritual nature, which recent research identifies as affecting the dynamics of participation.[74] For paraders, I will soon show, have their own reasons for participating that come from a source none of the other approaches considered: the varied benefits intrinsic to the very act of participation in a contentious ritual. In the next chapter, I detail these benefits and explain how they are provided by contentious rituals.

---

74. See the articles in the special issue of *Mobilization* 17, no. 3 (September 2012) introduced by Bert Klandermans, "Between Rituals and Riots: The Dynamics of Street Demonstrations," pp. 233–234; Klandermans, van Stekelenburg, Damen, van Troost, and van Leeuwen, "Mobilization Without Organization," p. 707; and María Inclán and Paul D. Almeida, "Ritual Demonstrations Versus Reactive Protests: Participation Across Mobilizing Contexts in Mexico City," *Latin American Politics and Society* 59, no. 4 (Winter 2017): 47–74.

CHAPTER 3

Parading Mainly for Fun and Process

Mark's passion for parades and parading is unmistakable. The technology entrepreneur was so eager to talk about parades and his experiences parading that, upon hearing about my study from someone else, he contacted me, volunteering to take part. We arranged to meet and, on the day before the Twelfth of July, I took the short train ride to Carrickfergus, a Protestant suburb just outside of Belfast. He picked me up from the train station and we drove to a nearby cafe, where we spoke over breakfast. Affable and enthusiastic, Mark talked to me about parading for the better part of two hours.

His love of parading began over forty-five years ago, when he was just a young boy. In the opening minutes of the interview he explained how he first paraded at the age of four, when his uncle, "a very strong member of the Orange Order," brought him to the Twelfth of July to hold the strings that hung from the lodge's banner. "I just knew this is where I was meant to be," he recalled. "It was almost as if it was my whole reason for being, to a certain degree—and that may sound very strange from a young child." He was hooked and has "been a member of the Orange Order ever since."

As Mark matured and learned more about what the Orange Order stands for, he saw that it is "exactly what I'm about. That is who I am." Speaking rapidly, he continued: "It's like asking a Jewish person, 'Why do you go to the synagogue?' Asking a Catholic person, 'Why do they go to Mass?' Why am I in the Orange? Because that is exactly what I am and it's—I don't do it to offend Catholics, to offend anybody. I am in the Orange simply because that's my identity and that's my belief." For Mark, participation is about his sense of self and how he understands his life and his world. It is a reflection of his deepest-held principles and priorities.

Parading is an expression of who he is and who he wants to be. It is so vital to his self-conception that he participates despite the potential detriment to his material well-being. "I've never faced any personal discrimination because of membership of the Orange Order," he said, "but let's put it this way":

> Because of my business now, I don't advertise it too much. That's the fear, that is the fear.... I've went to business meetings and listened to business speakers who stood on a platform and—some of them very, very good business speakers too—talked about how they're a member of their local GAA club [Gaelic Athletic Association, an Irish nationalist organization], and getting involved in the community and all the rest of it, and that's simply accepted. But I can bet you any money if it was myself standing up and I started talking about how I am a member of an Orange lodge and I am involved in my local community, that would be absolutely, totally frowned upon. Now it's always been demonized to such a degree that now it's no longer deemed acceptable to mention that you are a member of it.

And the prospect of losing business is not the only fear that keeps him quiet in some quarters. "The other thing you have to bear in mind, as well: it's only fifteen years ago that the IRA stopped killing us, for a while. So you certainly wouldn't want to go into certain areas and advertise that you are an Orangeman because you'd be putting a target on your own back, unfortunately." His fears came up throughout the interview—for his job, his future, his country. Many observers see parading as a way that men like Mark take a stand to prevent such terrifying futures—particularly the erosion of Protestant territory and power. But Mark does not.

The way he sees it, parades celebrate "that we are a distinct cultural group. And we're still here and we still adhere to old-fashioned British values of honesty and decency."

"So is that the primary message then?" I pressed.

"Eh, the message? I don't know." He hesitated before proceeding haltingly: "When I go out parading, do I go out to send a message? Hmm. Maybe it could be viewed upon that I am sending a message, but probably it's more of a statement of what I am." Mark normally spoke confidently in long, uninterrupted paragraphs, but my question knocked him off-balance. Despite just stating a plausible message ("we are a distinct cultural group . . ."), he was unsure how to answer. Parades are about his "identity"—"who I am," "what I am," "what I'm about." They are an "outward expression" of his beliefs. As a result, he generally does not—and perhaps cannot—think about them in terms of sending and receiving a message. Despite the overwhelming view among observers and opponents that parades send some message—whether affirmative or antagonistic—Mark, a lifelong parader, had no ready answer. He simply does not understand parades that way.

This is not to argue that instrumental, external, outcome-oriented reasons have no place in his thinking or acting. For instance, he acknowledged that parades have a political aspect because they are performed by people who support the union of Northern Ireland and Great Britain. "It is a political statement in that regard," he said. "Although, we don't set out— We simply set out to celebrate, 'This is what we are and this is what we stand for.'" He fully understands that a "political statement" gets broadcast when he parades, yet, he stresses, it is not his main intent.

Mark presents a very different account of the reasons to parade than what is commonly heard outside of the circles of paraders and their supporters. Whereas Mark focuses on the expression of his identity, the more familiar view, as I discussed in the previous chapter, is that paraders are motivated by bigotry and seek to insult and offend Catholics. A post on a popular Northern Irish political blog illustrates this perspective forcefully. "The sheer weight of evidence," the blogger writes, "makes it impossible to reach any logical conclusion other than that the 11th Night and Twelfth commemorations are used by a large section of loyalism to express their hatred, loathing and abhorrence of their catholic [*sic*], nationalist neighbours."[1] The gap between Mark's view and the blogger's could hardly be wider.

This chapter, as well as the next, explores reasons why this is the case. My analysis of interview, survey, and ethnographic data uncovers four central reasons for participation: collective identity expression, tradition, social and emotional pleasures, and external communication. The first three of these reasons, which are the most common in the data, are process-oriented and intrinsic to participation itself. I will show that participants are centrally concerned with the meanings and satisfactions inherent to the experience of parading, not the outcome-oriented motives frequently attributed to them by outsiders. It is not simply "either/or," however. The data suggest that intrinsic and instrumental reasons are complements, not rivals. My analysis will show that process- and outcome-oriented reasons have much in common, and can, at times, overlap. For the sake of clarity, I discuss the four reasons for participation separately, but we will see that the borders between them often blur.

REASONS FOR PARTICIPATING

People act collectively for a wide variety of reasons. Social psychologist Tom Tyler divides motivations for cooperative behavior into two types:

1. Chris Donnelly, "Grieving for a Lost Supremacism," *Slugger O'Toole*, July 15, 2013, http://sluggerotoole.com/2013/07/15/grieving-for-a-lost-supremacism/.

instrumental (external and material) and social (internal and non-material).[2] Bert Klandermans, also a social psychologist, suggests three motivations for collective action: instrumentality, identification, and expressiveness.[3] And rational choice theorist Jon Elster presents a typology of five motivations for contributing to collective action: rational, selfish, outcome-oriented; rational, selfish, process-oriented; rational, non-selfish, outcome-oriented with a positive orientation toward others (altruism); rational, non-selfish, outcome-oriented with a negative orientation toward others (envy and spite); and social norms.[4] But for many decades, most social science research on collective action has fixated on a single view of human decision-making: one that, in Elster's terms, is rational, selfish, and outcome-oriented.

For some time now, scholars of collective mobilization have pushed back against this simplistic view. For instance, in one effort to redress this imbalance, some pointed to the "new social movements" of the 1970s and 1980s to show that there are expressive movements, which seek to express an identity, in addition to instrumental ones, which seek to influence politics and society.[5] But approaches such as this drew too rigid a line between types of movements, activists' motives, and general modes of action. Newer research has demonstrated that it is more complicated. Instrumental action can impact the identities and emotions of participants.[6] Identities and emotions can be deployed for strategic, outcome-oriented ends.[7] The distinctions between purely expressive and purely instrumental movements are empirically untenable: all movements use both instrumental and expressive action and are oriented both internally and externally.[8] There is variation among actions and movements, but it is a matter of degree, not kind.

2. Tom R. Tyler, *Why People Cooperate: The Role of Social Motivations* (Princeton: Princeton University Press, 2011), esp. pp. 27–47.

3. Bert Klandermans, "Motivations to Action," in *The Oxford Handbook of Social Movements*, ed. Donatella Della Porta and Mario Diani (New York: Oxford University Press, 2015), pp. 219–228.

4. Jon Elster, *The Cement of Society: A Study of Social Order* (New York: Cambridge University Press, 1989), pp. 34–49, 97–151.

5. For example, Jean L. Cohen, "Strategy or Identity: New Theoretical Paradigms and Contemporary Social Movements," *Social Research* 52, no. 4 (Winter 1985): 663–716; and Alberto Melucci, *Nomads of the Present: Social Movements and Individual Needs in Contemporary Society*, ed. John Keane and Paul Mier (Philadelphia: Temple University Press, 1989).

6. For example, James M. Jasper, *The Art of Moral Protest: Culture, Biography, and Creativity in Social Movements* (Chicago: University of Chicago Press, 1997).

7. For example, Mary Bernstein, "Celebration and Suppression: The Strategic Uses of Identity by the Lesbian and Gay Movement," *American Journal of Sociology* 103, no. 3 (November 1997): 531–565; Francesca Polletta and James M. Jasper, "Collective Identity and Social Movements," *Annual Review of Sociology* 27 (2001): 283–305; and Deborah B. Gould, *Moving Politics: Emotion and ACT UP's Fight Against AIDS* (Chicago: University of Chicago Press, 2009).

8. Jasper, *The Art of Moral Protest*; and Verta Taylor and Nella Van Dyke, " 'Get Up, Stand Up': Tactical Repertoires of Social Movements," in *The Blackwell Companion to Social Movements*, ed.

The same is true for people's motives for collective participation. Most collective action is likely motivated by a mix of goals and reasons, including "values, norms, commitments, emotions, material interests, and aversions."[9] As Mark demonstrates, these concerns can vacillate and coexist within the same person.[10]

In my research with parade participants, I found both process-oriented and outcome-oriented reasons for action. People parade to express their identity, be part of tradition, experience the pleasures of participation, and communicate with external audiences. The first three reasons are process-oriented or intrinsic, each "depends on the process and not on the consequences" of parading;[11] the fourth reason is outcome-oriented or instrumental, it does depend on achieving a particular consequence of parading. And though process-oriented reasons appear more often in the data, outcome-oriented reasons matter too.

Motives, however, can be tricky things to study. They must be approached with caution, as there are at least three perils in asking participants about their motivations. First, people are not good at accurately reconstructing what motivated them to act. Psychologists warn that "much of the mind is inaccessible to conscious awareness." So when asked to identify their motives, people "generate reasons that are consistent with cultural and personal theories and are accessible in memory."[12] Second, there is the obstacle posed by the passage of time. Besides the simpler problem of basic forgetting, there is the problem identified by sociologist C. Wright Mills seven decades ago: motives are often provided "after the fact." As a result, our stated motives for past behavior are shaped by our current concerns, beliefs, and identities. In the case of social movements, observe Snow, Zurcher, and Ekland-Olson, "'motives' for joining and continued participation...arise out of a process of ongoing interaction" with the movement itself.[13] In other

David A. Snow, Sarah A. Soule, and Hanspeter Kriesi (Malden, MA: Blackwell, 2004), pp. 262–293.

9. Elisabeth Jean Wood, *Insurgent Collective Action and Civil War in El Salvador* (New York: Cambridge University Press, 2003), p. 231.

10. A further advantage of embracing multiple reasons for action is that it helps clarify the relationship between the elites who organize these events and ordinary, mass participants. Elites may well use parades and other contentious rituals instrumentally to augment their power, as the elite-manipulation argument maintains. But this does not mean that participants are similarly motivated. Contentious rituals, then, can emphasize both instrumental and non-instrumental action, depending on one's perspective and the level of analysis.

11. Wood, *Insurgent Collective Action*, p. 240.

12. Timothy D. Wilson and Elizabeth W. Dunn, "Self-Knowledge: Its Limits, Value, and Potential for Improvement," *Annual Review of Psychology* 55 (2004): 499, 505. The classic study is Richard E. Nisbett and Timothy DeCamp Wilson, "Telling More Than We Can Know: Verbal Reports on Mental Processes," *Psychological Review* 84, no. 3 (May 1977): 231–259.

13. David A. Snow, Louis A. Zurcher Jr., and Sheldon Ekland-Olson, "Social Networks and Social Movements: A Microstructural Approach to Differential Recruitment," *American*

words, the "motives" we list as critical to prompting our participation in a movement often result from the experience of participation—attending events, chatting with other activists, reading up on the cause—rather than precede it. Third, social psychological and sociological processes bias people toward reporting socially desirable motives over socially undesirable ones.[14] This desire to appear to conform to social norms and expectations could incentivize parade participants to emphasize motives such as the positive expression of identity rather than hostility toward Catholics, personal financial gain, or the desire to spark a riot.[15]

To address these concerns, I rarely asked people about their motives directly. Rather, following the recommendation of scholars of collective political action, I asked participants to recall the process through which they joined their parading organization; to recount specific recent events (usually the most recently parade they had walked in); and to describe concrete moments, interactions, thoughts, and feelings.[16] The data that result are imperfect, but necessary nonetheless. Despite all the known problems and biases, gathering and analyzing these first-person accounts are crucial to making sense of participants' actions from their own perspective.[17] At the very least, how participants remember and narrate their experiences "sheds light on what those experiences meant and the work they do in the source's understanding of the world."[18] Furthermore, such memories

---

Sociological Review 45, no. 5 (October 1980): 795, citing C. Wright Mills, "Situated Actions and Vocabularies of Motive," *American Sociological Review* 5, no. 6 (December 1940): 904–913.

14. For instance, Theresa J. Demaio, "Social Desirability and Survey Measurement: A Review," in *Surveying Subjective Phenomena*, vol. 2, ed. Charles F. Turner and Elizabeth Martin (New York: Russell Sage Foundation, 1984), pp. 257–282. This human tendency is but one example of our daily work of impression management in interactions with other people. See Erving Goffman, *The Presentation of Self in Everyday Life* (New York: Anchor, 1959).

15. Yet there is also a countervailing desire to report our own actions as rational and instrumentally pursued toward our desired ends, in which case people might be proud to relay that they were compensated for their efforts or that their contributions helped achieve an important outcome. See Jeff Goodwin, James M. Jasper, and Francesca Polletta, "Why Emotions Matter," in *Passionate Politics: Emotions and Social Movements*, ed. Jeff Goodwin, James M. Jasper, and Francesca Polletta (Chicago: University of Chicago Press, 2001), p. 15.

16. On asking about the process of mobilization, see Hahrie Han, *Moved to Action: Motivation, Participation, and Inequality in American Politics* (Stanford: Stanford University Press, 2009), p. 101. On asking about specific events, see Kay Lehman Schlozman, Sidney Verba, and Henry E. Brady, "Participation's Not a Paradox: The View from American Activists," *British Journal of Political Science* 25, no. 1 (January 1995): 10; and Jocelyn S. Viterna, "Pulled, Pushed, and Persuaded: Explaining Women's Mobilization into the Salvadoran Guerrilla Army," *American Journal of Sociology* 112, no. 1 (July 2006): 13–14. Schlozman, Verba, and Brady, "Participation's Not a Paradox," p. 10, also argue that we can be more confident in the accuracy of self-reported reasons when the action in question is important to the person, something which applies to parading.

17. See Wood, *Insurgent Collective Action*, pp. 39–40.

18. Erica S. Simmons, "Market Reforms and Water Wars," *World Politics* 68, no. 1 (January 2016): 68. See also Lee Ann Fujii, *Killing Neighbors: Webs of Violence in Rwanda* (Ithaca: Cornell

and interpretations of past behavior, as political scientists Kay Lehman Schlozman, Sidney Verba, and Henry Brady note, "surely have implications for activists' decisions to get involved again in the future."[19] As a result, following social movement scholars Lorenzo Bosi and Donatella Della Porta, I understand motivations less as "a psychological element," which my study, like theirs, "is unable to grasp, but rather [as] the *activists' per-ceived reasons for joining,* as they emerge in biographical accounts" given by participants.[20]

As a first, and rough, cut to explore paraders' motivations, I use a question from the survey—"In your opinion, what is the purpose of parades?"—to test whether participants are more likely to attribute process-oriented, rather than outcome-oriented, aims to parades.[21] Each open-ended response was coded with at least one of ten purposes, with some responses receiving multiple codes.[22] The codes were developed inductively to accurately capture the concepts conveyed by respondents. I grouped the purposes into two general categories based on their orientation: *Intrinsic* and *Instrumental.* Intrinsic purposes (culture, tradition, celebration, commemoration, social, and carnival) refer to the act itself. Instrumental purposes (taking a stand, displaying loyalty, promoting, and causing a negative outcome) focus on achieving some outcome of the act.

Simple statistical analyses (two-tailed t-tests) show that participants are significantly more likely to mention intrinsic purposes than instrumental purposes. The first row in table 3.1 displays the results for current participants (92 percent intrinsic versus 13 percent instrumental) and the second row shows the results for respondents who have ever paraded since age sixteen (88 percent intrinsic versus 14 percent instrumental). Current and former participants are significantly more likely to state that the purpose of parading is to "celebrate Protestant culture and tradition" or "to commemorate the victory of the Battle of the Boyne" than "marking territory" or "to make a statement." Interestingly, current paraders are also significantly more likely than nonparticipants to cite intrinsic purposes (92 percent versus 73 percent; p = .04). But still, nearly three-quarters of nonparticipants see the

University Press, 2009), esp. pp. 42–43; and Ziad W. Munson, *The Making of Pro-Life Activists: How Social Movement Mobilization Works* (Chicago: University of Chicago Press, 2009), p. 198.

19. Schlozman, Verba, and Brady, "Participation's Not a Paradox," p. 11.

20. Lorenzo Bosi and Donatella Della Porta, "Micro-Mobilization into Armed Groups: Ideological, Instrumental and Solidaristic Paths," *Qualitative Sociology* 35, no. 4 (December 2012): 364. My emphasis.

21. For a similar empirical approach, see Abby Peterson, Mattias Wahlström, Magnus Wennerhag, Camilo Christancho, and José-Manuel Sabucedo, "May Day Demonstrations in Five European Countries," *Mobilization* 17, no. 3 (September 2012): 281–300.

22. The definitions are in table C.1 in appendix C.

Table 3.1. PURPOSES OF LOYALIST PARADES REPORTED BY
PARTICIPANTS: INTRINSIC VS. INSTRUMENTAL (%)

	Intrinsic Purpose	Instrumental Purpose	Difference	P-Value (Two-Tailed)	N
Current participants	92%	13%	79%	.00***	24
Current and former participants	88%	14%	73%	.00***	64

Each response could take multiple codes, so rows do not sum to 100%.
*** *p<.001*

purpose of parades as intrinsic, suggesting that this notion is deeply embedded in the Protestant community.

The semi-structured interviews confirm that participants express more interest in the process of participation than its outcomes. These purposes and reasons were cited more often, with more vigor, and tended to be more immediate and more developed. Participants' understanding of parades focuses on the expression of collective identity, tradition, the social and emotional pleasures of participation, and external communication. The following sections explore each in turn.

"IDENTITY ISN'T A PRIVATE THING": EXPRESSING COLLECTIVE IDENTITY

For most, if not all, paraders, the central purpose of a parade is the expression and celebration of a multifaceted Protestant identity. In interview after interview, participants described parades as opportunities to articulate "what I am," to "show your identity," or to "express Protestant culture."[23] Expressing collective identity—"a shared sense of 'one-ness' or 'we-ness' anchored in real or imagined shared attributes and experiences . . . and in relation or contrast to one or more actual or imagined sets of 'others'"—is a significant reason why people act in general.[24] Scholars have found that

23. Interview with Mark, July 11, 2013; interview with Albert, August 20, 2012; and interview with Rachel, August 8, 2013.

24. David Snow, "Collective Identity and Expressive Forms" (working paper, Center for the Study of Democracy, University of California, Irvine, 2001), p. 2, https://escholarship.org/uc/item/2zn1t7bj. For discussions of the use of the concept in the social movement literature, see Polletta and Jasper, "Collective Identity and Social Movements"; Scott A. Hunt and Robert D. Benford, "Collective Identity, Solidarity, and Commitment," in Snow, Soule, and Kriesi, *The Blackwell Companion to Social Movements*, pp. 433–457; and Cristina Flesher Fominaya, "Collective Identity in Social Movements: Central Concepts and Debates," *Sociology Compass* 4, no. 6 (June 2010): 393–404.

collective identity is an important cause and consequence of mobilization in a range of movements.[25]

In the case of parading, there are several relevant, overlapping identities: Protestant, British, unionist, and loyalist. Protestant identity in Northern Ireland can refer both to an ethnic identity and a religious one. Parading itself, especially by the Orange Order and Royal Black Institution, reflects the two faces of the identity, as both ethnic and religious language and iconography are pervasive. But even the religious aspect of the Protestant identity in parades carries ethnic overtones, and parades' sense of Protestantism is directed to local believers, not a universal faith community. In the Northern Irish context, Protestant also implies a British, as opposed to Irish, national identity. The British identity of many Ulster Protestants, however, is more of an ethnic identity than the multinational, multicultural, civic-ethnic hybrid British identity found among most Britons, even after the Brexit referendum.[26] Related is the unionist identity, which is a political identity rooted in a desire to remain bound to Britain. Many paraders also hold a loyalist identity, which contains both political and cultural aspects.

25. For example, Verta Taylor and Nancy E. Whittier, "Collective Identity in Social Movement Communities: Lesbian Feminist Mobilization," in *Frontiers in Social Movement Theory*, ed. Aldon D. Morris and Carol M. Mueller (New Haven: Yale University Press, 1992), pp. 104–129; Bernstein, "Celebration and Suppression"; Bernd Simon, Michael Loewy, Stefan Stürmer, Ulrike Weber, Peter Freytag, Corinna Habig, Claudia Kampmeier, and Peter Spahlinger, "Collective Identification and Social Movement Participation," *Journal of Personality and Social Psychology* 74, no. 3 (March 1998): 646–658; Sheldon Stryker, Timothy Joseph Owens, and Robert W. White, eds., *Self, Identity, and Social Movements* (Minneapolis: University of Minnesota Press, 2000); P. G. Klandermans, "Identity Politics and Politicized Identities: Identity Processes and the Dynamics of Protest," *Political Psychology* 35, no. 1 (February 2014): 1–22; and Aidan McGarry and James M. Jasper, eds., *The Identity Dilemma: Social Movements and Collective Identity* (Philadelphia: Temple University Press, 2015).

26. Britishness has been multinational since its origins in the early eighteenth century; see Linda Colley, *Britons: Forging the Nation 1707–1837* (New Haven: Yale University Press, 1992). On the United Kingdom's commitment to multiculturalism after Brexit, even as the meaning of the concept continues to evolve, see Richard T. Ashcroft and Mark Bevir, "Multiculturalism in Contemporary Britain: Policy, Law and Theory," *Critical Review of International Social and Political Philosophy* 21, no. 1 (2018): esp. 6–7; Richard Ashcroft and Mark Bevir, "Pluralism, National Identity and Citizenship: Britain After Brexit," *The Political Quarterly* 87, no. 3 (July–September 2016): 355–359; and Tariq Modood, "Multiculturalism Can Foster a New Kind of Post-Brexit Englishness," *EUROPP: European Politics and Policy Blog*, August 11, 2016, http://blogs.lse.ac.uk/europpblog/2016/08/11/multiculturalism-can-foster-a-new-kind-of-post-brexit-englishness/. On the civic and ethnic dimensions of British identity, see Anthony F. Heath and James R. Tilley, "British National Identity and Attitudes Towards Immigration," *International Journal on Multicultural Societies* 7, no. 2 (2005): 119–132; and Zsolt Kiss and Alison Park, "National Identity: Exploring Britishness," in *British Social Attitudes: The 31st Report*, ed. Alison Park, Caroline Bryson, and John Curtice (London: NatCen Social Research, 2014), pp. 61–77, http://www.bsa.natcen.ac.uk/media/38893/bsa31_full_report.pdf. On the distinction of civic and ethnic models of national identity, see Rogers Brubaker, *Citizenship and Nationhood in France and Germany* (Cambridge, MA: Harvard University Press, 1992).

Finally, the organizational identity of the parading group that one belongs to is important to many.

Though the parades "spell out" each of these identities, the identities can hold varying meanings and weights for different participants.[27] Despite walking behind the same flags and banners to the beat of the same music, paraders bring their own understandings of the represented identities, their own attachments and emotional reactions to them, and their own sense of the reciprocal obligations entailed by them. Yet the meanings of the relevant identities for participants are not entirely free-floating or limitless. While there are differences among them, the paraders' understandings of the relevant identities share a great deal. As sociologist Geneviève Zubrzycki rightly observes, "Performative cohesion does not mean…that participants share a single common identity, but it does suggest a certain amount of consensus over what an ideal identity or way of life should be."[28]

Identity is front and center when speaking with paraders. George, for instance, states: "The overarching purpose [of parades] is to say to the world, 'Here we are.…Here we are as members of the Protestant, reformed, evangelical faith. This is our cause and we want the world to know.' I think that's the purpose." His actions are a declaration of his religious identity. He parades to publicly bear witness to his membership in a religiously defined group. But George's religious identity also demonstrates the ambiguities and overlaps among the collective identities at play in loyalist parades. For George, Protestantism is less about specific religious beliefs, practices, or values than "just the pride and the understanding of being a member of it." His Protestantism centers on belonging to a community. I pushed him to discuss the religious teachings that are important to him, but by his own admission, he was "hedging around the question because I can't really answer it."

> By my stumbling you can tell that's actually hard to say because people would tell you, of a much more Christian nature than what I am able to bring from myself, they would tell you about turning the other cheek and charity towards all men, regardless of who they are, and all the good things out of the church, which are right, but which are actually overtaken when you find that those who you are reaching out a hand of friendship to are grabbing you and then beating you around the head with it. That's a bit basic, but I'm trying to say that all the Christian values I would still maintain, but to try actually put them into practice with those who aren't members of the same faith has become increasingly difficult. In fact, at this point in time it's impossible.

27. Mary Ryan, "The American Parade: Representations of the Nineteenth-Century Social Order," in *The New Cultural History*, ed. Lynn Hunt (Berkeley: University of California Press, 1989), p. 133, quoted in Geneviève Zubrzycki, *Beheading the Saint: Nationalism, Religion, and Secularism in Quebec* (Chicago: University of Chicago Press, 2016), p. 25.

28. Zubrzycki, *Beheading the Saint*, p. 25.

In the end, George gave little more than the vague statement, "I believe in the teachings of the Protestant church.... It's all important to me." Far clearer to him was the fact that he is not Catholic: "I would be vehemently against the teachings of the Roman faith, where they are claiming to bring down God on Mass and his body and blood are being given in bread and wine. If that's not an abomination, I don't know what is." His sense of identity perfectly encapsulates Máiréad Nic Craith's argument that in Northern Ireland "identity is often based on our concept of the other or the enemy.... [W]e define ourselves as different from—or even in a simplistic fashion—as the opposite of another."[29] The essence of George's Protestantism is that it is *not* Catholicism.[30]

In large part, religion is serving as a marker of ethnic and political identities.[31] Religious beliefs, for George, define the boundaries of the group more than they seem to provide a theology or spiritual and ethical guidance. Though George defines his identity here in religious terms ("Protestant, reformed, evangelical"), he lacks a strong sense of the substance of that faith. In fact, he is the first to admit that living by some of the basic tenets of Christianity is a struggle for him, and that other people have "a much more Christian nature." What is most important is his deep attachment to one community and collective identity, and its distinction from the other. Parades are how George articulates his belonging to a collective identity, allowing him to declare that he is Protestant and not Catholic.

For Walter, parading is also about his religious identity—"it's all about being a Protestant," he said in response to a question about religion—but

29. Máiréad Nic Craith, *Culture and Identity Politics in Northern Ireland* (Houndsmill, UK: Palgrave Macmillan, 2003), p. 6.

30. I think this clarifies George's remark, "I believe in the teachings of the Protestant church." There is, of course, no one Protestant church. In fact, he belongs to a Presbyterian congregation, where the idea of a single, unified church is laughable. Rather, "the Protestant church" serves as the antithesis of the "the Catholic Church."

31. See John McGarry and Brendan O'Leary, *Explaining Northern Ireland: Broken Images* (Oxford: Basil Blackwell, 1995). Yet it is unfair to characterize George's Protestant identity as merely nominal identification with a religious community. He attends church, and religious ideas underpin his understanding of Protestant and Catholic social identities. As Claire Mitchell has demonstrated in several excellent works, "rather than just marking out identities, religion generally provides some substantive content to processes of social categorization and comparison in Northern Ireland." This is the case, she finds, even among people who do not attend church or consider themselves religious. As she write about Protestants who are "invisible in conventional measures of religiosity": "the concepts they use to understand social life are not just morally, but also pseudo-theologically, charged." Claire Mitchell, "Behind the Ethnic Marker: Religion and Social Identification in Northern Ireland," *Sociology of Religion* 66, no. 1 (Spring 2005): 3–21 (quotations are from p. 18); Claire Mitchell, *Religion, Identity and Politics in Northern Ireland: Boundaries of Belonging and Belief* (Aldershot: Ashgate, 2006); Claire Mitchell, "The Religious Content of Ethnic Identities," *Sociology* 40, no. 6 (December 2006): 1135–1152; and Claire Mitchell, "The Push and Pull Between Religion and Ethnicity: The Case of Loyalists in Northern Ireland," *Ethnopolitics* 9, no. 1 (March 2010): 53–69.

his focus is more on cultural and local identities. Parades are "about going out and showing our cultural identity—not through violence, but through music and through the pageantry of it all. And to show how well and respectful we can be." It is a way to express his Protestant and loyalist identities and demonstrate their worth. Loyalism is often associated with paramilitary violence and cultural inferiority. Parades are how Walter rebuts those stereotypes and asserts pride in being a loyalist. They are declarations of dignity.

In addition to the broader Protestant identity, Walter has a specific local identity that he also relishes showing off. "[Our neighborhood] is known throughout the land because of [our band]," he boasts. "It takes [the neighborhood's] identity everywhere: it's [printed] on our bass drum." Most members of his band are from the same small, tight-knit interface neighborhood, so the identities of the band and the community are intertwined. Walter even displays his attachment to his band on his body, with a tattoo on his leg. Half the band, he estimates, has done the same: "We have our band tattooed on us," he says. Local and organizational identities like these reinforce the wider collective identity as they tie individuals to a knowable segment of the larger group. Particularly in the case of ethnic movements, ties to an ethnic organization generate a concrete connection to the imagined community.

Expressing their deeply held collective identities in public is a source of process-oriented benefits that participants seek. It provides a satisfying reason to parade. In fact, as Friedman and McAdam argue, "One of the most powerful motivators of individual action is the desire to confirm through behavior a cherished identity."[32] Parading provides the opportunity to do just that. Parading is a way—perhaps *the* way—for participants to confirm their Protestant identity, to live its values and beliefs. It is, for many, what makes them Protestant.

And so, though it can be used instrumentally to effect an external outcome,[33] parade participants, for the most part, see expression itself as their purpose. For example, when I asked Albert what the goal of parading is, he replied: "Just to show your identity.... We are a parading organization and we parade as and when necessary." I asked why and he said, "That's the thing to do. You show it to your supporters, and if your non-supporters object, it's up to them." Responding to the same question, Robert said, the purpose of parading is "to show that we are members of the Protestant community." Albert's and Robert's statements about the goals of parading refer

32. Debra Friedman and Doug McAdam, "Collective Identity and Activism: Networks, Choices, and the Life of a Social Movement," in Morris and Mueller, *Frontiers in Social Movement Theory*, p. 169.

33. For example, Bernstein, "Celebration and Suppression."

inexorably back to the parade itself. Their reason for acting is the expression that is always already an element of parading.

Implicit in their comments is an idea that Ben makes explicit: "Identity isn't a private thing, it's a public thing." "Orangeism," he continues, "isn't something that we are just going to have in our wee halls and have our wee meetings and then go home again. Public expression of it is intrinsic to it, it's a value of it. It has to be public. It has to be a public manifestation of it."[34] In the eyes of Ben and many other Northern Irish Protestants, Protestant identity does not exist apart from its public display—there cannot be one without the other. Parading is so central to what it means to be an Ulster Protestant that Ben cannot imagine the identity without its public performances. Even among Protestants who choose not to parade, such as Matt, it is unthinkable: "It's just something that's always been part of my life, the bands and the parades. I couldn't even begin to imagine what it would be like if there wasn't any bands or parades, really to be honest. It's a way of expressing our identity and our expression."

Ben and Matt seem to intuitively understand the argument put forward by scholars attuned to the performative nature of identity: identities are "constituted by stylized acts, gestures, words, and deeds." Thus the very existence of an identity cannot be separated from its performance. "Viewed as performative," writes political scientist Lee Ann Fujii, "identities cease being states of being or properties that get triggered under the right conditions. Instead, identity amounts to the repeated and public actions, activities, and practices...that make them real."[35] This is an accurate account of the relationship between parading and Protestantism for many Ulster Protestants. Parading is not just what makes them Protestant; parading is what makes *Protestantism*. For many—especially those unable to articulate or elaborate what exactly the identity stands for or means—parading constitutes Protestantism in Northern Ireland. As Billy asserts, "The parades *are* my culture."[36]

A key manner of expressing—and thus constituting—collective identity is commemorating the collective past. Commemorations are a medium through which we assert, define, and contest current collective identities.

---

34. Compare to Sherry Ortner's summary of Geertz: "culture is not something locked inside people's heads, but rather is embodied in public symbols." Sherry B. Ortner, "Theory in Anthropology Since the Sixties," *Comparative Studies in Society and History* 26, no. 1 (January 1984): 129. See also Ann Swidler, "Culture in Action: Symbols and Strategies," *American Sociological Review* 51, no. 2 (April 1986): 273–286; and Ann Swidler, "Cultural Power and Social Movements," in *Social Movements and Culture*, ed. Hank Johnston and Bert Klandermans (Minneapolis: University of Minnesota Press, 1995), esp. pp. 26–27.

35. Lee Ann Fujii, "Performances of Identity and Violence" (paper prepared the RIGS paper seminar series, University of California, Irvine, 2010), p. 7.

36. My emphasis.

Though ostensibly about history, they are always about the present.[37] Many parades perform the memory of great moments in Ulster Protestant history, particularly military battles.[38] By honoring the men who gave their lives for the nation, paraders also honor the nation itself. Commemorative parades mark the Battle of the Boyne (1690) on July 12, the Battle of the Somme (1916) on July 1, and the Siege of Derry (1689) on the Saturdays nearest August 12 and December 18. Even non-commemorative parades, on account of their annual repetition, call the past to mind.[39] In parades, the work of the Protestant past is to articulate the Protestant present.

Yet this is not necessarily how participants understand their own actions. They do not see their commemorations as having an extrinsic purpose or as being a means for an external end.[40] For example, Albert told me, "The First of July [parade], it commemorates the Battle of the Somme [and] the 36th (Ulster) Division [in World War I], the Twelfth of July [parade] commemorates the Battle of the Boyne. They're all battles we remember."

"You do that to continue the memory?" I asked, probing his reasoning.

"Yes, to continue the tradition," he replied.

As Albert states, the purpose of marching is to maintain the memory of these great battles and the men who died in them. He understands his actions as part of a long line of war commemoration where the goal is wrapped up in the performance of tradition. Tradition is maintained in order to maintain tradition.

Kenny suggests a similar understanding: "You've got commemoration parades, like the Twelfth. That to me is all part of my history. People fought and died for that and I want to be part of it to keep it going." His interest is in maintaining the honor of those who gave their lives for his nation. The memory of the victories and sacrifices of Ulster Protestant history motivates Albert and Kenny. Though they are hazy on what exactly that past is or why it is valuable, they seek to honor and to preserve it. They are driven to gain the satisfaction of joining with friends to "keep it going."

Despite the internally oriented stated intentions of most participants, these acts of remembrance reverberate across society. The commemorated past is partial, selective, and exclusively Protestant. It is "ethno-history," or

---

37. See Paul Connerton, *How Societies Remember* (New York: Cambridge University Press, 1989).

38. Neil Jarman, *Material Conflicts: Parades and Visual Displays in Northern Ireland* (Oxford: Berg, 1997), p. 1, describes parades as "the performance of memory."

39. Connerton, *How Societies Remember*, p. 45.

40. A large literature from the past several decades has documented beyond question that elites use commemorations for present-day political purposes. See, for example, the seminal collection of essays in John R. Gillis, ed., *Commemorations: The Politics of National Identity* (Princeton: Princeton University Press, 1996). However, far less is known about the perspectives and motivations of the ordinary people who participate in these events.

as Kenny says more straightforwardly, "*my* history."[41] Catholics are almost always excluded—unless they appear as the villain. In their commemorations, participants remember, celebrate, and mourn the Protestant dead, which encourages communal divisions.[42] Commemorative parades for the Somme, for instance, are dedicated to the 36th (Ulster) Division of the British Army, ignoring the heavy casualties of the 16th (Irish) Division, mainly Catholic nationalists who also volunteered to serve the Crown. And despite the protestations by a few individuals that during parades they personally commemorate the sacrifices made by the 16th (Irish), the Catholic dead are publicly ignored in Protestant commemorations.[43]

This exclusiveness is common in national memories and commemorations, which seek to produce and sustain national myths. In multinational societies like Northern Ireland, argues historian John Gillis, this means that "memory tend[s] to divide rather than unite."[44] Commemorations reinforce ethnic boundaries instead of expanding the "community of memory."[45] Yet, as the participants cited here attest, most seek to honor their nation's dead, not to further divide Protestants from Catholics. But as with collective identity expression in any divided society, where unpacified cleavages set the boundaries of belonging and access to power, celebrating one community's past or present inevitably leaves the other community feeling excluded.[46] As the Northern Irish literary critic Edna Longley observes,

41. David Officer and Graham Walker, "Protestant Ulster: Ethno-History, Memory and Contemporary Prospects," *National Identities* 2, no. 3 (2000): 293–307.

42. Divisions that remain even after death—Belfast City Cemetery has an infamous underground wall that keeps Catholic and Protestant graves apart. See Peter Shirlow and Brendan Murtagh, *Belfast: Segregation, Violence, and City* (London: Pluto, 2006), p. 13.

43. See Jim McAuley, "Memory and Belonging in Ulster Loyalist Identity," *Irish Political Studies* 31, no. 1 (2016): 122–138; and James W. McAuley, *Very British Rebels?: The Culture and Politics of Ulster Loyalism* (London: Bloomsbury, 2016), pp. 104–106. Gareth Mulvenna, "Labour Aristocracies, Triumphalism and Melancholy: Misconceptions of the Protestant Working-Class and Loyalist Community," in *The Contested Identities of Ulster Protestants*, ed. Thomas Paul Burgess and Gareth Mulvenna (Houndmills, UK: Palgrave Macmillan, 2015), p. 172, points out the incongruity between Somme commemorations as celebrations of Ulster's role in protecting general British "freedoms and liberties" and as "essentially parochial remembering." At the battlefield in France, however, Protestant organizations have performed commemorations at the 16th (Irish) Division's monument. Brian Graham and Peter Shirlow, "The Battle of the Somme in Ulster Memory and Identity," *Political Geography* 21, no. 7 (September 2002): 889.

44. John R. Gillis, "Memory and Identity: The History of a Relationship," in Gillis, *Commemorations*, p. 7. See also Sara Dybris McQuaid, "Parading Memory and Re-member-ing Conflict: Collective Memory in Transition in Northern Ireland," *International Journal of Politics, Culture, and Society* 30, no. 1 (March 2017): 23–41.

45. Robert N. Bellah, Richard Madsen, William M. Sullivan, Ann Swidler, and Steven M. Tipton, *Habits of the Heart: Individualism and Commitment in American Life* (Berkeley: University of California Press, 1985), pp. 152–155.

46. Lorenzo Bosi and Gianluca De Fazio, "Contextualizing the Troubles: Investigating Deeply Divided Societies Through Social Movements Research," in *The Troubles in Northern*

"Commemorations are as selective as sympathies. They honour *our* dead, not *your* dead."[47] This dilemma begins to account for the starkly different visions of parades by Protestants and Catholics.

"THAT'S MY TRADITION"

"Tradition," observes anthropologist Neil Jarman, "is one of the most over-used words in contemporary Northern Ireland."[48] I often felt the same about the interviews I conducted. Participants repeatedly accounted for both the overall existence of parades and their own reasons for parading by invoking "tradition." The word rolled off their tongues as if it were simple, obvious, and the final, definitive answer. While the concept is sometimes cited without the term ("It's what we do; we've done it for years," says Albert), references to the term and its derivatives abound. Billy, for instance, joined because of "tradition"; Robert began parading because "it was part of the family tradition"; and Kyle got involved because "that was just a family tradition." The survey shows that one-third of men who ever participated cite tradition as a purpose of parades, and 30 percent say that tradition is what attracted them to join their specific lodge or band.

For the analyst, however, "tradition" poses a problem. What are we to make of the assertion of tradition as a reason for action? Communication theorist James W. Carey elaborates the difficulty: "Actions motivated by tradition, values, and affections pretty much escape our understanding and end up as the human interest exotica."[49] Though tradition has long been a key concept in the social sciences and humanities, prominent scholarly approaches are little help. For Weberians, tradition is non-rational. In fact, it "lies very close to the borderline of what can be called meaningfully oriented action."[50] For constructivists, tradition is "invented," rather than "genuine," and so it is not really a valid reason for behavior.[51] For Marxists,

Ireland and Theories of Social Movements, ed. Lorenzo Bosi and Gianluca De Fazio (Amsterdam: Amsterdam University Press, 2017), p. 11.

47. Edna Longley, "The Rising, the Somme and Irish Memory," in *Revising the Rising*, ed. Máirín Ní Dhonnchadha and Theo Dorgan (Derry, Northern Ireland: Field Day, 1991), p. 29, quoted in Guy Beiner, *Remembering the Year of the French: Irish Folk History and Social Memory* (Madison: University of Wisconsin Press, 2006), p. 304. Italics in the original.

48. Jarman, *Material Conflicts*, p. 25.

49. James Carey, "The Dark Continent of American Journalism," in *James Carey: A Critical Reader*, ed. Eve Stryker Munson and Catherine A. Warren (Minneapolis: University of Minnesota Press, 1997), p. 181.

50. Max Weber, *Economy and Society: An Outline of Interpretive Sociology*, trans. and ed. Guenther Roth and Claus Wittich (Berkeley: University of California Press, 1978), p. 25.

51. Eric Hobsbawm and Terence Ranger, eds., *The Invention of Tradition* (Cambridge: Cambridge University Press, 1983).

modernization theorists, and other Whigs, tradition is backward and constraining, but bound to disappear.[52] Though these are some of the most
influential perspectives on tradition, none of them explain why so many
people continue to find tradition so appealing.

There are two additional problems when trying to understand tradition
as a reason for action. First, participants could be merely mimicking the
official language of parading organizations. That is, interviewees might be
giving me "little more than organizational slogans repeated as personal
beliefs."[53] And "tradition" certainly is an important slogan for parading
organizations: Dominic Bryan finds that it is "the dominant discourse used
to legitimize the parades."[54] If this is the case, "tradition" is not a reason so
much as a justification, and a memetic one at that.

Building on this is a second problem: participants could be using the language of tradition to mask their "true" motives. If so, tradition does not
reflect participants' beliefs, but is cleverly used by them to deceive observers and interlocutors (American social scientists very much included). The
contributors to Hobsbawm and Ranger's famous volume *The Invention of
Tradition* demonstrate that appealing to tradition is an important way to
confer legitimacy on actions and institutions in the present.[55] From this
perspective, invoking tradition is a red flag whose present-day purpose of
political and social control must be exposed. But this story of elite invention ignores the non-elite participants who take part in traditions.[56] The
very reason why Hobsbawm and Ranger's critique of tradition is so powerful is that traditions do not appear to be invented to most people most
of the time; they appear traditional. For the men and women who take part
in a "traditional act," the feel and appeal of tradition can be strong and
authentic. In analyzing their motives, we need not be so suspicious of
the invocation of tradition for fear that it is invented—knowing full well
that it is. Rather, we should investigate what participants mean by it and
how it operates.

52. On Marx, see Craig Jackson Calhoun, "The Radicalism of Tradition: Community
Strength or Venerable Disguise and Borrowed Language?" *American Journal of Sociology* 88, no.
5 (March 1983): 887–888. On modernization theory, see Nils Gilman, *Mandarins of the Future:
Modernization Theory in Cold War America* (Baltimore: Johns Hopkins University Press, 2003),
esp. pp. 9–12.

53. Kathleen Blee, *Inside Organized Racism: Women in the Hate Movement* (Berkeley:
University of California Press, 2002), p. 201.

54. Dominic Bryan, *Orange Parades: The Politics of Ritual, Tradition, and Control* (London:
Pluto, 2000), p. 155.

55. Hobsbawm and Ranger, eds., *The Invention of Tradition*.

56. See related critiques in Ian McBride, "Memory and National Identity in Modern Ireland,"
in *History and Memory in Modern Ireland*, ed. Ian McBride (Cambridge: Cambridge University
Press, 2001), p. 9; and Guy Beiner, "The Invention of Tradition?" *The History Review* 12
(2001): 6–8.

Investigating tradition as a reason for parading reveals three layers of significance for participants. They mean it is a personal, family, and communal
tradition. Each layer adds depth to the meaning of participation in parades
by conveying a sense of continuity with the past. The desire to be part of the
continuation at each level is a powerful motive for participation.

As a personal tradition, parading is something that people have often
done for many years. Starting to parade at age five or six is not uncommon,
and parents even bring infants to parades. For nearly all paraders, their
engagement with parading culture began young. The survey shows that
99 percent of participants attended parades in their childhood, and 60 percent belonged to the Junior Orange Order or a marching band before they
turned sixteen. As Ben recalls, "It was always just a part of life. It's what we
did." Part of what makes current experiences so valuable is that they are
saturated with years of accumulated personal memories of past experiences. It is undoubtedly heartening to gather with the same people, don the
same attire, hear the same tunes, and see the same people cheering in the
same place they stood last year and the year before that. Such memories
accompany participants as they march today.[57]

As a family tradition, parading can link participants to fathers, grandfathers, and beyond. It gives participants the opportunity to take part in a
ritual that was held dear by ancestors.[58] As Joseph remarks: "When I parade
with the very same band that my great-grandfather was in, that my father
paraded in, there is a sense of continuity. There's a sense of continuing
something, which is something to be proud of." Parading allows Joseph to
walk in his ancestors' footsteps and sustain something that he knows was
dear to them. Billy feels similarly: "Carrying on the tradition is important,"
he explains. "My tradition is going back generations in my family. So I think
that it's important that I keep that going. I think it's important that it doesn't
fall by the wayside because somebody couldn't be bothered to take an interest in it." A family history of parading also contributes to a personal history,
since it shapes the environment in which one is raised—providing memories of watching one's father on parade, for instance.[59] This commitment to

57. On biographical continuity, see Doug McAdam, "The Biographical Consequences of
Activism," *American Sociological Review* 54, no. 5 (October 1989): 744–760; and Robert
W. White, "Structural Identity Theory and the Post-Recruitment Activism of Irish Republicans:
Persistence, Disengagement, Splits, and Dissidents in Social Movement Organizations," *Social
Problems* 57, no. 3 (August 2010): 341–370.

58. Mary C. Waters, *Ethnic Options: Choosing Identities in America* (Berkeley: University of
California Press, 1990), describes how people weave together identities and traditions from
their family and their ethnic group.

59. On family background influencing activism, see Hank Johnston, "New Social Movements
and Old Regional Nationalisms," in *New Social Movements: From Ideology to Identity*, ed. Enrique
Laraña, Hank Johnston, and Joseph R. Gusfield (Philadelphia: Temple University Press, 1994),
p. 271; Sidney Verba, Kay Lehman Schlozman, and Henry Brady, *Voice and Equality: Civic*

family can be an important motive for some. It provides a meaning and a purpose that is filled with love and loyalty to family, and, through family, to the Protestant people of Northern Ireland.

As a communal tradition, participating is a way to connect with the broader Protestant collectivity, past, present, and future. Participants recognize parades as "something my community has always done," which leads to reverence and a desire to continue.[60] Thus Craig says, "There's tradition involved in it...and it's a way of life." And Frankie asserts, "[We've] been doing this for hundreds of years.... It's part of our make-up, it's part of what we do." As both suggest, traditional action is intertwined with identity: "it's a way of life" and "part of our make-up." In this way, the authority of tradition, as Weber argues, is legitimate because its "mores [are] sanctified."[61] Tradition motivates participation because people have "piety for what actually, allegedly, or presumably has always existed."[62] Because it is long-established, and hence sanctified, parading is seen as "an inviolable norm of conduct" to participants.[63] Jamie sums it up this way: "[Parading is] just a massive, massive part of my life. It's part of my upbringing and almost who I am, if that makes sense. It's so ingrained into me. That's our history; that's our culture; and that's something we need to keep alive and keep going."

The desire to follow tradition at all three levels provides an important reason for action. Weber suggests as much by placing traditional action among his four types of meaningful social action (along with instrumentally rational, value rational, and emotional action). He is, however, generally unsympathetic to traditional action and authority, viewing it as non-rational and "determined by ingrained habituation." "Strictly traditional behavior," he continues, "...is very often a matter of almost automatic reaction to habitual stimuli."[64]

Voluntarism in American Politics (Cambridge, MA: Harvard University Press, 1995), p. 437; White, "Structural Identity Theory and the Post-Recruitment Activism of Irish Republicans," p. 354; Bosi and Della Porta, "Micro-Mobilization into Armed Groups," pp. 368–372; and Robert W. White and Tijen Demirel-Pegg, "Social Movements and Social Movement Organizations: Recruitment, Ideology and Splits," in Bosi and De Fazio, *The Troubles in Northern Ireland and Theories of Social Movements*, pp. 129–146.

60. Interview with Kyle, June 11, 2014.
61. Max Weber, "Politics as a Vocation," in *From Max Weber: Essays in Sociology*, trans. and ed. H. H. Gerth and C. Wright Mills (New York: Oxford University Press, 1972), p. 78. See also J. G. A. Pocock, "Time, Institutions and Action: An Essay on Traditions and Their Understanding," in *Politics, Language, and Time: Essays on Political Thought and History* (Chicago: University of Chicago Press, 1989), p. 237; and David Gross, *The Past in Ruins: Tradition and the Critique of Modernity* (Amherst: University of Massachusetts Press, 1992), p. 10.
62. Max Weber, "The Social Psychology of World Religions," in *From Max Weber*, Gerth and Mills, p. 296.
63. Ibid.
64. Weber, *Economy and Society*, pp. 24–26 (quotations are from p. 25); see also pp. 4–5; Calhoun, "The Radicalism of Tradition," p. 895; and Arnold M. Eisen, "Constructing the Usable

Parade participants share Weber's distinction between instrumental rationality and tradition, but without disparaging the latter. In fact, they tend to treat tradition as a superior mode of and reason for action. Both Tom and Kyle exhibit the contrast between instrumental action and tradition. I asked Tom what the overall goal of parading is and he replied: "The overall, uh— It's part of our tradition, it's part of what we've always done, what we do, who we are." The question about goals seemed to throw him off and he stumbled for an answer—like Mark at the beginning of the chapter. His response suggests that he sees no goal outside the action itself. Parades for Tom are "what we've always done, what we do, who we are," not "this is what we want, these are our demands." They represent Protestant identity, values, and community, rather than outcome-oriented, instrumental goals. Parades are fundamental to how he understands himself and his place in the world, so thinking about them in terms of "goals" is nonsensical; it literally does not make sense to how he thinks and feels about parades.

Kyle similarly distinguishes tradition from instrumentalism. In response to a question about whether parades send a message, Kyle said, "I wouldn't say so. I'd say it's a celebration of culture, it's heritage, it's something we've always done." Sending a message is instrumental, but parading is something else: tradition. For both Tom and Kyle, "tradition" means action that is done for its own sake, for its own intrinsic value. It is not goal oriented. Tradition is action whose rewards are found in the pleasures and meanings of collective participation in a beloved inheritance.

This emphasis on the meaningfulness of tradition conflicts with a prevalent Weberian understanding of tradition as almost Pavlovian. Paraders repeatedly recount that the choices to begin parading and to remain active were made deliberately, not unconsciously. They all have stories to tell about how they joined, and these stories emphasize that for them parading is not "automatic" or "ingrained habituation," as Weber insists. Frankie, for instance, recalls that though membership in the Orange Order goes back several generations in his family, his father had quit at some point. Joining the organization was therefore "completely a choice on my part" and not simply continuing down a path determined by his family. Tom also sees conscious decisions, not habit, as why he has remained active for so many decades. "My own choice," he says, "was to stay in the Order. I could have left when I [got a new job] and became a Christian, but at each step I made a conscious decision to stay." And though mobilization stories that highlight personal agency over structural factors may not be entirely

Past: The Idea of Tradition in Twentieth-Century American Judaism," in *The Uses of Tradition: Jewish Continuity in the Modern Era*, ed. Jack Wertheimer (New York: Jewish Theological Seminary of America, 1992), p. 451n7.

accurate, they indicate how participants understand parading and the decision to parade.[65] What they reveal is that participants, in contrast to many skeptics of tradition, do not perceive parading as a habit or other thoughtless behavior.

Tradition, contra Marx, does not always weigh "like a nightmare on the brain of the living" or compel action by eliminating conscious choice.[66] In some circumstances, to be sure, tradition constrains behavior; but in others, such as loyalist parading, tradition motivates it. By imbuing action with meaning rooted in the feeling of being "part of something continuous," tradition encourages mobilization.[67] Understanding parades as tradition connects participants to their past at the levels of biography, family, and community. It gives them the opportunity to take part in the preservation of a treasured history—to be, as historian David Gross writes, "a link in a chain stretching back in time."[68] Tradition thus motivates by providing an appealing sense of continuity and the privilege of carrying something important into the future. Through parading, participants can dive into the stream of history to swim alongside forefathers and fading memories of their youth. These layers of history and memory as well as the accompanying feelings of continuity ensure that parading is not merely habit, but action saturated with memory, identity, family, and culture. Attaining the experience of living with history, of carrying the past into the present and even the future is what participants mean when they say they parade because of tradition.

"WHY NOT? IT'S GOOD FUN": THE PLEASURES OF PARTICIPATION

Almost all participants I interviewed happily talked on and on about how much they loved to parade. Their enthusiasm was palpable. And their discussions about parades and what parades mean to them kept returning to

65. See also the emphasis on personal choice in mobilization decisions among female Salvadorian rebels in Jocelyn Viterna, *Women in War: The Micro-Processes of Mobilization in El Salvador* (New York: Oxford University Press, 2013), p. 105.

66. Karl Marx, "The Eighteenth Brumaire of Louis Napoleon," in *The Marx-Engels Reader*, ed. Robert C. Tucker (New York: Norton, 1978), p. 437.

67. Gross, *The Past in Ruins*, p. 10. On tradition as a mobilizing force, see Blee, *Inside Organized Racism*, p. 169; Calhoun, "The Radicalism of Tradition"; Dean C. Hammer, "Meaning and Tradition," *Polity* 24, no. 4 (Summer 1992): 564–565; and Michael Walzer, *The Paradox of Liberation: Secular Revolutions and Religious Counterrevolutions* (New Haven: Yale University Press, 2015), p. 28. As Jarman, *Material Conflicts*, p. 10, writes about loyalist parades: "The apparent historical continuity of ritual is an important feature of its power, the unchanging form is itself a major attraction, to join in and carry on a tradition, to follow in one's father's footsteps, or to wear 'the sash my father wore.'" See also his discussion on pp. 25–28.

68. Gross, *The Past in Ruins*, p. 10.

the pleasures of participation. These pleasures are varied, but the two most prominent sources are the other people who participate and the emotions experienced while parading.

The social benefits of parading come from the opportunity to spend meaningful time with friends and family to articulate shared values together.[69] For Sammy, there is an element of pure enjoyment in it: "Why not [join a band]? It's good fun. I enjoy traveling throughout Northern Ireland, being out with my brothers, many of them are in the various loyal orders with me, and just meeting new people and talking to different people and traveling to different towns and cities. And we go to mainland UK as well: like we've been to London, been to Corby; we go to Southampton. And to me that's what it's about. It's about fun and making new friends."

What made Michael's most recent parade "fantastic" was "just being part [of it] and just spending the day with people of like-minded views and showing your cultural identity. It makes me very proud. It excites me." He enjoys the company of friends and acquaintances and the connection he feels with them. Being surrounded by so many other Protestants also concretizes his collective identity and makes him feel part of something bigger. Parades and other mass gatherings are visual evidence for participants and various audiences that the performers—and what they represent—are, as Tilly puts it, worthy, united, numerous, and committed.[70] Taking part in such a large, collective event, where people feel bound together by ideology, faith, and tradition, is exhilarating for many.

Rich also recalls the gratifications of experiencing togetherness. "When you're walking up the street in an Orange parade," Rich reminisces, "... waving at people you know and being part of something, there's a sense of belonging and being owned and owning something. It's so hard to define.... It's an undefinable quality of belonging."[71] This feeling of collective belonging is "part of why it's so hard to leave" parading, yet Rich did just that. He quit the Orange Order fourteen years earlier, after the signing of the Agreement, because he disagreed with what he saw as the confrontational and sectarian stances taken by the Order during the peace process and Drumcree crises of the mid-1990s. Rich remains critical of parades and parading organizations—but the power of the experience is still

69. See James M. Jasper, "The Emotions of Protest: Affective and Reactive Emotions In and Around Social Movements," *Sociological Forum* 13, no. 3 (September 1998): 418.

70. For instance, Charles Tilly, *Contentious Performances* (New York: Cambridge University Press, 2008), pp. 72, 122–126. See also Jesus Casquete, "The Power of Demonstrations," *Social Movement Studies* 5, no. 1 (May 2006): 45–60.

71. Psychology research shows that humans have a deep psychological need to belong to groups. See Roy F. Baumeister and Mark R. Leary, "The Need to Belong: Desire for Interpersonal Attachments as a Fundamental Human Motivation," *Psychological Bulletin* 117, no. 3 (May 1995): 497–529.

unmistakable to him. Years later, the powerful social satisfactions that come from taking part in a parade continue to resonate with him. "Once you're in it, you feel it," he says.

As the interviewees' discussions of the social experience of participation suggest, a significant part of that experience is emotional.[72] Indeed, many of the social pleasures are rooted in the "reciprocal emotions" of activism, "the emotions generated in a social movement... [that] concern participants' ongoing feeling toward each other. These are the close, affective ties of friendship, love, solidarity, and loyalty, and the more specific emotions they give rise to."[73] This affect manifests in multiple ways and encourages both mobilization and commitment. Walter, for instance, illustrates the role of reciprocal emotions in maintaining commitment and persistence. "The band has been my main love all the years," he says. It is "an extended family" to whom he is loyal. As a result, "It's not only something that you do for a year or two years. It's something that'll stay with you all your life." For Walter, this has meant thirty years of parading with the same band.

Of the many emotions experienced by participants, pride is one of the most common and widespread in the interviews.[74] Pride and its opposite, shame, are what sociologist Thomas Scheff calls "master emotions": they are strong motives for human action.[75] I found three primary sources of pride among paraders: publicly demonstrating their culture; the public approval they receive; and their grand, distinguished appearance on parade.

Participants are proud of their cultural heritage and of collectively displaying it to fellow Protestants and beyond. Walter explains:

> I love to get out there and show people what I can do and how proudly I can do it; how well I look and how well I sound when I do it. It's a pride thing, probably, for me. And it's an identity thing, showing my identity as a loyalist to everyone— And I'm not just showing it to loyalist people: I'm showing it to nationalist people, I'm showing it to people who really don't care.

---

72. On the role of emotions in activism and conflict, see Jasper, "The Emotions of Protest"; Goodwin, Jasper, and Polletta, eds., *Passionate Politics*; Roger D. Petersen, *Understanding Ethnic Violence: Fear, Hatred, and Resentment in Twentieth-Century Eastern Europe* (New York: Cambridge University Press, 2002); Helena Flam and Debra King, eds., *Emotions and Social Movements* (London: Routledge, 2005); Gould, *Moving Politics*; James M. Jasper, "Emotions and Social Movements: Twenty Years of Theory and Research," *Annual Review of Sociology* 37 (2011): 285–303; and Wendy Pearlman, "Emotions and the Microfoundations of the Arab Uprisings," *Perspectives on Politics* 11, no. 2 (June 2013): 387–409.

73. Jasper, "The Emotions of Protest," p. 417.

74. This is not surprising, for as Jasper (ibid., p. 418) writes: "articulating one's moral principles is always a source of joy, pride, and fulfillment."

75. Thomas J. Scheff, *Bloody Revenge: Emotions, Nationalism, and War* (Boulder, CO: Westview, 1994).

Showing off his loyalist identity "to everyone" fills Walter with pride. He is also proud of demonstrating his personal accomplishments. Parades give him the chance to demonstrate "what I can do...how well I look and how well I sound when I do it." His public performances bear witness to his talents and his commitment to his community. This "pride thing" is a significant source of participants' desire to express their collective identity discussed above. It is an emotional aspect of publicly identifying with a cherished identity and community.[76]

Participants are also proud of the recognition they receive for their efforts. Just as the performance itself is a source of pride, so too are the responses from their audiences. As Tom describes, "There's a pride in walking, there's a pride in marching. There's a pride in the crowd, it's cheering and supportive and clapping. There's that pride walking around." A positive reception such as cheering is a typical cause of pride, which "we feel...with achievement, success, and acceptance."[77] Walter explains how it feels to attract the attention of tourists:

> We get Japanese people or American people or people from all over the world coming over and asking, "Can I have [my] photo taken with you?" So you're doing something, [otherwise] why would they want their photo taken with you?...They want their picture taken with somebody who looks well....I mean you're standing and you're smart, your uniform's clean, your boots are shining.

All the positive attention stands in contrast to routine life, when he knows that no stranger would approach him to snap a photo. The positive recognition he gets from visitors makes him proud and confirms that he is doing something worthwhile.

Along with the anonymous cheers from the crowd and recognition from tourists, pride is enhanced by personal connections to supportive audience members. Along the parade route, participants greet and are greeted by friends, family, neighbors, and acquaintances. "It's a fairly proud and enthralling moment," George says, "because you can't walk down the street without someone shouting out at you who knows you." Participants' faces light up as they shout hello, wave, nod, point, and occasionally jump out of the parade for a handshake or hug. Many interviewees mentioned that since audience members tend to stand in the same place year after year, they expect to see certain friends and family at specific locations along the parade route. Tom, for instance, explains: "I can go down that route and

---

76. Jasper, "The Emotions of Protest," p. 415, argues that collective identity itself "is an emotion, a positive affect toward other group members on the grounds of that common membership."

77. Scheff, *Bloody Revenge*, p. 39.

know where family will stand and friends will stand, or where they no longer stand because they're dead.... I know where my mother's cousin will stand with his wife. I know where a woman who worked in a store when I was a kid will have a can of Coke for me, still."[78] After months of fieldwork, even I got the occasional wave from paraders I got to know as I stood in the crowd of spectators lining the street.

These exchanges between participants and supporters illustrate that the social and emotional elements of parading are entwined. Many of the peak emotions of the action are generated in interaction with other participants and with the audience.[79] Mabel Berezin captures the experience of parading well: "Public political rituals," she writes, "create 'communities of feeling.'"[80] The emotions that arise from the verbal and non-verbal exchanges among participants and between participants and the audience help underpin, condense, and concretize the political identity being enacted and affix it to a visible, felt body politic congregated in the streets.[81]

Participants, lastly, are proud of their dignified self-presentation. Parades are an opportunity to dress up in dark suits and collarettes for loyal order members and colorful, elaborate, often military-style uniforms for band members. "We go out and we're all in nice suits and nice collarettes—a lot of money spent—and you're going out and you're proud ... and your friends and family are proud to see you," states Mikey, further demonstrating the social and interactional roots of emotions. Billy hones in on the role of fine and ceremonial clothing:

> I enjoy the parades. The Twelfth of July you feel proud. You like to wake up on the
> Twelfth morning and you get your best suit on, and get your best clothes on. You get
> your bowler hat out. You get your coat and hat out. You get your white gloves out. You
> get your cuffs out. You go on parade. You turn out your best to do the organization

78. Iddo Tavory, "The Private Life of Public Ritual: Interaction, Sociality and Codification in a Jewish Orthodox Congregation," *Qualitative Sociology* 36, no. 2 (June 2013): 127, 126, argues that these "predictable forms of interaction" are a common feature of "public worship and ritual."

79. Gordon Ramsey vividly narrates instances of this dynamic throughout *Music, Emotion and Identity in Ulster Marching Bands: Flutes, Drums and Loyal Sons* (Bern: Peter Lang, 2011). For example: "We entered the packed city centre, to the tune *Billy Boys*. As we struck up the chorus, there was a cheer from the crowd and a massive wave of sound as the packed street started to sing: *Hallo! Hallo! We are the Billy Boys!* As hundreds of fists punched the air to roars of *Hallo! Hallo!* I felt a wave of emotion as powerful as the wave of sound—a feeling of communal oneness—a communion. I could see other bandsmen trying not to smile and lose their embouchure" (p. 165). See also Ramsey's thoughtful reflections on the instinctive nature of his "moment of pure pleasure" born in "a blatantly sectarian tune." "No ideological commitment was necessary," he writes, "just bodily participation" (p. 172).

80. Mabel Berezin, "Emotions and Political Identity: Mobilizing Affection for the Polity," in Goodwin, Jasper, and Polletta, *Passionate Politics*, p. 93.

81. Ibid.; Jasper, "The Emotions of Protest"; and Casquete, "The Power of Demonstrations."

proud. And it's just a feeling of [being] so proud of the tradition, the culture,...and the history of the village, keep[ing] the history going.

Looking sharp, respectable, and dignified on parade fills Billy, a truck driver by profession, with pride. Moreover, wearing clothing with a history connects him to that history. The pride in wearing a bowler hat and white gloves comes not from adopting the latest fashions, but in dressing in a manner that consciously invokes the past.[82] As Hobsbawm remarks, "The wigs of lawyers could hardly acquire their modern significance until other people stopped wearing wigs."[83] The same is true for the Orangeman's outdated outfits. Its significance lies in its obsolescence. Dressing and acting in a deliberately formal and expressive manner produces pride. As Michael summarizes, "It's always a proud moment to be on parade."

The pride, excitement, and other positive, satisfying emotions are energizing and encourage sustained participation.[84] Craig describes the invigorating aspect of parades:

> It's not routine to me. It's a totally refreshing day. It's one of those days when after you've walked twenty-two miles, you finish up with a load of energy. You're on a high, so you are. And it's thoroughly enjoyed, thoroughly enjoyed. If I was to walk five miles there today, I'd have sore feet and blisters. There's something magical about being in the band and playing your flute. I never have a blister.

Craig ends the day refreshed and full of energy despite being on his feet for many hours and even more miles. And though he might exaggerate the magical ability of parades to prevent blisters, he certainly conveys his sentiment. The face-to-face interactions, large cheering crowds, music, and feeling of doing something important and right all contribute to the visceral excitement that Émile Durkheim calls "collective effervescence" and Randall Collins identifies as "emotional energy." Durkheim noticed the energizing features of collective gatherings, arguing that all groups need to

---

82. See Connerton, *How Societies Remember*, pp. 45, 48, on how commemorative rituals deliberately refer to the past.

83. Eric Hobsbawm, "Inventing Traditions," in Hobsbawm and Ranger, *The Invention of Tradition*, p. 4.

84. Many scholars of collective action have argued the rituals and the emotions generated by them are a central method for maintaining the enthusiasm and commitment of participants. The case of loyalist parading, however, shows that disengagement rates can still be high even when the organization's primary form of mobilization is an emotionally rich collective ritual. For example, Rosabeth Moss Kanter, *Commitment and Community: Communes and Utopias in Sociological Perspective* (Cambridge, MA: Harvard University Press, 1972); Jasper, *The Art of Moral Protest*, esp. pp. 183–209; Jasper, "The Emotions of Protest," p. 418; Sharon Erickson Nepstad, *Religion and War Resistance in the Plowshares Movement* (New York: Cambridge University Press, 2008), pp. 99–103.

convene occasionally so that members may "renew their common faith by making a public demonstration of it together." Face-to-face conventions have this effect, he holds, because "in the midst of an assembly that becomes worked up, we become capable of feelings and conduct of which we are incapable when left to our individual resources."[85] This certainly seems the case in parades.

Building on Durkheim and others, Collins argues that emotional energy is the outcome of successful "interaction rituals"—"momentary encounters among human bodies charged up with emotions and consciousness because they have gone through chains of previous encounters."[86] Emotional energy, Collins writes, "makes the individual feel not only good, but exalted, with the sense of doing what is most important and most valuable.... [It] has a powerful motivating effect upon the individual; whoever has experienced this kind of moment wants to repeat it."[87] Parade participants, it seems, would agree.

Enhancing the energy of parades is the music that thunders through them. The music played by loyalist marching bands tends to have a military rhythm designed for marching.[88] The beat sets a pace for the marchers and reverberates across the city, town, or village. Both marching together and music, Jasper argues, "have unusual capacities to make people melt into a group in feelings of satisfaction, perhaps because so many parts of the brain and body are involved at once."[89] Walter and Rachel illustrate this point well. Walter reports that "if your band's playing well and your bass drums sound loud, the hair on the back of your neck actually lifts! Crowds cheer when you're coming back and people acknowledge your band and say, 'There's [our band]!' You can feel that coming inside you. It's a fantastic feeling." Rachel describes the experience of a "blow out," when two bands march past each other and play as loud and hard as they can. "It's the height

85. Émile Durkheim, *The Elementary Forms of Religious Life*, trans. Karen E. Fields (New York: Free Press, 1995), pp. 211–212.

86. Randall Collins, *Interaction Ritual Chains* (Princeton: Princeton University Press, 2004), p. 3. Though Collins's interaction rituals differ from what I call rituals, I believe the mechanism he identifies remains relevant.

87. Ibid., pp. 38–39.

88. For analyses of the musical elements of parading, see Ramsey, *Music, Emotion and Identity*; Gordon Ramsey, "Band Practice: Class, Taste and Identity in Ulster Loyalist Flute Bands," *Ethnomusicology Ireland* 1 (February 2011): 1–20; Ray Casserly, "Blood, Thunder, and Drums: Style and Changing Aesthetics of Drumming in Northern Ireland Protestant Bands," *Yearbook for Traditional Music* 45 (2013): 142–163; and Ray Casserly, "Parading Music and Memory in Northern Ireland," *Música e Cultura* 9 (2014). On music and movements in general, see, for example, Ron Eyerman and Andrew Jamison, *Music and Social Movements: Mobilizing Traditions in the Twentieth Century* (New York: Cambridge University Press, 1998); and William G. Roy, "How Social Movements Do Culture," *International Journal of Politics, Culture, and Society* 23, nos. 2–3 (September 2010): 85–98.

89. Jasper, "Emotions and Social Movements," p. 294.

of being out with the band," she explains. "The adrenaline rush that comes through you when two competing bands playing opposite tunes just start passing each other and blasting it out and the bass drummer is going absolutely mental playing the tune. Yeah, your adrenaline goes up." In both the case of acclaim and the case of competition, the intensity of the musical experience generates a physical reaction among participants, demonstrating the mental and bodily aspects of parading to music.

The positive emotions and energy of parading also explain why Craig feels that something so often repeated is "not routine." Conventional outcome-oriented approaches to participation find rituals difficult to explain in part because they expect that people would get bored or tired of repeating the same action, especially when there is no external goal or material reward.[90] They predict that the experience of repeated action would feel routine because the sole benefit is assumed to be received only upon its successful completion. But as Craig observes, this is not the case. The allure of parading and other rituals is in the action itself. The appeal *is* the experience: the pride, excitement, and energy; the quality time with respected friends and comrades; the tangible connection to the past. These are what encourage mobilization and sustained activism in a collective ritual.[91]

The sense of pride and energy, attained in the company of friends and family, is a prime experience of parade participation. My findings resonate with Gordon Ramsey's ethnographic conclusion that marching in loyalist bands is motivated in large part by the "emotional rewards of participation."[92] More generally, they match what Elisabeth Wood calls "emotional in-process benefits," the "emotion-laden consequences of action experienced only by those participating in that action."[93] Feelings like this make it unsurprising that, despite the lack of personal or collective material gains, participants choose to return time after time.

Overall, the interviews demonstrate that parading is itself a desired benefit for participants. They look forward to parades, talk about them with

90. For instance, Charles Tilly, *Regimes and Repertoires* (Chicago: University of Chicago Press, 2006), p. 41, remarks that in "contentious claim-making...perfect repetition from one performance to the next breeds boredom and indifference on the part of claimants and objects alike."

91. This effect is also seen in William McNeill's well-known recollection of aimless marching during basic training in the US Army during World War II. Though marching around in the blistering Texas sun seemed pointless at the time, decades later his main memory is that he "rather liked strutting around....Words are inadequate to describe the emotion aroused by the prolonged movement in unison that drilling involved." William H. McNeill, *Keeping Together in Time: Dance and Drill in Human History* (Cambridge, MA: Harvard University Press, 1995), pp. 1–2.

92. Ramsey, *Music, Emotion and Identity*, p. 223.

93. Elisabeth Jean Wood, "The Emotional Benefits of Insurgency in El Salvador," in Goodwin, Jasper, and Polletta, *Passionate Politics*, p. 268.

their friends, and many, if not most, come to structure their lives around them. Some participants even told me about damaging romantic relationships or missing family functions in order to parade. Yet they certainly do not view parading as a cost—on the contrary, as I showed in chapter 2, they actually pay for the privilege to parade their identity and moral vision alongside dear friends and compatriots. It is something they would not miss for the world. As Billy says of friends who do not parade, "That's their loss.... You know, they're missing out."

"WE'RE STILL HERE": SENDING A MESSAGE
TO PROTESTANTS AND CATHOLICS

External communication is the fourth reason for participation frequently discussed by paraders. Many—though not all—paraders seek to send a message to fellow Protestants or to Catholics.[94] Scholars have long theorized ritual as a communicative device.[95] According to Mary Douglas, for instance, "Ritual is pre-eminently a form of communication."[96] But ritual is an imprecise form of communication.[97] The ambiguity inherent in the meaning of symbols and rituals leaves room for Protestant and Catholic audiences to receive a different message from the same parade.

For members of the Protestant in-group, the primary message is unity. Irish Protestants have long believed that remaining united is essential for their strength and survival on an island where they are a minority. But unity has often been seen as elusive for a group rent by religious denomination, class, and political allegiances.[98] By gathering large crowds and icons of the community, parades not only represent Protestant unity, but can cause it as well. Parading, like all communal rites, is a way to renew community

94. Parades have also been interpreted as sending messages to other paraders, the British government, and unionist political parties and elites, but I rarely, if ever, heard these targets discussed by participants. See Jarman, *Material Conflicts*; Bryan, *Orange Parades*; and Lee A. Smithey and Michael P. Young, "Parading Protest: Orange Parades in Northern Ireland and Temperance Parades in Antebellum America," *Social Movement Studies* 9, no. 4 (November 2010): 402.

95. Other students of ritual, conversely, maintain that ritual is a rare example of purely expressive action that contains no external orientation whatsoever. The most extreme position is taken by Frits Staal, "The Meaninglessness of Ritual," *Numen* 26, no. 1 (1979): 9, who argues, "Ritual is pure activity, without meaning or goal....Things are either for their own sake, or for the sake of something else....My view is that ritual is for its own sake."

96. Mary Douglas, *Natural Symbols: Explorations in Cosmology* (London: Routledge, 1970), p. 20.

97. Anthony P. Cohen, *The Symbolic Construction of Community* (London: Routledge, 1985), p. 21.

98. Lee A. Smithey, *Unionists, Loyalists, and Conflict Transformation in Northern Ireland* (New York: Oxford University Press, 2011), pp. 208–210.

members' commitment and sense of solidarity.[99] Parades were and are understood as a way to unify the community.[100]

A number of participants I interviewed share this diagnosis and solution. For example, Robert believes that parades help unify Protestants across denomination and class because they "bring a lot of people…together" and, crucially, "show that we're together." By assembling so many people from across the Protestant religious and socioeconomic spectrums—"a lot of clergy from different denominations…[and] people from the humblest person, a bus driver, a member of the Loyalists [paramilitaries] to a doctor and professors…a high court judge…and a lot of our MLAs and politicians"— parades create a sense of community that might otherwise be lacking. Indeed, according to one band member quoted by local researcher Michael Hall, "The unionist community is more and more fragmented, and bands are the only thing which is holding the Protestant working-class community together at the present moment."[101]

The primary message to members of the Catholic out-group, by contrast, is one of opposition. Parades are a way that participants express opposition to a united Ireland, republican violence, and perceived losses in Protestant power and prestige in past decades. Vocalizing this opposition takes two forms: an expressive desire to vent and an instrumental desire to change the situation.

Since the end of unionist hegemony in 1972, and especially since the peace process of the 1990s, many Protestants have resented the changes in Northern Irish society and felt humiliated by them.[102] The transition from ethnic dominance to a more level playing field is bound to cause pain in the formerly dominant community. The Protestant experience, finds sociologist Lee Smithey, has been framed "in terms of loss or the perpetual potential for loss."[103] Making matters worse, many Catholic elected officials were IRA combatants not long ago. For many Protestants, this is an attack on their moral vision and their fundamental sense of right and wrong. As Mark characterizes it: "Would David Cameron [or] Barack Obama bring…Osama bin Laden in? Give him a place in government? Because that's what we are expected to do here." Making matters even worse, the republican politicians "who had murdered and maimed and destroyed this country" use their power to try to restrict non-violent parades because these ex-terrorists find

---

99. See Durkheim, *The Elementary Forms of Religious Life.*

100. For example, Bryan, *Orange Parades;* and Jarman, *Material Conflicts.*

101. Michael Hall, *Towards a Shared Future (5): Ulster's Marching Bands* (Belfast: Island Publications, 2014), p. 30. See also Ramsey, *Music, Emotion and Identity,* p. 147.

102. Petersen, *Understanding Ethnic Violence,* esp. pp. 40–61, argues that resentment is the natural emotional response to a reordered ethnic status hierarchy.

103. Smithey, *Unionists, Loyalists, and Conflict Transformation,* p. 66.

them offensive.[104] For many, if not all, participants, the contradiction is sickening. "Why can a convicted bomber tell me that I can't walk down the road because I've got a flute?" Mikey asks with indignation.

Parading provides the opportunity for some participants to express defiance and moral outrage toward the perceived attacks on their way of life by republicanism. Defiance is "a refusal to acquiesce," writes Wood. "Its value [is] not contingent on success or even on one's contributing to the likelihood of success."[105] Its value, rather, lies in the act of expression. Parades are thus a way to take a stand, voice their disgust, and defy those who want to stop them. George, for instance, says: "Now I don't mean that to be antagonistic, but [my intention is] to say, 'We've always been here and we're not going away.'" His action is rooted in the "inner moral obligation" to express his opposition to the moral outrages he sees in his society.[106] Yet George's comments exemplify how process-oriented and outcome-oriented reasons can blur together. I earlier quoted George's view that parades are an expression of his religious identity. The purpose of parades, he holds, "is to say to the world... 'Here we are as members of the Protestant, reformed, evangelical faith. This is our cause and we want the world to know.'" It can be hard to discern how these two statements are so different. Expressing a politically salient identity, especially in a divided, post-conflict society, has external consequences. Regardless of intentions, proclaiming "here we are" in such circumstances always carries the external message "...and we're not going away."

At a massive parade in Markethill, County Armagh, Sammy, who brought me along on his band's bus, repeatedly pointed out bands to tell me that the town or village they are from used to have a Protestant majority, but now only a few are left. Yet, he would proudly say, they still have a marching band. The band's purpose is not to defend the Protestant community against the violence of the republican paramilitaries, nor is it designed to entice Protestants back. The Protestant minority still supports a band, he argued, to defy what he views as the ethnic cleansing of those towns. They parade to show that they still can.

But not all expressions of opposition are just venting without concern for consequence. Some participants choose to parade in order to effect change. They see their actions in part as means toward an external end. For instance, Isaac recalls that "the impetus to join was probably political." In

104. Interview with George, August 14, 2012.
105. Wood, *Insurgent Collective Action*, p. 233. Also Jasper, *The Art of Moral Protest*, pp. 37–38.
106. Klandermans, "Motivations to Action," p. 225. See also James M. Jasper and Jane D. Poulsen, "Recruiting Strangers and Friends: Moral Shocks and Social Networks in Animal Rights and Anti-Nuclear Protests," *Social Problems* 42, no. 4 (November 1995): 493–512.

the early 1970s, at the height of violence, he did two things "as a way of say-ing, look, I'm British": he joined the part-time police force and he joined the Orange Order. For Isaac, law enforcement and ritual action were linked in their mutual opposition to republicanism. Joining the security forces was a way to defend his community and values from those who threatened them. Parades were a way to publicly and proudly express what he stood for and against. It was, for Isaac, another way of defending his community. Becoming a police officer and an Orangeman were different sides of the same coin.

Importantly, the oppositional message, though read as aggressive by Catholics and other outsiders, is generally expressed by participants as defensive. This defensive message is encapsulated in a phrase repeated by many interviewees: "We're still here." As Mark explains, after the decades of "attacks that have been placed on our community," parades say, "We're still here, we're still living, we're still breathing." Joseph elaborates:

> "We're here, we exist..." Not necessarily meant to be threatening or intimidating any-body, but, "We exist." It's a simple message, "We exist." We see ourselves at the heart of our community and heart of the town, heart of the village and we don't want to be mar-ginalized and excluded.... Certainly there's been a lot of times in the past where I have paraded... just to say, "Listen, we're here, we're not going to threaten you, but we're here, we exist."

"We don't want to be marginalized and excluded" is not the message of a community that feels dominant, but one that feels under siege. It is the mes-sage of a community that has experienced change as loss. The message also demonstrates the natural ambiguity of public expression. While Joseph sees "We're here" as a defensive cry, he also recognizes that others under-stand it as "threatening or intimidating." Despite his explicit rejection of the rival understanding, the same words are interpreted very differently by dif-ference audiences. As a result, what is internal and process-oriented expres-sion to one can be external and outcome-oriented communication to another.[107]

Ben expands on Joseph's sentiment. The message of parades, Ben states, are "that we exist. We are a community, we exist, and we have things to celebrate and remember." But, he believes, that is not how Catholics view them:

---

107. Javier Auyero, "The Judge, the Cop, and the Queen of Carnival: Ethnography, Storytelling, and the (Contested) Meanings of Protest," *Theory and Society* 31, no. 2 (April 2002): 167, finds similar explicit denials of "competing understandings" in his interviews with Argentine rioters.

You see, the thing is they are trapped in a mindset [that Protestants are politically domi-
nant]. What have I got to be dominant about? I was born in 1973, a year after Stormont
fell....Unionists have not run Northern Ireland since 1972. What have I got to celebrate? Martin McGuinness [of Sinn Féin] should have been hung for treason against the
British state for organizing and developing an attempt to overthrow the power of
the United Kingdom....That hasn't happened. He is now sitting in government as the
deputy First Minister in the government of Northern Ireland. He helped murder
dozens of people. He's never been made amenable to justice. What have I got to be
dominant about? But I'm still somehow sending this superior message that I'm better
than them!

Ben is baffled and exasperated. Through his eyes, the past decades have
been patently awful for Protestants, and he cannot understand how anyone
could see otherwise. The chasm between his experience and outside perceptions is simply unintelligible to him. As he sees it, paraders are accused
of triumphalism that they do not, indeed cannot, actually feel.

Some paraders, such as Isaac and Joseph, readily participate in order to
send a message to Catholics. But unlike collective identity expression, tradition, and the pleasures of participation, external communication is not a
reason that all paraders would recognize. Several interviewees do not
believe that their actions even send a message. We saw this above in the
doubt and hesitations from Mark, Tom, and Kyle when asked about
parades' message, and the distinction Mark drew between sending a message and collective self-expression. We can see it again in Steven's comment
about what to call parades. The Orange Order often refers to its Twelfth
parades as demonstrations, because they march to a "demonstration field"
where there are speeches and benedictions. Steven, however, is not comfortable with this term. "I hate the word *demonstration* being used," he says.
"To me it should be *celebration*, as opposed to *demonstration*. We're not
demonstrating anything, we're celebrating our culture and heritage."
Demonstration connotes protest or deliberately sending a message, which is
not how he sees parades. The celebration of culture, he argues, is not a demonstration to Catholics or anyone else.

But even participants who see parades as a means for external communication believe that there are some messages that parades absolutely do not
send. The firm consensus among paraders is that their actions do not broadcast a message of hate or intolerance that is meant to intimidate or provoke
Catholics.[108] On the contrary, they vigorously distance themselves from

---

108. Table C.5, model 1 in appendix C shows that participation is not predicted by agreeing
with the statement "sometimes Catholics need to be reminded that they live in the United
Kingdom."

the divisive consequences of parades. In interview after interview, paraders emphasized that their actions are not intended to offend or antagonize anyone.[109] Isaac, for example, told me with all seeming earnestness, "I don't think we're going out to make an offensive statement. Certainly, anything that ever I have been personally involved in, I haven't seen any particularly offensive actions or anything that anybody could take as offensive." Kyle recognizes that some Catholics do view parades as offensive, but, he maintains, it is the result of a misinterpretation: "There's the perception that the bands go out to offend Catholics and to assert dominance over them, but it's not the case. I mean we don't go out on parade to dominate anybody or to claim anything is ours or to intimidate anybody."

This argument—that parades are not offensive, demeaning, provocative, or whatnot because participants do not intend them to be—hinges on a specious assumption about the nature of meaning in public performances. It supposes that paraders control the publicly held meaning of their actions. Yet we know from literary theory that authors cannot control the meaning of their texts and authorial intent does not dictate a reader's interpretation.[110] Likewise, participants' intentions do not determine how the audience interprets the meaning of a parade. Even if Kyle truly does not "go out on parade to dominate ... or to intimidate anybody," he does not have the ability to impose a specific meaning on an audience.[111] Observers bring their own expectations and presuppositions when they judge the meaning of a cultural object like a parade. These characteristics of the observer interact with characteristics of the object to generate meaning. An individual's expectations and presuppositions, moreover, emerge from their social and cultural environment, and so an individual's perceptions are shaped by their group's "distinctive way of seeing."[112]

109. Offense and division may be unintended consequences, but they are not unanticipated consequences—an important distinction explored by Frank de Zwart, "Unintended but Not Unanticipated Consequences," *Theory and Society* 44, no. 3 (May 2015): 283–297.

110. As one important essay argues, "The poem ... is detached from the author at birth and goes about the world beyond his power to intend about it or control it." W. K. Wimsatt Jr., and M. C. Beardsley, "The Intentional Fallacy," *The Sewanee Review* 54, no. 3 (July–September 1946): 470.

111. Paraders can, however, *try* to improve their reputation through both word and deed. Smithey, *Unionists, Loyalists, and Conflict Transformation*, pp. 125–149, documents and analyzes recent attempts by the Orange Order "to improve its image and to reach out to other sectors, domestic and international," including public relations, dialogue, education, outreach, and better behavior (quotation is from p. 126). See also Brian Kennaway, "The Re-Invention of the Orange Order: Triumphalism or Orangefest?" in Burgess and Mulvenna, *The Contested Identities of Ulster Protestants*, pp. 70–82.

112. Wendy Griswold, "The Fabrication of Meaning: Literary Interpretation in the United States, Great Britain, and the West Indies," *American Journal of Sociology* 92, no. 5 (March 1987): 1077–1117 (quotation is from p. 1081).

Yet parade participants insist that outsiders judge them based on criteria promoted by insiders. That is, they hold that people from another community, who approach parades with different presuppositions and experiences, ignore their own historically formed ways of seeing, and adopt the paraders'. For instance, when Isaac says, "I haven't seen… anything that anybody could take as offensive," he is insisting that his view on what is and is not offensive is authoritative and universal. But since paraders cannot unilaterally assert the social meaning of their public actions, this program is bound to fail. The very fact that there is controversy over parades is evidence that the program *has* failed.

Several participants, including Kyle, also point out that they put a lot of time and effort into parades, and if the goal was simply to antagonize Catholics, there would be easier ways to do it. "I mean we practice I would say on average twice a week all year round," he says about his band. "We don't do that to offend anybody." (David put it more bluntly: Why does his band spend thousands of pounds on instruments and uniforms when, if he was looking to offend someone, he could "throw a brick for free"?) The time I spent with a marching band in West Belfast provides further support for Kyle's two points (he was not a member of this band). Participants did spend time and effort in practicing. At the weekly sessions, they often rehearsed a single part of a song repeatedly until the musical director was pleased. And, as best I could tell, most if not all members could read music. This dedication is unremarkable from the point of view of a musical ensemble, but seems unnecessary if the (only) goal is to provoke a riot or flip the musical bird.

What is more, there were never any discussions among bandsmen about insulting, intimidating, or provoking Catholics. In fact, I never heard an overtly sectarian discussion at all. I specifically listened for any mentions of Catholics or communal politics in the privacy of the band practices, but they never came up.[113] Indeed, the two most illuminating episodes in this regard feature the *absence* of sectarian politics.

The first is a recurring episode. Each practice session concluded with the band playing "God Save the Queen," the United Kingdom's national anthem. This was generally the only remotely explicit political or nationalist moment during the ninety-minute practice. When played on the streets,

113. My observations are likely impacted by the fact that the band practices I attended were of a melody band, not a blood and thunder band. Melody bands require more musical skill and practice and they do not have as aggressive a reputation as blood and thunder bands. That said, I am near certain I have seen this band in clear contravention of a legally binding Parades Commission decision by loudly playing music as they marched by a Catholic church. It is also possible that they softened their language and behavior because I was present. Yet given what they did let me witness (ribaldry, roughhousing, one member mooning the rest of the band— and that was just the first practice I attended), I doubt they held much back in my presence.

where Irish nationalists can hear it, "God Save the Queen" can take a pro-vocative or defiant flavor. In the privacy of a clubhouse, however, it does not. Playing the anthem was never an excuse or opportunity for so much as a snide remark about Catholics or "Lundies," as traitors to unionism are called. They generally played it rather perfunctorily, I thought, as it was the final task before they could go home. It seemed to me more "banal nation-alism" or "everyday nationhood" than the "contrived occasions for the crys-tallization of national awareness" that often spill into the streets of Belfast.[114] National symbols are so highly charged in Northern Ireland that the out-wardly mechanical performance of the national anthem was striking.[115]

The second episode involved a T-shirt. At the last practice before the Twelfth of July in 2013, Dan, one of the band leaders, wore a T-shirt with a cartoon image of a potato and the words, in all capital letters, "THE FAMINE IS OVER SO WHY DON'T YOU GO HOME." These are the lyrics of the expressly sectarian "Famine Song," which mocks the Irish Potato Famine and caused much controversy outside St. Patrick's Catholic Church in Belfast the previous year. The shirt looked brand new—I noticed that the sleeves were still creased, as if just purchased—so I guessed that Dan had worn it specifically for the band practice. Yet despite the jokes and laughs I imagine he was hoping to inspire, I never heard any. Even with this invitation to mock Catholics or discuss the intimidation or provocation of them, I heard no comments by other band members. I was not following Dan the whole night so I could have missed private conversations, but nothing was said in front of the band as a whole. Furthermore, he wore the shirt in a private, Protestant forum, not in public, where Catholics could see it. Does this make the act less insensitive? Likely no. But wearing it was not an attempt to offend Catholics, who were not a potential audience for this private act.

Given the prevailing unfavorable stereotypes about loyalist bands, the absence of sectarian conversations around these episodes is striking. But Ramsey reaches a similar conclusion in his long-term ethnographic study of three marching bands:

114. Michael Billig, *Banal Nationalism* (London: Sage, 1995); and Jon E. Fox and Cynthia Miller-Idriss, "Everyday Nationhood," *Ethnicities* 8, no. 4 (December 2008): 536–563 (quota-tion is from p. 545). Historian Max Bergholz reminds us that "moments of intensely felt collec-tive solidarity and the antagonistic collective categorization of others are not constant and enduring features of local life." Max Bergholz, "Sudden Nationalism: The Microdynamics of Intercommunal Relations in Bosnia-Herzegovina After World War II," *American Historical Review* 118, no. 3 (June 2013): 703.

115. David Cairns, "The Object of Sectarianism: The Material Reality of Sectarianism in Ulster Loyalism," *Journal of the Royal Anthropological Institute* 6, no. 3 (September 2000): 448–449, comes to an alternative interpretation. In his ethnography of loyalist marching bands, he understands the playing of "God Save the Queen" at the end of band events (in his case, parties) as a much more charged, sectarian act.

> Participating in a loyalist parade is almost universally seen by outsiders as a display of political and religious allegiance, an act of power or resistance with a political goal. Some within the band may accept such characterization to some degree.... Yet... in six years of intensive involvement in the band scene, spanning some of the most politically controversial events of the peace process, I have never heard politics or religion discussed seriously in a bandroom.[116]

The playing of the national anthem and the non-reaction to the wearing of a potentially offensive T-shirt hint that participants are often not consciously looking to provoke or intimidate Catholics. The closest that any participants I interviewed got to acknowledging a connection between parades and these outcomes were the few interviewees who mentioned that *other* participants want to cause trouble. Members of the loyal orders tended to blame bands, while band members tended to blame other bands or the "blue bag brigade," inebriated young men who follow a parade drinking loads of cheap alcohol. Ramsey similarly describes how the bandsmen he knew referred "to *other* bands as political bands, by which they meant those bands with paramilitary affiliations."[117]

A central reason why participants do not intend to offend Catholics is that they do not believe that Catholics are actually offended. Instead, participants believe that Catholic objections to parades are all disingenuous cant manufactured by the republican movement. As they see it, the controversy is invented, Catholics feign the offense, and any violence that may follow a parade is, therefore, unrelated to the parade itself. "We're not causing the trouble," Sammy stresses. "It's violent republicans who are causing the trouble." These widely held beliefs suggest that many participants are not deliberately trying to offend Catholics or polarize the communities. Since participants do not believe that Catholics genuinely get offended, it is unlikely that they act with the goal of offending them. There is much more to say on this issue and I will address it in detail in the next chapter, where I argue that participants' understanding of culture and cultural action helps them to disassociate parades from their consequences.

116. Ramsey, *Music, Emotion and Identity*, p. 163. In contrast, Cairns, "The Object of Sectarianism," pp. 447–448, finds that it is precisely behind closed doors, at loyalist social events, where he "was able to develop a fuller appreciation of sectarianism": "[sectarian] attitudes and beliefs may be on display at the main Orange ritual events themselves, but this is not the primary site of their formation, nor the place in which loyalist symbolism is impregnated with its sectarian significance: it is the loyalist social occasion which provides an opportunity for identity formation and reinforcement, a site for the discourse to work itself into person and object alike."

117. Ramsey, *Music, Emotion and Identity*, p. 226. Emphasis in the original.

CONCLUSION

Parades have significant social and political effects in Northern Ireland. Among other things, they represent the Protestant community, promote Protestant solidarity, offend Catholics, intensify communal friction, and occasionally trigger violence. These outcomes, particularly the more aggressive ones, are seen by many outsiders as the goals of parading. But this chapter has tried to show that paraders, for the most part, are uninterested in the prospect of achieving these consequences. Their reasons for participating are found elsewhere, in the experience of parading itself. The rewards that motivate them—the social and emotional satisfactions of expressing a collective identity and being part of a cherished tradition—are mostly intrinsic to the process of acting collectively. Parading in order to send a message—a more externally oriented, instrumental reason—can be an important motive, too. But, on balance, for most paraders most of the time, intrinsic benefits prevail.

The mix of reasons that bring people to action suggests that purely expressive and purely instrumental accounts of collective mobilization are not realistic. A binary viewpoint, at least in this case, oversimplifies to the point of distortion. Many explanations of loyalist parading, however, still adopt a purely instrumental approach: outsiders tend to assume that participants are motivated by the expected achievement of the divisive consequences that follow from parades. Contrary to this perspective, I did not find evidence that participants are motivated to achieve any of the well-known deleterious outcomes of parades, such as insulting Catholics or provoking riots (though we must not confuse the absence of evidence for evidence of absence). Of course, Protestants have strong incentives to say that they do not intend to effect these harmful consequences, even if it is untrue. (We must therefore also be suspicious of purely expressive explanations proffered by paraders and their supporters.) Nevertheless, my formal interviews and informal conversations with a broad range of participants and observations at many parades and related events overpowered my strong skepticism and I believe that most of them are sincere.

Yet doubts surely remain. In a final effort to assuage lingering suspicions, note that paraders privilege the intrinsic benefits of parading over its outcomes even when the outcomes are uncontroversially positive. For example, when I asked Mikey if parading has a goal, he replied in a similar fashion to so many others: "It's not a goal as such." But he then acknowledged the public service they provide: "There's hundreds of parades going on in Northern Ireland and people like to go out and watch them, it's a spectacle. People like to listen to bands. People like to see their brothers and sisters, their family walking. People like to see it." And people who attend parades agree wholeheartedly. Sophie, an enthusiastic attender, describes being at parades this way: "Love it.... You just feel more of your cultural identity. You're all together and it gives you a wee bit of hope for the future." Or as a band member interviewed by Michael Hall recalls, "One woman [at a community meeting in East Belfast] said, 'We struggle all year to make ends meet, and watching the bands is the only bit of holiday time we get.'"[118]

So why do many participants write off the joy that they bring to their own communities? Why do they de-emphasize the plainly positive outcomes that they can be justifiably proud of? While these are a satisfying byproduct of parading, they told me, they are not why they act. Both Michael and Howie, for instance, make this point. Michael states, "It's our right to do it. It's our belief to do it. The crowds and the spectators are an added bonus to us. We will walk the streets whether there is one person watching us or one hundred million people watching us. It's our right, it's our identity. It's our reason we exist." Howie agrees: "[When there is a large crowd] it's just nicer. But if there wasn't as many of a crowd there it wouldn't bother me.... I've been to parade where there hasn't been many people watching it, but it's still an honor and a privilege for me to walk with the Apprentice Boys."

My observations confirm their claims: on occasion, I was the only person on the street watching the parade, particularly when it was early on a weekend morning or it was pouring rain. A crowd of cheering supporters certainly creates a livelier atmosphere, but, as Michael and Howie make clear, entertaining the community is not what drives them. Honor, privilege, fulfilling a right, acting on a belief, carrying on a tradition, living their identity: these are their reasons. And so they will parade whether or not the streets are brimming with spectators.

Above all, participants seek the experience, not the consequences, of parading. Participation is about the sights and sounds, the thoughts and feelings, the memories and people, not the social, political, or economic results, be they personal or collective. As Jack, a Methodist minister who was in a band as a young man but quit parading years ago, reflects, "It's not simply a parade, there's a multiplicity of issues:...identity, religion, self-worth, self-esteem, nostalgia, family members.... There's so many competing emotions spilling into what looks like a normal day out:...music, crowds, the ritual, symbolism, memory, past, pain." All of these elements, and more, join together to generate the thrilling and meaningful experience of marching down a road to the sound of flutes and drums in Northern Ireland.

---

118. Hall, *Towards a Shared Future (5)*, p. 9.

CHAPTER 4

Culture, Politics, and the Paradox
of Anti-Politics

A curious feature of the discourse surrounding loyalist parades in
Northern Ireland is the impassioned insistence of many Protestants
that parades are apolitical. At the center of this claim is a paradox:
parades have patently and widely recognized political causes and consequences, yet many parade participants maintain that they are not just
apolitical, but anti-political—that parades transcend politics and exist
apart from it. How is it that parades, which from the outside look so clearly
to be political activism, are imagined and encountered as non-political
by participants? To seek an answer, we must examine how participants
construct, understand, and experience social categories such as politics
and culture. Through this we can see how they try to remove parading
from the realm of politics, making it "inaccessible to deliberation or
contestation."[1]

This attempt to shrink the political arena sits in marked contrast to the
efforts of scholars and activists to expand it. Through both argument and
action, many have worked to widen society's view of what counts as politics.
For instance, an influential strand of scholarship in recent decades has pos-
ited and demonstrated that seemingly ordinary acts of everyday life can be
freighted with political meaning. Examining the daily lives of powerless
people around the globe, scholars have identified how small, seemingly
prosaic actions are deliberately used to make political claims challenging

---

1. Nina Eliasoph and Paul Lichterman, "Making Things Political," in *Handbook of Cultural Sociology*, ed. John R. Hall, Laura Grindstaff, and Ming-Cheng Lo (New York: Routledge, 2010), p. 483.

the status quo that they are unable to pronounce in open protest.[2] Likewise, the second-wave feminist movement argued that places previously thought to be apolitical were actually replete with politics. Under the slogan "the personal is political," they demonstrated the political aspects of private life: "that power relations shaped life in marriage, in the kitchen, the bedroom, the nursery, and at work."[3] But this work to redefine the boundaries of politics goes in the other direction as well, and many institutions and movements try to narrow the limits of public contestation. This chapter shows that contentious rituals, which straddle both culture and politics, are important sites of conflict over what is understood as political and what is not.

I begin by demonstrating the contours of the paradox in the interviews I conducted with parade participants. The interviews show that many participants fully recognize the politics ingrained in parades, while at the same time maintaining that parades have nothing to do with politics. Parades, they argue, are about culture, a social category they see as mutually exclusive to politics. I then explain why this paradox matters. In particular, I argue that it allows participants to maintain positive personal and collective identities, and that there is political power in the claim of anti-politics. It shapes outcomes by shifting the debate away from bargaining and compromise, thereby making the conflict over parades more intractable. Third, I probe how this seemingly untenable contradiction is maintained by the ritual nature of parades. As rituals, parades provide participants with apolitical reasons to participate and their symbolic ambiguity allows for multiple interpretations of the events. Together, these two features create the behavioral and attitudinal environment that sustains the idea of anti-politics, thereby perpetuating this aspect of the Northern Irish conflict.

THE PARADOX OF ANTI-POLITICS

Though they have served varying political projects over their two-century history, as I argued in chapter 1, Protestant parades in the north of Ireland have been thoroughly political since their earliest days.[4] Their political character remains to this day—that is, parades "striv[e] to influence the distribution of power...among groups within a state"—and is evident to

2. For example, James C. Scott, *Weapons of the Weak: Everyday Forms of Peasant Resistance* (New Haven: Yale University Press, 1985); and James C. Scott, *Domination and the Arts of Resistance: Hidden Transcripts* (New Haven: Yale University Press, 1990).

3. Ruth Rosen, *The World Split Open: How the Modern Women's Movement Changed America*, rev. ed. (New York: Penguin, 2006), p. 196.

4. Neil Jarman, *Material Conflicts: Parades and Visual Displays in Northern Ireland* (Oxford: Berg, 1997), pp. 25–79; and Dominic Bryan, *Orange Parades: The Politics of Ritual, Tradition, and Control* (London: Pluto, 2000), pp. 29–96.

nearly all outside observers.[5] Marc Howard Ross's observation, for example, is quintessential: "Parades in Northern Ireland... are political statements—provocations and challenges, rights claims, assertions of power, and public acts of commitment."[6] In calling parades political, I refer to two specific characteristics: they make political claims and they have political consequences.

The primary political claim made by parades is that Northern Ireland should remain part of the United Kingdom. Agreement or disagreement with this principle marks the paramount political, social, and cultural cleavage in the province. The conflict between unionism and nationalism sets the sides and terms of politics, from policy debates to political violence. Parades always proclaim political loyalty to the UK at least implicitly, using symbols such as the Union Flag or "God Save the Queen," though at times they make it explicit, such as in speeches on the Twelfth of July. Through these means, each loyalist parade makes a claim about the most important political question in Northern Ireland.

In addition to claims about the constitutional question, parades make—or, more precisely, are understood as making—several other, no less charged, political claims. As sociologists Lee Smithey and Michael Young argue, "Orange parades have operated as expressions of loyalty and dissent across at least three relational domains: between Protestants and Catholics, between Protestant unionists and British governments, and within unionist politics."[7] Between Protestants and Catholics, parades make claims about power, status, ethnic hierarchy, and territorial control.[8] Most participants object to this characterization, but most Catholics certainly see parades this way. Between unionists and British governments, parades make claims about the interests of the unionist community, primarily ensuring that London does not abandon them to drift toward Dublin. Finally, within unionist politics, parades make hardline claims on unionist political parties, often serving to narrow their bargaining position. Rival loyalist paramilitary organizations have also used parades to assert power and claim territory on a local level. And despite their self-promoted appearance as a

5. Max Weber, "Politics as a Vocation," in *From Max Weber: Essays in Sociology*, trans. and ed. H. H. Gerth and C. Wright Mills (New York: Oxford University Press, 1972), p. 78.

6. Marc Howard Ross, *Cultural Contestation in Ethnic Conflict* (New York: Cambridge University Press, 2007), p. 88.

7. Lee A. Smithey and Michael P. Young, "Parading Protest: Orange Parades in Northern Ireland and Temperance Parades in Antebellum America," *Social Movement Studies* 9, no. 4 (November 2010): 402.

8. See, for instance, Joseph Ruane and Jennifer Todd, *The Dynamics of Conflict in Northern Ireland: Power, Conflict, and Emancipation* (New York: Cambridge University Press, 1996), p. 109; Jarman, *Material Conflicts*, p. 79; and Allen Feldman, *Formations of Violence: The Narrative of the Body and Political Terror in Northern Ireland* (Chicago: University of Chicago Press, 1991), pp. 29–30.

timeless, traditional ritual, parades and their claims have changed over time in response to shifting social and political conditions across all of these relations.

Using parades for political claim-making is not unique to Northern Irish Protestants. In fact, parades are "common features of contentious politics."[9] Historian Susan Davis argues that "as public representations, parades and public ceremonies are political acts: They have pragmatic objectives, and concrete, often material results."[10] Parades are frequent arenas for contesting authority, generating legitimacy, challenging policies, forging new political identities, confronting rival groups, asserting dignified personhood, and claiming citizenship.[11] They are an important part of the modern repertoire of contention.[12]

The second political feature of parades is their political consequences. Parades are hotly debated by politicians in the Northern Ireland Assembly and local government councils, as well as in the media. Protestant politicians have been using parades to connect with voters en masse since the mid-nineteenth century,[13] and still today, politicians are perennial speakers at Twelfth of July parades and events such as the protests over the parade dispute in North Belfast in 2013 through 2016. But while the history of politicking at parades is long, the history of Protestant-Catholic violence is longer. The sustained relationship between parades, disorder, and violence began in the earliest days of Protestant parading in the late eighteenth century and has not yet ended. Parades have proved particularly assertive and likely to stir unrest during periods of Catholic political mobilization, such as the campaign for emancipation in the 1820s and the civil rights movement of the late 1960s. As a result of this combustibility, historically and today, the performance of parades often requires the coercive apparatus of the state—police, riot police, and, until 2006, the British military. Yet

9. Smithey and Young, "Parading Protest," p. 394.

10. Susan G. Davis, *Parades and Power: Street Theater in Nineteenth-Century Philadelphia* (Philadelphia: Temple University Press, 1986), p. 5.

11. In addition to the studies of Northern Irish parades that I cite throughout, see, for example, Natalie Zemon Davis, "Rites of Violence: Religious Riot in Sixteenth-Century France," *Past and Present* 59 (May 1973): 51–91; Davis, *Parades and Power*; Mona Ozouf, *Festivals and the French Revolution*, trans. Alan Sheridan (Cambridge, MA: Harvard University Press, 1988); Mary Ryan, "The American Parade: Representations of the Nineteenth-Century Social Order," in *The New Cultural History*, ed. Lynn Hunt (Berkeley: University of California Press, 1989), pp. 131–153; Mabel Berezin, *Making the Fascist Self: The Political Culture of Interwar Italy* (Ithaca: Cornell University Press, 1997); Holly J. McCammon, " 'Out of the Parlors and into the Streets': The Changing Tactical Repertoire of the U.S. Women's Suffrage Movements," *Social Forces* 81, no. 3 (March 2003): 787–818; and Geneviève Zubrzycki, *Beheading the Saint: Nationalism, Religion, and Secularism in Quebec* (Chicago: University of Chicago Press, 2016).

12. See Charles Tilly, *Contentious Performances* (New York: Cambridge University Press, 2008).

13. Bryan, *Orange Parades*, pp. 44–46; and Jarman, *Material Conflicts*, pp. 61–62

even in the absence of overt physical violence, parades polarize the two communities and heighten tension between them, thus restricting politicians' room to compromise and communities' efforts to reconcile.

The parade participants themselves often recognize one or both of these political characteristics of parades—though, as I will soon demonstrate, they resolutely refuse to recognize parades as political action. In particular, three themes emerged in my interviews with participants that betray a political interpretation of parades. First, some participants readily acknowledge that parades make a political claim about the sovereignty question. For example, Jesse, an Orangeman and DUP elected official, articulates this view forcefully. He mentioned that he got involved in the Orange Order through his political activism, so I asked him to explain the relationship between parades and politics:

> Well there is [a relationship] when it comes to identity. There is when you consider— And, so it's not party political. So you'll not find the Orange Order advocating for the political position of the Ulster Unionist Party, the Democratic Unionist Party, the Progressive Unionist Party, or whatever. But on those big-ticket items, on Northern Ireland being a part of the United Kingdom, on reverence for the monarchical system that we have and our head of state, it is, it is political.

Here Jesse makes clear his view that parades are political because of their message about the "big-ticket items," namely remaining in the United Kingdom. Though, note how he begins by qualifying his remarks, stating that parades are not political in the sense of party politics.

Jesse also illustrates a second theme: some participants argue that parades help the political prospects of unionism by unifying the Protestant community. Parades are politically useful "not only [in] energizing people, getting the people on the streets, but [in] showing that there's such level of support for political aspiration, for a political goal." As a politician, he understands the strategic uses of large, public demonstrations: parades mobilize citizens, excite them about the unionist cause, and symbolize and help create Protestant unity and communal solidarity. These "public enactments of worthiness, unity, numbers, and commitment" can even influence people who do not attend parades.[14] By "showing that there's such level of support," parades demonstrate to participants, attenders, and those who do not attend that the ideology has great and deep backing. This is an important message for both advocates and opponents of unionism. Protestants see that unionism is alive and well—which might forestall electoral defection—while

14. Tilly, *Contentious Performances*, p. 120.

Catholics (along with the British and Irish states) see that it remains a formidable political force.

Other paraders speak more explicitly about sending a message to Catholics, a third political theme. For them, parades are a ritualized means of communication with nationalists and republicans. Through the display of symbols—flags, collarettes, uniforms, music, banners—and the physical presence of the marchers, parades say to Irish nationalists, "We're still here."[15] As discussed in the previous chapter, this message of defiance and opposition is not recognized by all participants, but some do see their action this way. Kenny, for example, states that parades are "about making the stand that we can't just be forced out of our own country." "I look at it as not simply about a parade," John says, "but it has to do with civil liberty. It has to do with tyranny. It has to do with [not] giving into the violence, giving in to the people who want to take away your civil rights, which I would look upon as republicanism." By parading, this clergyman takes a stand against Irish republicanism.[16] For participants like Kenny and John, the communication with nationalists is an intentional political strategy.

While many participants acknowledge these claims and consequences of parades, they nevertheless generally refuse to accept that their participation in them is in any way political. We can begin to see the tension caused by this paradox in Mark, who suggests that parades are inherently political and used politically, but will not characterize them as political actions. Instead, he identifies the Northern Irish context as why parades are considered political. He first explains that parades are political because they commemorate political events. "Obviously there is a political part," Mark says. "I mean the Battle of the Boyne was won in 1690 by the king of England, which in a way heralded a change in almost the constitution of the United Kingdom that guaranteed the rights of everybody." Moreover, he argues, parades today make an explicit political claim: "You know, the parades are almost a statement of what we stand for, and we stand for the union between Northern Ireland and the United Kingdom. . . . It is a political statement in that regard." To "stand for the union between Northern Ireland and the United Kingdom" is, of course, to take a position on the predominant question in Northern Irish politics.[17]

---

15. For an anthropological analysis of the relationship between Orange Order icons and the body, see Feldman, *Formations of Violence*, pp. 57–58.

16. See also the bandsman's statement recorded in Michael Hall, *Towards a Shared Future (5): Ulster's Marching Bands* (Belfast: Island Publications, 2014), p. 27: "Our band culture is the last obstacle standing in the way of militant Irish Republicanism."

17. It is worth recalling that in the opening pages of the previous chapter Mark contended that though a political message is sent, it is not his purpose in parading: "It is a political statement in

But then Mark's view shifts. He suggests that parades are not by nature political, but *made* political by the local context, providing two comparisons as evidence. First, while Protestant parading in Northern Ireland says, "We're still here," Orange parades in the Republic of Ireland carry a different meaning because "they have a different set of problems to deal with." In other words, there is nothing inherent in parades that makes them claim "We're still here"; it results from the context. What is more, parades have "political connotations...because...you are carrying the Union [Flag]." "This is the difference in thinking, Jonathan," he told me. "If there was a parade by a religious group in the United States and they flew the Star Spangled Banner on the parade, would you deem that parade as being political? Probably not. But if you fly the Union Jack in Northern Ireland, it's political." Again, it is the vexed politics of Northern Ireland that renders parades political, not parades' actual character. Mark here is torn between his understandings of the sources of parades' politics. He cannot seem to decide whether parades are political by nature (which would qualify them as political action in his mind) or whether Northern Ireland's social, political, and historical context made them so (which means they do not qualify). His reluctance to accept the politics of parades is not unfounded. In fact, it is deeply rooted in the Protestant public discourse around parades. For most participants, there is not even a question.

Many, if not most, participants forcefully assert that parades are in no way political.[18] In fact, for many participants, parades are anti-political— they exist outside the realm of politics. By identifying paraders' claims and rhetoric as anti-political, I intend to highlight their view that parades are not merely not political, but above and beyond politics. Anti-political is a stronger, more extreme stance than apolitical. Being apolitical is to be passively not political; being anti-political is to take an active and antagonistic stance against politics and the political. Things that are anti-political are not on the same spectrum as things that are political; there is an absolute difference in kind.

To understand how parades are anti-political, we must first know how participants view politics. Politics, for most paraders, is the domain of elite

that regard. Although, we don't set out— We simply set out to celebrate, 'This is what we are and this is what we stand for.' "

18. See also Gordon Ramsey, *Music, Emotion and Identity in Ulster Marching Bands: Flutes, Drums and Loyal Sons* (Bern: Peter Lang, 2011), pp. 226–227; and Ray Casserly, "The Fyfe and My Family: Flute Bands in Rathcoole Estate," *Irish Journal of Anthropology* 13 (2010): 11. As recently as the 1990s, when he conducted his fieldwork, Bryan, *Orange Parades*, pp. 106, 107, found that only "a few Orangemen will go so far as to argue that Orangeism is not political at all, but simply religious." He further observed: "The relationship between the 'religious' and the 'political' is not lost on members of the Orange Order; indeed that relationship is seen by many as fundamental."

and electoral competition. It is politicians and political parties jockeying for advantage, challenging each other, and competing for votes. This is a narrow, but not incorrect, conception of political life.[19] By this definition, contemporary parades are not especially political, particularly when compared to parades in earlier decades, when the Orange Order was tightly linked to the ruling Ulster Unionist Party and parades were effectively party rallies. In contrast, parading organizations today do not advocate for a particular party, and their memberships reflect the panoply of unionist political parties.[20] As Rachel reports, "We avoid bringing up politics in band because it's a very, very, very sensitive issue.... It just takes one snide comment and a whole band can be torn apart."[21] So at least in this confined, partisan sense, parades are not political.

But this is not the main reasoning that drives participants' argument. Rather, participants claim that parades are not political because they are *cultural*, which they see as mutually exclusive categories. Culture and politics are often juxtaposed by participants and defined in contrast to each other.[22] As Craig states, parades "wouldn't be seen as political from anybody coming from a parading side. It's a cultural thing." Robby contrasts the two concepts as he compares himself to his brother. His brother loves politics: "He can't not watch the news every night and he was a member of the DUP party and stuff. He was quite politically minded." Robby, however, has "no real interest" in politics. Instead, he is interested in parades: "As [for] what I do as in the Orangeism and the band scene and stuff like that ... I'm more culturally minded to politically minded." Culture and politics are seen as distinct,

19. In fact, many political scientists might agree. For a discussion of varying approaches to "politics" and "the political," see Andrew Mason, "Politics and the State," *Political Studies* 38, no. 4 (December 1990): 575–587. The "elite competition as politics" approach I find in the interviews is even narrower than what Mason calls the "narrow approach," which is anything having to do with government. For an important discussion of how observers should approach "the political" and navigate the differences between their own views and the "native" view, see Nina Eliasoph, *Avoiding Politics: How Americans Produce Apathy in Everyday Life* (New York: Cambridge University Press, 1998), pp. 14–15, 278.

20. See Jocelyn A. J. Evans and Jonathan Tonge, "Unionist Party Competition and the Orange Order Vote in Northern Ireland," *Electoral Studies* 26, no. 1 (March 2007): 156–167; Jon Tonge, Jocelyn Evans, Robert Jeffery, and James W. McAuley, "New Order: Political Change and the Protestant Orange Tradition in Northern Ireland," *British Journal of Politics and International Relations* 13, no. 3 (2011): 400–419; and Eric P. Kaufmann, *The Orange Order: A Contemporary Northern Irish History* (New York: Oxford University Press, 2007), esp. pp. 202–235.

21. See also Ramsey, *Music, Emotion and Identity*, p. 145.

22. See also ibid., p. 227. Brian Kennaway, "The Re-Invention of the Orange Order: Triumphalism or Orangefest?" in *The Contested Identities of Ulster Protestants*, ed. Thomas Paul Burgess and Gareth Mulvenna (Houndmills, UK: Palgrave Macmillan, 2015), pp. 70–82, suggests that the Orange Order has emphasized the centrality of "culture" since the middle of first decade of the new millennium in contrast to its previous emphasis on "faith." This repositioning, he argues, is part of an attempt to appeal to a broader segment of society.

even opposing, points of view. For Robby, culture replaces politics: while his brother lives and breathes politics, Robby lives and breathes culture.

Rachel makes the contrast between the cultural and the political explicit:

> Any time it's said that the Twelfth of July is making a political statement, no, it's not. It's a cultural statement. The only time that it would be making a political statement [is] if it's a protest against [something], like say a flag protest, or if it's a civil rights march, then that's political. But if it is cultural, it's not.

There is no overlap between culture and politics in Rachel's mind. Politics is protests and "trying to score political points against other unionist parties," as she says several moments later; culture is parades, tradition, music, history, and the like. And if it is one, it cannot be the other. As a result, politics does not enter parades: "I am DUP through and through," she declares, "but when I'm out parading I'm not doing it for the DUP." Parades are cultural, so politics is left outside.

In addition to making definitional and conceptual distinctions, paraders present comparative evidence to support the argument that parades are cultural, not political. One piece of evidence that several interviewees cited to me is that parades are not political because they are a widely enjoyed cultural practice. Parades in Northern Ireland cannot be political, they reason, because they are simply one example of a global means of self-expression and celebration that elsewhere is apolitical. Edward is certainly correct that "people all around the world celebrate with parades. It's not unique to Orangemen, to Northern Ireland, or to Britain." So is Mikey: "The army has parades, schools in America have parades, they have parades on St. Patrick's Day. People want to parade." And in all of those cases, he argues, there are no political challenges. Therefore, parades in Northern Ireland are not political either.

What is more, parades are a tradition, by which they mean that parades have been practiced for centuries—which, again, is true. The conclusion that participants draw is that since their parades have existed for a long time, they cannot have relevance to contemporary politics. Traditions, by definition, are unchanging: their "object and characteristic... is invariance," as Eric Hobsbawm argues.[23] Thus, a tradition that began in the eighteenth century and has, perforce, continued unchanged to the present cannot speak to today's political debates. "How can there be a political parade," Dan asks, "when it's been walking that road for one hundred years?"

---

23. Eric Hobsbawm, "Inventing Traditions," in *The Invention of Tradition*, ed. Eric Hobsbawm and Terence Ranger (Cambridge: Cambridge University Press, 1983), p. 2. As Jarman, *Material Conflicts*, p. 9, notes, repetition in and of rituals "enhances the feeling that they never change."

Participants relatedly maintain that parades are not only from the past, they are *about* the past: they are commemorative. The subject of parades is historical, so they are detached from present-day politics. If anything, some argued, the era that many major parades memorialize was a time when Catholics and Protestants were united against a common enemy. As a number of interviewees pointed out to me, the pope supported William of Orange in 1690.[24]

Yet even the staunchest defender of parades' anti-politics recognizes that parades today are hotly disputed. So how do they explain why, if parades are not political by their origins or their subject, they are contested? How did parades become the subject of such intense political controversy? The nearly universally held answer among participants and their supporters is that parading was strategically *politicized* by the republican movement during the Troubles. Sinn Féin, the Provisional IRA, and others deliberately transformed parades into political subjects: they made them "into topics of public deliberation or contestation."[25] By doing so, republicans inserted politics where it did not belong and had never been before. And their campaign of politicization succeeded: parades today remain "not political, but they're perceived as political."[26] This explains why events that, from participants' perspective, are and always have been cultural are at the center of today's political battles.

Again and again, interviewees told me the following history.[27] For centuries, parades passed uncontested. In fact, they were attended and enjoyed by Protestants and Catholics alike. Many participants recall childhood

24. This myth is *almost* true. The pope in 1690, the short-lived Alexander VIII, did not support William. But his predecessor, the more important Innocent XI—who died in 1689—did back the Prince of Orange. James II was allied with Innocent's chief rival, Louis XIV of France, so the pope favored James's ouster in the Glorious Revolution. Alexander, by contrast, was less hostile to France and, therefore, James (though his support for James seems reluctant). Even without the pope's blessing, William was supported by the Catholic leaders of the Holy Roman Empire, Spain, and Bavaria, and his victory at the Boyne was celebrated in Vienna's cathedral and other Catholic churches. See J. G. Simms, "Remembering 1690," *Studies: An Irish Quarterly Review* 63, no. 251 (Autumn 1974): 231–233; Craig Rose, *England in the 1690s: Revolution, Religion and War* (Oxford: Blackwell, 1999), p. 115; and Steven Pincus, *1688: The First Modern Revolution* (New Haven: Yale University Press, 2009), pp. 122–124, 139, 345.

25. Eliasoph and Lichterman, "Making Things Political," p. 483, define politicizing as "action, collective or individual, that makes issues or identities into topics of public deliberation or contestation."

26. Interview with Craig, December 12, 2012.

27. The history is also recounted by parading's senior leaders in public addresses. See, for example, Grand Secretary of the Grand Orange Lodge of Ireland Drew Nelson's speech of January 17, 2014, excerpted in "Is the Long War on the Orange Order Over" http://www.grandorangelodge.co.uk/news, accessed February 9, 2014. Neil Southern, "Territoriality, Alienation, and Loyalist Decommissioning: The Case of the Shankill in Protestant West Belfast," *Terrorism and Political Violence* 20, no. 1 (2007): 79–80, finds a very similar narrative in his interviews with Protestant clergy and paramilitaries.

Catholic friends who wanted to join the parade with them, or Catholic neighbors coming over on the morning of the Twelfth to pin flowers to their fathers' lapels.[28] This all changed around the 1980s and 1990s. In those years, Sinn Féin and the IRA developed a strategy to turn the Catholic population vehemently against parades in order to delegitimize Protestant culture in Northern Ireland. The intensity of this campaign increased during the peace process, as the IRA began demobilizing troops and combatants were released from prison. The republican leadership suddenly needed something beyond armed conflict for these men and women to do. So they placed operatives in Catholic communities to manufacture anti-parade sentiments and orchestrate local protests. Sinn Féin president Gerry Adams himself boasted as much in 1997: "Do you think Drumcree happened by accident?" he asked rhetorically, in a quote often referenced by interviewees. As protests mounted and succeeded in a particular place, republicans moved their attention to new parade routes, with the intention of one day banning all parades in Northern Ireland.[29] The tactics might be new, but the

---

28. See also Jack Santino, *Signs of War and Peace: Social Conflict and the Uses of Symbols in Public in Northern Ireland* (New York: Palgrave, 2001), p. 34; and James W. McAuley, Jonathan Tonge, and Andrew Mycock, *Loyal to the Core?: Orangeism and Britishness in Northern Ireland* (Dublin: Irish Academic Press, 2011), p. 174. Bryan, *Orange Parades*, pp. 69–70, points out that the postwar era (1945 to mid-1960s), when parades were relatively harmonious, was the formative period for the generation who became loyal order leaders during and after the Troubles. Friendlier times were within their living memories, which shaped their reaction to growing Catholic opposition.

29. Parts of this account are accurate. There was a republican strategy that began in those years, which aimed to target parades, and Adams was reported to have stated the question at a Sinn Féin party meeting in Athboy, Ireland. See Malachi O'Doherty, *The Trouble with Guns: Republican Strategy and the Provisional IRA* (Belfast: Blackstaff, 1998), pp. 173–176, 183; Martyn Frampton, *The Long March: The Political Strategy of Sinn Féin, 1981–2007* (London: Palgrave Macmillan, 2000), pp. 126–127; James Dingley, "Marching Down the Garvaghy Road: Republican Tactics and State Response to the Orangemen's Claim to March Their Traditional Route Home After the Drumcree Church Service," *Terrorism and Political Violence* 14, no. 3 (Autumn 2002): 42–79; Ed Moloney, *A Secret History of the IRA* (New York: Norton, 2003), pp. 466–468; and Kevin Bean, *The New Politics of Sinn Féin* (Liverpool: University of Liverpool Press, 2007), p. 120. Nevertheless, Dominic Bryan, "Parade Disputes and the Peace Process," *Peace Review* 13, no. 1 (2001): 45, cautions that we should not give too much credit to the strategic view that "underestimates the local community dynamics that have long existed in places such as the Garvaghy Road and the political space the peace process created for public opposition to parades." For the recent dynamics of residents groups and their place in republican politics, see Martyn Frampton, *The Return of the Militants: Violent Dissident Republicanism* (London: International Centre for the Study of Radicalisation and Political Violence, 2010), pp. 20–21; Henry Patterson, "Beyond the 'Micro Group': The Dissident Republican Challenge," in *Dissident Irish Republicanism*, ed. P. M. Currie and Max Taylor (New York: Continuum, 2011), pp. 75–76; and Sophie A. Whiting, *Spoiling the Peace?: The Threat of Dissident Republicans to Peace in Northern Ireland* (Manchester: Manchester University Press, 2015), p. 189.

Despite the elements of historical truth, my interviewees' idealized interpretation of the years before the 1980s is the result of selective memory that ignores the long history of sectarian conflict at and over loyalist parades. (This selective memory has its own interesting history: for example, just days before July 12, 1969, Northern Irish prime minister James Chichester-Clark

anti-parade protests these provocateurs stirred up were simply the latest chapter in the long republican campaign to unite the island.[30]

This narrative, in varying degrees of detail, is ubiquitous among my interviews. As Dan remembers:

> Twenty years ago on the Twelfth day, Catholics used to come out. Now it's all been IRA orchestrated to try to stop bands going where they want to go. The bands used to go by Catholic areas and they [the residents] would turn the radio up: live and let live, it'll be by in a minute. But now they're out in the streets trying to stop parades. It has changed.

In Isaac's rosy memories of a bygone era, "neighbors lived at peace with each other. What has happened is that we've all become contentious now. You know, you didn't need a Parades Commission before the Troubles." Craig insists, "The reality is people have marched down the same road there for umpteen years...without causing offense until Sinn Féin/IRA politicized it." Or, in Mark's telling:

> During the thirty years [of the Troubles] the republican community weren't interested in parades, because they had other things on their mind: how they were going to plan their next atrocity, who they were going to murder next. They seem to have changed tactics and come away from that. "Ok, let's pick a soft target now during the peace process," which is a parade.

The story they tell is of a helpless Protestant community being acted on by conniving republicans.[31] Protestants are not agents in their view of this history: politicization happened to them. According to Craig, parades were "pulled into politics" by "a very serious negative propaganda attack from Sinn Féin." "The situation has been politicized," Isaac comments. As these examples illustrate, when speaking of parades, participants tend to use the passive voice; but when talking about republicans, their verbs are active, and their language is the language of conspiracy: "There was a deliberate

and the Inspector-General of the Royal Ulster Constabulary "were assuring the General Officer Commanding in the Province...that Orange marches had never been a source of communal strife." Richard Bourke, *Peace in Ireland: The War of Ideas* [London: Pimlico, 2003], p. 99.) Yet my point is not to dismiss my interviewees' understanding of history; it is to investigate how their understanding of the past works in the present. What kind of power does this narrative have and how does it affect behavior? For a general account of cultural polarization following political polarization, see Ann Swidler, *Talk of Love: How Culture Matters* (Chicago: University of Chicago Press, 2001), pp. 169–175. She specifically addresses ethnic conflict on p. 259n10.

30. Neil Jarman, "From Outrage to Apathy?: The Disputes over Parades, 1995–2003," *The Global Review of Ethnopolitics* 3, no. 1 (September 2003): 94.

31. It is common for groups to view their rivals as far more organized and unified than themselves, or than the rival actually is. See Robert Jervis, *Perception and Misperception in International Politics* (Princeton: Princeton University Press, 1976), pp. 319–342.

policy formulated by Sinn Féin/IRA...when they were in prison"; parades become contentious when "republicans deem them to be contentious"; republicans "sectarianize the unionist tunes"; "they're going out of the way to cause problems."[32] Billy summarizes the sentiment: "It's all orchestrated. It's created, deliberately created conflict where there was no conflict."[33]

A conclusion drawn from this narrative is that all anti-parade sentiment is artificial.[34] The only people who are offended by parades are those who choose to be offended by parades. For many Protestants, parades are a synecdoche for their community, so to be offended by parades is to be offended by the Protestant community—and to challenge parades is to challenge the community's very existence.[35] So those who choose to be offended by parades do so because they hate Protestants and want to drive them off Ireland. Any and all opposition to parades, consequently, is illegitimate.[36]

32. Interview with Craig, December 12, 2012; interview with Mark, July 11, 2013; interview with Sammy, July 9, 2013; and interview with Howie, August 13, 2012. For interpretations of the conspiratorial elements of loyalist ideology, see Ronnie Moore and Andrew Sanders, "Formations of Culture: Nationalism and Conspiracy Ideology in Ulster Loyalism," *Anthropology Today* 18, no. 6 (December 2002): 14–15. More generally, see the classic analysis of the "paranoid style" of politics in Richard Hofstadter, *The Paranoid Style in American Politics, and Other Essays* (New York: Vintage, 2008), pp. 3–40. Hofstadter's discussion of the paranoid's view of "the enemy" is particularly relevant (p. 31).

33. Significantly, interviewees are now using "politics" differently than they did before. Recall that when discussing unionist politics, they use the term narrowly to mean intra-unionist party politics. Now, when discussing nationalist politics, they use the term much more broadly to mean contestation.

34. Beyond artificial, some interviewees suggested that anti-parade feelings are actually coerced. As Billy told me: "I had very good friends in there who are Catholics and talking to them and chatting like the way we are, they would say, 'The parade's been going down here for a lifetime. It didn't annoy me, because I didn't go to see it. But I didn't tell you that. I can't openly say that. If I openly say that, I would be told to get out.' So they'd be under pressure for that." And Steven says: "I have been told by Catholic friends that they were visited by Sinn Féin activists and told that if they got anywhere near Orange parades, the Twelfth of July, well, the repercussions would be fair.... So then they stopped coming." Whether or not these stories are true, they are part of the dominant narrative among paraders and their supporters.

35. Ross, *Cultural Contestation in Ethnic Conflict*, esp. pp. 22–26, provides a rich cultural theory of this dynamic, with a specific analysis of loyalist parading in chapter 4, "Loyalist Parades in Northern Ireland as Recurring Psychocultural Dramas"; and in Marc Howard Ross, "Psychocultural Interpretations and Dramas: Identity Dynamics in Ethnic Conflict," *Political Psychology* 22, no. 1 (March 2001): 157–178.

36. For an alternative interpretation of this dynamic of ethnic conflict, see Sherill Stroschein, *Ethnic Struggle, Coexistence, and Democratization in Eastern Europe* (New York: Cambridge University Press, 2012), p. 238. Stroschein finds that in Romania and Slovakia, people also tend to blame out-group ethnic mobilization on manipulation by the other group's elites, but concludes that this is a mechanism to reduce tensions in the daily interactions with members of the other ethnicity. Rather than blame your neighbors for contentious mobilization, you can blame their elites for manipulating them. This way you can continue to shop at their stores and say hello on the street. I interpret this tendency to blame rival elites in Northern Ireland very differently. Rather than facilitate good relations, I see it as stripping "the enemy" of their own autonomy and agency. It transforms the other group into one undifferentiated whole who are slaves to their masters. In the context of Protestant-Catholic relations this builds from and feeds into

For all of these reasons, participants understand parades not just as non-political, but in contradistinction to politics, despite their widely known political claims and consequences. The paradox of anti-politics is most clearly evident in individuals who explained to me the patently political functions and effects of parades, but ardently refused to call them political. A case in point is this exchange with Robert, a retired factory worker very active in the Orange Order in West Belfast:

J.B.: *Now is parading at all political?*

ROBERT: Well I don't think so. Now there was a time it would have been termed that [because of the connection to the Ulster Unionist Party], but I'm thinking over the last thirty years it's not. It used to be [every parade] had to [have] a politician on the field, but you find a lot of places [where] that wouldn't be. Yes, there's members of the Orange Order that are politicians and they'd maybe speak, but normally they've done away with the political agenda.

J.B.: *So does parading help to maintain the union?*

ROBERT: Yes, it does let people see we're still here and we haven't gone away and I think that's one of the main things.

J.B.: *What's one of the main things?*

ROBERT: That we see that we maintain the union with Great Britain. [It] lets people see we're still very strong in numbers...

J.B.: *So if parading relates to unionism, is that not political? Or is that—*

ROBERT: Not really. I would say most of the Orangemen would— Alliance [Party] people not many and some, well, quite a lot of independents, but most of the Orangemen would be of a unionist family background. No, I wouldn't, I wouldn't say it was political.

Robert had just told me that helping to maintain the union between Northern Ireland and Great Britain is "one of the main things" about parades. It is also clearly *the* main thing in Northern Irish politics. But then when I asked him about the politics involved in that action he demurred and returned to a discussion of party politics.

---

the old idea that Catholics are servile (and therefore "Home Rule means Rome rule"). This idea is at least partially rooted in perceptions of theological differences between the two faiths, where Protestantism is seen as rooted in personal choice, while Catholicism is rooted in submission. See John Bell, *For God, Ulster or Ireland?: Religion, Society and Security in Northern Ireland* (Belfast: Institute for Conflict Research, 2013), pp. 5, 7, 61–71, 106. See also general strategies of assigning blame in James M. Jasper, *Getting Your Way: Strategic Dilemmas in the Real World* (Chicago: University of Chicago Press, 2006), pp. 48–53.

The same dynamic occurs with Walter, the bandsman from a West Belfast interface community. He first argues that parades are not political on the grounds that they are unrelated to political parties:

J.B.: *So some people would argue that parading in general is political. I'm assuming you would disagree.*

WALTER: Well we don't have any political agenda.

[...]

WALTER: I don't really know any bands that are [political]. The DUP probably would have had—

J.B.: *Well maybe not party political, but political in the most basic sense of the sovereignty issue or the constitutional issue. Does that play—*

WALTER: No.

J.B.: *That plays no role in it?*

WALTER: No, not to a great extent. A lot of people believe that they want to be British, but it wouldn't be played out in a role within a band. The band wouldn't play a role of being—of wanting to keep the union, if you know what I mean.

Political agendas, according to Walter, are things that politicians and political parties have. Cultural organizations, such as his band, do not have them. In fact, individual members even suppress their political beliefs in the context of the band. But then later in the interview, I asked Walter if parading has a goal, and he replied:

I think it has. It shows that we're still here. It shows that the people still want to be part of Ulster. They want to remain loyalist, they don't want to be part of anything else, just our own— This is our wee country. This is our band's walk on the streets to show that we can do [it], how many of us there is, and that's the support there is for our cause, which is loyalism.

In Walter's eyes, though he wants to "be part of Ulster," opposes a united Ireland, and supports the cause of loyalism, he insists that he does not "have any political agenda." The contradiction appears glaring, but there are several strong reasons for Walter and many others to construct and maintain it.

THE POWER OF THE PARADOX OF ANTI-POLITICS

Thus far I have demonstrated that the anti-political discourse of parades promoted by participants is paradoxical. But, to paraphrase religion scholar

Lori Beaman, the interesting and important question is not whether parades are political, but "what is achieved [and] which power relations [are] shifted and preserved, by recasting" parades "as 'cultural' rather than" political?[37] What is achieved by the anti-politics paradox, I argue, is the creation of a powerful political tool to be wielded by parade participants and their allies. Specifically, the paradox provides them with two advantages. First, it protects participants' self-concept as good people. Participants' approach to politics is shaped by an understanding of the world where culture is inherently good and politics is inherently bad. By separating culture from politics, the language of anti-politics places parades and paraders on the moral high ground. It is part of an ongoing project to construct and maintain a positive sense of their personal and collective identities. Second, there is political power in the discourse of anti-politics. This discourse shapes debates and political outcomes because if parades are not political, they are immune from critique and protected from compromise. The logic of anti-politics, in other words, can be used to silence democratic opposition. Participants, therefore, want parades to be outside of politics because, ironically, there is political power in the claim of transcending politics.[38] These two features of the anti-politics discourse help explain why there is such strong and sustained resistance to thinking of parades as political.[39]

Are these not just post hoc rationalizations of their behavior? I believe they are not. Rather, the elements of the anti-politics paradox are what sociologists Gresham Sykes and David Matza call "techniques of neutralization." Sykes and Matza argue that techniques of neutralization are commonly "viewed as [justifications] following deviant behavior and as protecting the individual from self-blame and the blame of others after the fact. But there is also reason to believe that they precede deviant behavior and make deviant behavior possible."[40] Thus the discourse of anti-politics more than just rationalizes controversial parading behavior; it *enables* it.

For most participants, as previously discussed, politics and culture are separate spheres of life. Politics is the sphere of politicians, their parties, and

37. Lori G. Beaman, "Battles over Symbols: The 'Religion' of the Minority versus the 'Culture' of the Majority," *Journal of Law and Religion* 28, no. 1 (April 2012): 79.

38. See also Bryan, *Orange Parades*, esp. pp. 155–172; and Camille O'Reilly, "The Politics of Culture in Northern Ireland," in *Peace at Last?: The Impact of the Good Friday Agreement on Northern Ireland*, ed. Jörg Neuheiser and Stefan Wolff (New York: Berghan, 2002), pp. 168–187, who succinctly describes this political power as "Culture = Tradition = Legitimacy" (p. 169).

39. Ramsey, *Music, Emotion and Identity*, p. 228, suggests a third reason why bandsmen, in particular, resist a political label: "music defined as 'political' is devalued *as music*" (emphasis in the original).

40. Gresham M. Sykes and David Matza, "Techniques of Neutralization: A Theory of Delinquency," *American Sociological Review* 22, no. 6 (December 1957): 666. See also Marvin B. Scott and Stanford M. Lyman, "Accounts," *American Sociological Review* 33, no. 1 (February 1968): 46–62.

their competition for power. Culture, meanwhile, is the sphere of faith, tradition, and heritage. Layered on top of this distinction is an implicit normative ranking: culture is good, politics is bad.[41] Culture is pure, politics is corrupt. Culture is about communal identity, politics is about individual greed. Culture is traditional, politics is instrumental (and, as I showed in the previous chapter, paraders value tradition over instrumental action).

The negative view of politics emerges in interviewees' choice of language and arguments. Parades are "tarnished as being political," Rachel told me. Politics is dirty and soils parades. For one thing, politics is about naked self-interest. As George sees it, parades "crept into the political realm because various politicians have used the political network to assist their own ends." He blames Sinn Féin, but then also criticizes "our political people, who have used it for their own ends when needed."

Part of this conceptual division is the idea that "we" do culture, but "they" do politics. Interviewees argue that nationalists have even inappropriately pushed politics onto their own cultural heritage. Irish nationalists politicized elements of Irish culture such as the Irish language and St. Patrick's Day, and thereby excluded Protestants from them.[42] Steven com-

41. For a general analysis, see Colin Hay, *Why We Hate Politics* (London: Polity, 2007); see also Eliasoph, *Avoiding Politics*. Northern Irish public opinion surveys consistently show that politicians are strongly disliked, and that Protestants are especially disenchanted with their elected representatives. In a 2009 poll, 87 percent of Protestants stated that they did not trust politicians. In a 2003 poll, 75 percent agreed that "those we elect lose touch with people pretty quickly" and 77 percent agreed that "parties are only interested in people's votes, not in their opinions." Most of the people I interviewed were also thoroughly angry at or disappointed by unionist politicians, particularly at the national level (local officials were often rated more highly). A question about whether there were political leaders they admired frequently prompted sighs or laughter. Survey data: ARK, *Northern Ireland Life and Times Survey, 2009*, distributed by ARK, 2009, http://www.ark.ac.uk/nilt/2009/Political_Attitudes/POLTRUST. html, accessed March 6, 2015. ARK, *Northern Ireland Life and Times Survey, 2003*, distributed by ARK, 2003, http://www.ark.ac.uk/nilt/2003/Political_Attitudes/LOSETCH.html; and http://www.ark.ac.uk/nilt/2003/Political_Attitudes/VOTEINTR.htm, accessed March 6, 2015.
42. Interview with Frankie, December 4, 2012; and Interview with Steven, December 5, 2012. Many scholars share the assessment that the Irish nationalist movement has used and continues to use the Irish language and St. Patrick's Day for political gain. See, for example, Mike Cronin and Daryl Adair, *The Wearing of the Green: A History of St. Patrick's Day* (London: Routledge, 2002), esp. pp. 175–179; and Camille C. O'Reilly, *The Irish Language in Northern Ireland: The Politics of Culture and Identity* (New York: St. Martin's Press, 1999). Some nationalist activists agree as well. For example, Gerry Adams, *Free Ireland: Towards a Lasting Peace* (New York: Penguin, 1995), p. 139: "The revival of the Irish language … is a central aspect of the reconquest." For a broader historical discussion of the role of Irish culture in Irish nationalism, see John Hutchinson, *The Dynamics of Cultural Nationalism: The Gaelic Revival and the Creation of the Irish Nation State* (London: Allen & Unwin, 1987). But my interviews are likely most familiar with the criticisms of the politicization of Irish culture, especially language, coming from Protestant leaders. For instance, Grand Master of the Belfast County Orange Lodge George Chittick warned that Protestants should not learn the Irish language because "it's part of the republican agenda." According to the BBC, "He said the Irish language had not been 'political' in the past, but this had been changed in recent times by republicans." Similarly Gregory

plains that the politicization of the Belfast St. Patrick's Day parade upsets him, and so he avoids it—despite how much he enjoys "as they say, the diddly-dee music." "If I wanted to be offended I could go in there and see tricolors flying all over the place, and as I say to my Catholic friends, What has the tricolor got to do with St. Patrick? The tricolor was never brought into use until 1922 as such. . . . I says, so St. Patrick didn't even know about a tricolor, why is it waved?" And just as republicans turned Irish culture political, they also made loyalist parades political to serve their political agenda. Dan sums up the general thinking. He was telling me that protests are orchestrated by the IRA, so I asked him, "Why is the IRA interested in this?" "They want to break the loyalists down. They want a united Ireland," he replied.

All of the protests, all of the anger, all of the restrictions are, to Dan, part of the republican agenda to unite Ireland. And their ongoing success is because republicans are brilliant strategists and excellent manipulators: "The republican media/PR machine has been so good," as Mark puts it. Protestants, on the other hand, are just plain-spoken, honest folk who did not stand a chance. This move—complimenting one's opponent for being a fantastic speaker—is a classic rhetorical strategy, because it implies they can trick the audience into believing lies. As Tom explains:

> They're better at manipulating the press, they're better at spin. . . . We're blunt and straight to the point. . . . We call a spade a spade, that's what it is. We don't flower it up or dress it up, and sometimes that straight truth needs dressing up. Republicans dress it up, so people tend to believe what republicans are saying.

So "they," with their sophisticated "propaganda machine,"[43] play politics, while "we" do what we've always done: culture.

In bemoaning the politicization of parades, participants also yearn for the lost innocence of the "good old days," a mythic past of Protestant-Catholic harmony under unionist rule. The contrast between memories of friendly parades in the halcyon, pre-political era and today's anger and hyper-contestation could not be clearer. Scott told me that when unionists controlled the country (an era well before his birth), they could parade

Campbell, the DUP MP for East Londonderry, stated that he will "expose [Sinn Féin's] . . . politicising of the Irish language." See, respectively, Mark Simpson, "Orangeman Says Protestants Should Not Learn Irish Language," *BBC News Online*, February 1, 2014, http://www.bbc.co.uk/news/uk-northern-ireland-26000146, accessed February 5, 2014; and Jennifer O'Leary, "Why Is Irish Language Divisive Issue in Northern Ireland?" *BBC News Online*, December 17, 2014, http://www.bbc.com/news/uk-northern-ireland-30517834, accessed December 17, 2014.

43. Interview with Robert, November 28, 2012. Relatedly, there is a widespread sentiment among my interviewees that the media is out to get Protestants, in general, and parades, in particular.

anywhere they liked. During those years, he said, there was no such thing as a contentious parade. Isaac, who did live though this period, recalls the era when "the RUC [Royal Ulster Constabulary, an all-Protestant police force] policed all those parades and there never was really any trouble." But these statements inadvertently reveal the truth. The earlier era was not pre-political; parades were *always* tied up with politics and political power. It is just that interviewees used to support the politics, since it permitted them, and in fact actively helped them, to parade wherever they wanted. The very reason that parading is so much more prominent among Protestants than Catholics is that the state promoted Protestant parades while using expansive legislation to suppress Catholic ones.[44] Even some paraders recognize that the notion of a time before politics is a myth. Tom, for instance, questions the veracity of his fellow Protestants' memories of the Orange Order in their grandfathers' generation: "They think it was a great organization then because [the Orange Order] weren't into all this politics—they were into politics. People look back with rose-tinted glasses."

This earlier era was defined by unionist political dominance—so much so that Northern Ireland was known to critics as "the Orange state."[45] The general mood was captured in a well-known statement by Northern Ireland's first prime minister, James Craig: "I have always said I am an Orangeman first and a politician and Member of this Parliament afterwards....All I boast of is that we are a Protestant Parliament and a Protestant State."[46] The Orange Order, along with the other institutions of unionist hegemony, actively worked to exclude Catholics from political power and labor markets, thereby maintaining their second-class status.[47] Parades under Stormont's unionist governments served not only to symbolize Protestants' privileged position, but, at times, to maintain it in concrete ways as well. For instance, during the late 1960s, loyal orders would preempt civil rights demonstrations by organizing "annual parades" for the

---

44. Bryan, *Orange Parades*, p. 61; and Jarman, *Material Conflicts*, p. 72. One of the laws used to restrict Catholic parades was the Civil Authorities (Special Powers) Act of 1922, about which an apartheid-era South African Justice Minister said that he would "trade all the coercive powers at his disposal 'for one clause of the Northern Ireland Special Powers Act.'" Bourke, *Peace in Ireland*, p. 46.

45. Michael Farrell, *Northern Ireland: The Orange State* (London: Pluto Press, 1976).

46. Parliamentary Debates, Northern Ireland, 1933/34, vol. 16, columns 1091 and 1095, April 24, 1934. The Hansard record is available online at http://stormontpapers.ahds.ac.uk/.

47. A Northern Irish human rights organization, the Pat Finucane Centre, *For God and Ulster: An Alternative Guide to the Loyal Orders* (Derry: Pat Finucane Centre, 1997), http://www.patfinucanecentre.org/god-and-ulster-alternative-guide-loyal-orders, points out the bitter irony that while the loyal orders extol and exercise their own rights and liberties, their "political involvement...has often served to deny civil, religious and political liberties to others."

same time and location, forcing the government to prohibit both marches in order to prevent violent confrontations.[48]

In Protestant memory, however, this history is forgotten. Memory, as the French historian Pierre Nora writes, "only accommodates those facts that suit it."[49] As I argued above, participants' general understanding of the historical shift from Catholic quiescence to protest is that Catholics' attitudes changed, not that the political opportunity structure changed. This is reflected in the heartfelt desire expressed by several participants that one day Catholics would come to love parades as much as Protestants do. As Walter says: "I wish they could feel the passion that we feel." Howie states:

> I would love the day—and I think it probably does happen, but it's not being reported—
> I want to see the day when the Catholic community can come out and enjoy it. Enjoy the
> spectacle of it and enjoy the music of the bands. That's the way it used to be whenever I
> was growing up.... We would have traveled into Belfast, whenever we were young teen-
> agers, and them guys [Catholic friends] would come with us to watch the parade.

If only the future would be like the past, everything will return to normal. For many paraders, the only solution to current problems surrounding parades is a cultural one: for Catholics to accept, or even embrace, loyalist parades, just like they did in their personal and collective nostalgias.

The problem with this vision of the past is that, like all nostalgia, it is idealized and passes over blemishes, such as the long history of Catholic exclusion and mistreatment. "Nostalgia," comments literary scholar Svetlana Boym, "is an abdication of personal responsibility, a guilt-free homecoming, an ethical and aesthetic failure."[50] Espousing parades' anti-politics means holding onto this ideal vision of the past and present, and ignoring or dismissing any contradictory evidence. But, as Boym further observes, "The danger of nostalgia is that it tends to confuse the actual home and the imaginary one."[51] It prevents participants from recognizing

---

48. Jarman, *Material Conflicts*, 76–77; and Charles Tilly, *The Politics of Collective Violence* (New York: Cambridge University Press, 2001), p. 125. Also Eric Kaufmann, "Demographic Change and Conflict in Northern Ireland: Reconciling Qualitative and Quantitative Evidence," *Ethnopolitics* 10, nos. 3–4 (September–November 2011): 381–382.

49. Pierre Nora, "Between Memory and History: *Les Lieux de Mémoire,*" *Representations,* no. 26 (Spring 1989): 8. Importantly, such remembering and forgetting is the product of "memory work" by "agents of memory," which include the parading organizations themselves. On these concepts, see Robert S. Jansen, "Resurrection and Appropriation: Reputational Trajectories, Memory Work, and the Political Use of Historical Figures," *American Journal of Sociology* 112, no. 4 (January 2007): 953–1007; and Vered Vinitzky-Seroussi, "Commemorating a Difficult Past: Yitzhak Rabin's Memorials," *American Sociological Review* 67, no. 1 (February 2002): 30–51.

50. Svetlana Boym, *The Future of Nostalgia* (New York: Basic Books, 2001), p. xiv.

51. Ibid., p. xvi.

that most Catholics *cannot* embrace parades, because for them, parades were not and are not fun, happy times. As Northern Irish novelist and essayist Glenn Patterson asserts:

> It is time the Orange Order stopped being disingenuous. The Twelfth demonstration and the three thousand smaller parades are not folk festivals capable of being enjoyed by all sections of the community. The fact that some Catholics do not take exception to the parades, might even come out to watch them…, does not give the lie to this. The Orange Order *is* hostile to Catholicism and Catholicism cannot be distinguished from the individuals who follow it.[52]

Nostalgia contributes to participants' sense that they need not accept responsibility for the fact that their beloved parades are sincerely reviled by many members of their society.

Ernest Gellner argues that in the age of nationalism, society worships itself "openly" and "overtly," rather than "adore[] its own camouflaged image…covertly," as Durkheim suspected. But, he warns, this transparency "does not mean that the current style is any more veridical than that of a Durkheimian age….Nationalism has its own amnesias and selections which…can be profoundly distorting and deceptive."[53] This is surely the case for many Ulster Protestant paraders and their allies. Though they regularly engage in naked self-worship in a society split along national lines, they resist coming to terms with what that fully entails. The anti-political frame that renders parades cultural and only cultural means that they do not have to. In Patterson's poignant phrasing: "'Culture' too often, and perversely, is our sick-note out of self-examination and change."[54]

The language, concepts, comparisons, histories, and memories that paraders think with sustain a broader narrative that distinguishes "good, cultural us" from "bad, political them." It weaves a comprehensive story of people celebrating their culture by practicing a generations-old tradition, despite the machinations of bad people trying to stop their tradition and destroy their culture. The story excises any elements of politics. They maintain the paradox of anti-politics despite overwhelming evidence to the contrary in part because the "narrative construction" as anti-political is central to participants' personal and collective identities.[55] In the stories they tell about their past and their present to themselves, to each other, to the media, and to interviewers, paraders construct "the sense of who they are, i.e., their

---

52. Glenn Patterson, *Lapsed Protestant* (Dublin: New Island, 2006), p. 21.
53. Ernest Gellner, *Nations and Nationalism* (Ithaca: Cornell University Press, 1983), pp. 56, 57.
54. Patterson, *Lapsed Protestant*, p. 21.
55. This sentence paraphrases a sentence from Francesca Polletta, "'It Was Like a Fever…':
Narrative and Identity in Social Protest," *Social Problems* 45, no. 2 (May 1998): 153.

'self-understandings.'"[56] In her study of the African American student sit-ins of the 1960s, sociologist Francesca Polletta finds that activists repeat-edly recounted their actions as "spontaneous," despite their acknowledged planning and coordination. "Narratives of the sit-ins," she argues, "described student activists and potential activists to themselves and, in the process, helped to create the collective identity on behalf of which students took high-risk action."[57] The narratives of spontaneity were not simply designed to strategically persuade outsiders, or even themselves, that their actions were politically efficacious and untainted by "outside agitators." Rather, "narratives help to *constitute* new strategic actors."[58] They "establish who we are."[59]

The same narrative processes of identity formation are also found on the other side of the civil rights divide. Sociologist Kristen Lavelle reports that white Southerners who lived through the civil rights movement create and protect their positive sense of self through narratives of racial innocence and victimhood. By downplaying racial oppression under Jim Crow and highlighting their own feelings of threat and vulnerability during black protests and desegregation, elderly white Southerners construct a "White victim narrative" whose function is to "distance themselves from the segregation era altogether in order to assert their racial goodness."[60] In building a sense of the past and present, the victim narrative "allows White Southerners to establish *lifelong* racial innocence and morality while reflect-ing on a life lived on the favored side of racial domination."[61] This narrative produces and preserves "notions of self-as-virtuous, and other-as-threat" that "safeguard positive identities," despite wider American narratives that cast white Southerners as backward and racist.[62]

As a rule, we all want to think of ourselves as good, moral, respectable people.[63] So we construct narratives of the self that maintain a favorable self-image. We include events that align with our positive vision of our-selves and pass over events that do not. As a result, we are not neutral arbi-ters of the self—as psychologist Jerome Bruner suggests, "The Self as

56. Javier Auyero, "The Judge, the Cop, and the Queen of Carnival: Ethnography, Storytelling, and the (Contested) Meanings of Protest," *Theory and Society* 31, no. 2 (April 2002): 154.

57. Polletta, "'It Was Like a Fever…,'" p. 138.

58. Ibid., p. 154.

59. Ibid., p. 141. See also Francesca Polletta, "Contending Stories: Narrative in Social Movements," *Qualitative Sociology* 21, no. 4 (December 1998): 419–446.

60. Kristen M. Lavelle, "Under Siege in Any Era: White Threat and Victim Memories of the Civil Rights Movement," *Du Bois Review* 14, no. 2 (Fall 2017): 516.

61. Ibid., p. 530. Emphasis in the original.

62. Ibid., p. 531.

63. This paragraph is indebted to Jens Rydgren, "The Power of the Past: A Contribution to a Cognitive Sociology of Ethnic Conflict," *Sociological Theory* 25, no. 3 (September 2007): 225–244, esp. pp. 229–233.

narrator not only recounts but justifies."[64] In our daily quest to reduce cognitive dissonance and evaluate our own lives in a good light, we adjust autobiographical "facts." The same logic applies to our social in-groups as well. Our sense of self, social identity theory suggests, is rooted in part in our relationships to the groups we identify with and their members. As a result, "people generally evaluate their in-group membership positively as a way of achieving a positive self-evaluation—sometimes by actively denigrating out-groups to which the in-group is compared."[65]

Such selective storytelling certainly occurs in Northern Ireland. For paraders, describing themselves and their actions as anti-political is a way of constructing their identity, a way of saying, "This is who we are." More specifically, by thinking and talking about themselves as separate from politics, they claim and promote a positive self-identity. Stories, examples, and descriptions of anti-politics are therefore central in the construction of the parade *and* the paraders.[66] It is a way of constituting themselves as good, pure, and cultural—the opposite of their enemies, who are bad, corrupt, and political. By narrating the past and present of parading as anti-political, participants define themselves as virtuous and moral. The paradox of anti-politics, then, is not only a tool for persuasion. Like the parades themselves, talking about parades anti-politically is a way in which participants form, maintain, and express their collective identity. The anti-political narrative is a vision of who they are and who they want to be.

The language of anti-politics and the logic of depoliticization has a second aspect as well: there is political power in anti-politics. This power is premised on the idea that culture transcends politics and is therefore exempt from the practices of democracy, such as critique, debate, and compromise. Culture and cultural practices, as anti-political phenomena, are simply beyond the reach of democratic processes and procedures. The discourses of culture and tradition are thereby a free pass to act in ways that would not normally be acceptable in society. As traditional cultural practices, parades simply have to be accepted. This aspect of parades' anti-politics does not succeed as well as the first one—paraders and their allies simply are not in the hegemonic position to enforce their view on the whole society. But, they still try to use it to shape political outcomes. This second face of anti-politics suggests that, just like the parades it describes, the posture is simultaneously expressive and instrumental.

64. Jerome Bruner, *Acts of Meaning* (Cambridge, MA: Harvard University Press, 1990), p. 121.

65. Rydgren, "The Power of the Past," p. 229. On social identity theory, see Henri Tajfel, *Human Groups and Social Categories: Studies in Social Psychology* (Cambridge: Cambridge University Press, 1981).

66. This sentence paraphrases a sentence from Auyero, "The Judge, the Cop, and the Queen of Carnival," p. 154.

To show how the discourse of anti-politics tries to silence criticism and dismiss compromise, I focus on two statements by parade participants. The first is from Alexander, a senior member of the Orange Order. Sitting in his comfortable living room, sipping milky tea his wife had served us, I asked him, "Are parades at all political?" Alexander replied:

> I don't think that they seem to be political. Some can be. I mean, there have been political processions in Belfast, but the Orange parade is not a political parade as such. The speeches designated by the Grand Lodge, the resolutions to which the speakers are asked to speak as to loyalty, as citizens to the United Kingdom. *That could be perceived as political if you don't like the United Kingdom.* [My emphasis.]

Alexander first distinguishes Orange parades from political parades, differentiating culture from politics. Then he states that the resolutions proclaimed at parades are not political, they are merely about citizenship and loyalty to the state. His last quoted sentence, however, is the most revealing: "That could be perceived as political if you don't like the United Kingdom." Seeing politics where there is not any is a pathology caused by hatred of the union, he posits. It has nothing to do with the parades themselves. In other words, protesters do not have a legitimate political position, they are simply driven by hate. By calling parades political, this Orange doyen argues, the opponents of parades show their true cards.

The second remark comes from Rachel, a university-educated, female flute player. I quoted a piece of it earlier, but reproduce the entire statement here:

> They're tarnished as being political because the other side would see that as being political, but when you're in them with your other friends, they're not political, they're cultural. One thing that keeps getting told is that . . . this is a political problem. It's not a political problem, it's a cultural problem. But it's ingrained in the minds of people that it's a political problem because Sinn Féin always puts it down as being over politics. I don't see—You know, fair enough, people see Ardoyne as being a political tension point because who's the first people to come out and stand by? It's politicians. *But it's cultural: they're not respective of our culture.* [My emphasis.]

Here she identifies what is for her the crux of the issue: "they're not respective [*sic*] of our culture." Parades are cultural, so any problems that others have with parades must be because they have a problem with the culture. In other words, republicans do not like Protestants, end of story. The implication being that no political solution is possible, because there is no political problem to solve. Therefore, it will be not be fixed by reason, dialogue, or compromise. These are political hammers that simply cannot move this cultural nail. The logic of anti-politics leads to no other conclusion. Opponents cannot have a legitimate problem with parades because as cultural events there is nothing to object to, unless you object to the very presence of Protestants and Protestant culture. This is made clear in a large banner I saw carried by a group of women in the 2013 July Twelfth parade and displayed by parade supporters in Ardoyne in 2012: "END HATRED OF ORANGE CULTURE." The conclusion is unmistakable: opposition to parades is nothing more than hatred of Protestant culture.

The discourse of tradition and cultural anti-politics does a lot of work for participants. It constructs and maintains a positive collective identity. It justifies their actions and delegitimizes opposition. It explains why other people object to them and simultaneously dismisses their objections from the agenda, thereby shaping the political arena. Acknowledging the politics embedded in parades opens the door to a number of distasteful outcomes, including a tarnished self-conception and compromising a cherished tradition.[67] The platform of anti-politics, conversely, keeps the door tightly sealed. Therein lies its power.

THE RITUAL FOUNDATIONS OF THE PARADOX OF ANTI-POLITICS

It seems inconceivable to many outsiders that participants and supporters can maintain the paradox of anti-politics. Strong personal and political incentives to sustain it notwithstanding, how can they determinedly refuse to understand parades as political actions given the political claims and consequences of parades that many of them all but outright acknowledge? The foundation of the paradox, I argue, is the ritual nature of parades. While there are other ways to maintain such contradiction, some of which I will address later, for parading, the role of ritual is central. As rituals, parades provide participants with alternative (and genuinely apolitical) reasons to participate as well as with symbolic ambiguity that supports multiple and conflicting interpretations of the events. Further, the repetitive and formal qualities of rituals suffuse parades with a feeling of invariance and connection to history, feeding the idea that parades never were and are not now political events. These features of ritual sustain the paradox of anti-politics among participants and supporters against evidence to the contrary. And without the claim to anti-politics, paraders and like-minded Protestants could not take advantage of the defense mechanisms enumerated above.

67. Further, Ross, *Cultural Contestation in Ethnic Conflict*, p. 14, notes that "each side deeply fears that recognizing the claims of the other invalidates their own." Jennifer Todd, "Two Traditions in Unionist Political Culture," *Irish Political Studies* 2, no. 1 (1987): 19, finds that this trait is especially acute among unionists.

Thus, the intractability of the conflict over parades—and all of the hostility and violence that has resulted from it—is supported by parades' ritual nature.[68]

Parades, like all rituals, provide process-oriented motives to participate.[69] In particular, as I argued in the previous chapter, participants' central reasons for parading are expressing their collective identity, tradition, the pleasures of participation, and the like. As a result, participants' own understanding of why they participate is rooted in the very process of participation and is unrelated to the political effects of their actions, such as ethnic polarization, protests, damage to the peace process, and sometimes violence. In other words, participants understand their own motives as apolitical. Even if these are not their "real," underlying motivations as many observers might see them, they undoubtedly shape how participants understand what it is that they are doing. Their personal motivations to parade have nothing to do with politics, so in their eyes parades are not political.

Rituals also provide participants with politically useful ambiguity. Since every symbol "may stand for many things," Protestants and Catholics can hold different, even contradictory interpretations of parades.[70] Parades may be a proud display of a shared heritage for participants, and, at the same time, a nasty spectacle of triumphalism for protesters. Both interpretations can be read from the *"range* of meanings" contained in parades.[71] Parades' symbolic ambiguity means that they can be both things and more. An important conclusion is that just because many Catholics believe that parades are sectarian and hateful does not mean that Protestants see them the same way.[72]

68. Psychological mechanisms likely also support participants' understanding of parades as anti-political. In particular, psychologists have consistently found that people exhibit a "self-serving bias," attributing positive outcomes to personal capabilities and efforts and negative outcomes to forces outside the self. This common ego-protecting bias reflects both cognitive and motivational processes. See James Shepperd, Wendi Malone, and Kate Sweeny, "Exploring Causes of the Self-Serving Bias," *Social and Personality Psychology Compass* 2, no. 2 (March 2008): 895–908.

69. See, for example, Arnold van Gennep, *The Rites of Passage*, trans. Monika B. Vizedom and Gabrielle L. Caffee (Chicago: University of Chicago Press, 1960); Victor Turner, *The Ritual Process: Structure and Anti-Structure* (Ithaca: Cornell University Press, 1969); Paul Connerton, *How Societies Remember* (New York: Cambridge University Press, 1989); Émile Durkheim, *The Elementary Forms of Religious Life*, trans. Karen E. Fields (New York: Free Press, 1995); and Randall Collins, *Interaction Ritual Chains* (Princeton: Princeton University Press, 2004).

70. Victor W. Turner, *The Forest of Symbols: Aspects of Ndembu Ritual* (Ithaca: Cornell University Press, 1967), p. 50.

71. Anthony P. Cohen, *The Symbolic Construction of Community* (London: Routledge, 1985), p. 15. Emphasis in the original.

72. Ross, *Cultural Contestation in Ethnic Conflict*, p. 63, emphasizes the role of "divergent group psychocultural narratives" in producing such contradictory interpretations of events.

The ritual nature of parades also supports participants' understanding of the politicization of parading. Recall the narrative that paraders tell to explain current controversies: parades were peaceful for centuries until the republican movement decided to whip up opposition during the Troubles. This story, which has the effect of exculpating parades and deflecting blame for the unrest of the last decades, is buttressed by certain features of ritual. Since parades and other rituals project a sense of invariance and continuity with the past, they imply that any change could not possibly have been internal.[73] The changes must have originated outside the parading community.

Together all of these features make possible and validate participants' experience of parades as anti-political. As Rachel made clear in her earlier remark, "When you're in them with your other friends, they're not political, they're cultural." Parades do not feel political, they feel cultural, traditional, and ritualistic—the opposite of political. Therefore the accusations made by others that parades are sectarian, intimidating, triumphalist, or provocative—that is, political—do not resonate with participants' own experience.

Paraders, for example, understand that many Catholics think that parades are about confronting Catholics, but their own experience tells them that this is not true.[74] As Ben says: "The Catholic community has got it in its head [that] it's all about them: this is us stating our dominance over them.... [But, it's not.] It's just basically us being us. It's as simple as that." Ben's language inadvertently echoes a distinction that political economist Alexander Schuessler makes between instrumental and non-instrumental behavior. Instrumental behavior, Schuessler argues, is characterized by "*Doing*—individuals perform X in order to *do* Y"—whereas non-instrumental, expressive behavior is characterized by "identification, attachment, or *Being*—individuals perform X as this is how they *become* X-performers."[75] Ben thus unwittingly illustrates the distinction between instrumental politics and non-instrumental parading by contrasting "us stating our dominance over them"—quintessential Doing—with "us *being* us."

One element of the parading experience emphasized by several interviewees is that when they are marching, Catholics do not even cross their

---

73. Connerton, *How Societies Remember*, p. 45.

74. In this way, the paraders' experience is shaped in part by the reaction of opponents and the ongoing "contentious conversation" between them (and other players). Even as they deny the Catholic interpretation, it still impacts their understanding of their own actions. As Auyero, "The Judge, the Cop, and the Queen of Carnival," pp. 153, 154, points out, "constructing the experiential meaning of events" is a "deeply relational/dialogical process." See also Charles Tilly, "Contentious Conversation," *Social Research* 65, no. 3 (Fall 1998): 491–510.

75. Alexander A. Schuessler, *A Logic of Expressive Choice* (Princeton: Princeton University Press, 2000), p. 30.

mind—except for the few minutes it may take to walk past any protesters.[76] Mikey, for instance, describes what he thinks about when on parade:

> You're out with your friends.... It's a social thing. It's not us going, "Yea, we're going to annoy the Catholics! Yo! We're all Protestants! Yo!" It's not like that.... The parade is like a gathering of friends.... There's this perception [among] nationalists and republicans— I don't know whether it's Catholics in general— ... that I'm getting up in the morning and I go to bed on a [Friday] night and wake up Saturday morning a sectarian bigot, and I'm going down to annoy Catholics. You don't care about that. Nobody cares about their religion. I don't care about them, I'm not thinking of anything. I'm not even thinking of the Protestant religion. I'm getting up and I know I'm going out... with my [Orange] lodge, with all my friends.

For Mikey, the contrast between the perception of parades and the actual experience of parades is stark. Like Ben, he is fully aware of the Catholic interpretation of parades, but has never observed it in his own involvement. Parades are an enjoyable time spent with friends; Catholics do not enter the equation. Thus, to paraders like Ben and Mikey, parades do not feel in any way political.[77]

This experience of parades as anti-political is, I believe, genuine—as are the apolitical motivations and meanings that participants carry. They reflect what religion scholar Catherine Bell calls "the power of ritualization." Ritual, in this view, is a technique of emphasizing difference. It is not a category of action, but a strategy: "a way of acting that is designed and orchestrated to distinguish and privilege what is being done in comparison to other, usually more quotidian, activities."[78] The perception of difference may be a deliberate construct, but when successfully achieved, it is powerful. Among many Northern Irish Protestants, this strategy has succeeded: parade participants and their supporters buy the work that ritualization is doing. They understand parades as different from other, "more quotidian" actions, such as politics. From inside their social and cultural system, it is very difficult to look beyond the successful ritualization of parades and see

76. This common statement provides a notable contrast to Walter's discussion in chapter 2 of the pride and pleasure he feels from the recognition he receives from tourists. The views of visitors seem to count more than those of fellow citizens: they embrace foreign cheers, but ignore, even dismiss, local jeers. In this way, paraders define the audiences they care about. See Kathleen Blee and Amy McDowell, "Social Movement Audiences," *Sociological Forum* 27, no. 1 (March 2012): 1–20.

77. See also Ramsey, *Music, Emotion and Identity*, p. 163.

78. Catherine Bell, *Ritual Theory, Ritual Practice* (New York: Oxford University Press, 1992), p. 74; also pp. 197–223. See also Jonathan Z. Smith, *To Take Place: Toward Theory in Ritual* (Chicago: University of Chicago Press, 1987), p. 109; and Caroline Humphrey and James Laidlaw, *The Archetypal Actions of Ritual: A Theory of Ritual Illustrated by Jain Rite of Worship* (Oxford: Clarendon Press, 1994), esp. pp. 5, 73.

them as undistinguished, instrumental, or political. As a result, paraders' motivations to parade, the meanings parades hold for them, and their experiences of parading all point to parades being anti-political.[79] The accusation of politics, therefore, does not make sense.

For many Catholics, however, the ritualization of parades has failed. They do not see parades as distinct or privileged behavior. Loyalist parades, in their eyes, are like any other political demonstration. This chasm between the beliefs of paraders and protesters often leads the groups to talk past each other and misattribute the goals of the other. Paraders think, "We are being cultural, so if they are against us, they must be against our culture"; while protesters think, "They are being political and we oppose their politics." Coming to an agreement is so difficult, in part, because Protestants and Catholics do not even agree on what it is that they disagree about.[80]

Of course, ritual is not the only way to create or maintain a politics of anti-politics. The human rights movement, for instance, has generated an ideological (and perhaps pragmatic) anti-politics premised on a "moral discourse centered on pain and suffering."[81] Political theorist Wendy Brown writes that human rights:

> generally presents itself as something of an antipolitics—a pure defense of the innocent and the powerless against power, a pure defense of the individual against immense and potentially cruel or despotic machineries of culture, state, war, ethnic conflict, tribalism, patriarchy, and other mobilizations or instantiations of collective power against individuals.[82]

It is human rights' very anti-politics, she argues, that allows it to pursue political projects (such as "liberal imperialism") unquestioned. Historian Samuel Moyn also finds that the human rights movement and its predecessors mobilized the language of anti-politics to their advantage. For example,

---

79. The same is true of Protestant spectators. Their motivations, meanings, and experiences related to attending parades also point to parades' anti-politics. The successful work of ritualization extends beyond the individuals who actually walk in parades to large parts of the Protestant community.

80. This disagreement is yet another piece of what McGarry and O'Leary call Northern Ireland's "meta-conflict," the "conflict about what the conflict is about." John McGarry and Brendan O'Leary, *Explaining Northern Ireland: Broken Images* (Oxford: Basil Blackwell, 1995), p. 1.

81. Wendy Brown, "'The Most We Can Hope For…': Human Rights and the Politics of Fatalism," *South Atlantic Quarterly* 103, nos. 2/3 (Spring/Summer 2004): 453.

82. Ibid. On the anti-politics of human rights' cousin, humanitarianism, see Michael Barnett, *Empire of Humanity: A History of Humanitarianism* (Ithaca: Cornell University Press, 2011), esp. pp. 212–219.

he describes Eastern European dissident movements of the 1970s as "based on a politics that worked precisely by claiming to transcend politics."[83]

The moralism of human rights that Brown and Moyn identify as anti-political has been similarly observed in other social movements. Sociologist Deborah Gould identifies and theorizes the role of moralism in the fracturing of the direct-action AIDS group ACT UP. She finds that moralism can supplant real political dialogue, since moralizing claims question the very essence of your opponent. Flooding an issue with moralizing rhetoric removes it from the possibility of political debate, persuasion, bargains, or compromise.[84]

In *The Anti-Politics Machine*, anthropologist James Ferguson argues that economic development officials in Lesotho cultivated an anti-politics based on scientific authority. He finds that the anti-political, technocratic rhetoric of economic development is a source of significant power for the development industry. He concludes that "the 'development' apparatus" is an "anti-politics machine" whose feat is "the suspension of politics from even the most sensitive political operations." By using its variation on Midas's Touch, "a 'development' project can end up performing extremely sensitive political operations involving the entrenchment and expansion of institutional state power almost invisibly, under the cover of a neutral, technical mission to which no one can object."[85]

Presenting an issue as anti-political operates in the three approaches to power identified by scholars.[86] Within Robert Dahl's one-dimensional approach to power, the discourse of anti-politics can be used to influence decision-makers.[87] It is a resource to be wielded by *A* in her bargaining with *B* to resolve a conflict over issue *X*. Within the two-dimensional approach to power elaborated by Peter Bachrach and Morton Baratz, claiming an

---

83. Samuel Moyn, *The Last Utopia: Human Rights in History* (Cambridge, MA: Harvard University Press, 2010), p. 137. Looking specifically at the Polish opposition, David Ost, *Solidarity and the Politics of Anti-Politics: Opposition and Reform in Poland Since 1968* (Philadelphia: Temple University Press, 1990), pp. 16–17, argues that not only did they need to reject state-centered politics, they wanted to abandon state-centered politics in favor of civil society. "Anti-politics ... is not a negation of politics," he writes, "but a relocation of the political public from state to society. It is this 'anti-political' project that is crucial to understanding Solidarity's practice."

84. Deborah B. Gould, *Moving Politics: Emotion and ACT UP's Fight Against AIDS* (Chicago: University of Chicago Press, 2009), pp. 378–392.

85. James Ferguson, *The Anti-Politics Machine: "Development," Depoliticization, and Bureaucratic Power in Lesotho* (Minneapolis: University of Minnesota Press, 1990), p. 256.

86. My understanding was greatly improved by the discussion in John Gaventa, *Power and Powerlessness: Quiescence and Rebellion in an Appalachian Valley* (Champaign: University of Illinois Press, 1980), pp. 5–20.

87. Robert A. Dahl, "The Concept of Power," *Behavioral Science* 2, no. 3 (July 1957): 201–215.

issue as anti-political is a way to keep it off the agenda in the first place.[88] The second face of power is where this discourse's influence really takes shape. There may still be a conflict between *A* and *B* over *X*, but since *X* is not considered a political issue, *B* is prevented from ever raising the issue in political fora. Within the three-dimensional approach to power theorized by Steven Lukes, the discourse of anti-politics affects *B* so profoundly that she does not even consider *X*, which is objectively detrimental to her, to be a political problem.[89] Here too the power of anti-politics can be great. *B* cannot even get to the point of conceiving of *X* as detrimental because she understands *X* as belonging outside the realm of political conflict.

This source of power is not lost on many groups and causes who try to use it to their advantage in the defense of culture and traditional practices. The rhetoric of anti-politics is commonly used in an attempt to influence political outcomes related to cultural issues. For example, historian David Hollinger argues that Americans tend to "give religious ideas a pass," meaning that they follow the "convention of protecting religious ideas from the same kind of critical scrutiny to which we commonly subject ideas about almost everything else." This convention is not only founded on the "virtues of decency and humility" but also a "constitutional tradition that does indeed treat religious ideas as a distinct category... [and] a history of religious diversity that renders silence a good way to keep the peace."[90] The result of this convention is that American politicians frequently justify their positions on religious grounds and their critics cannot question their reasoning. Religion is a "conversation-stopper," as philosopher Richard Rorty suggests.[91] More broadly, proponents of controversial practices around the world, such as female genital cutting and flying the Confederate flag, also appeal to culture and tradition to defend their actions.[92] By shifting the debate to culture and tradition, these actors are arguing that society needs to give them a pass. And in so doing, they are moving the debate away from politics.[93]

---

88. Peter Bachrach and Morton S. Baratz, "Two Faces of Power," *American Political Science Review* 56, no. 4 (December 1962): 947–952.

89. Steven Lukes, *Power: A Radical View* (London: Macmillan, 1974).

90. David A. Hollinger, "Religious Ideas: Should They Be Critically Engaged or Given a Pass?" *Representations* 101, no. 1 (Winter 2008): 145–146.

91. Richard Rorty, "Religion as Conversation-Stopper," *Common Knowledge* 3, no. 1 (Spring 1994): 1–6, cited in Hollinger, "Religious Ideas," p. 145.

92. See Rogaia Mustafa Abusharaf, "Virtuous Cuts: Female Genital Circumcision in an African Ontology," *differences: A Journal of Feminist Cultural Studies* 12, No. 1 (Spring 2001): 112–140; and John M. Coski, *The Confederate Battle Flag: America's Most Embattled Emblem* (Cambridge, MA: Harvard University Press, 2005).

93. In this sense, culture and tradition are similar to the rhetorical "god terms" analyzed in James M. Jasper, "The Politics of Abstractions: Instrumental and Moralist Rhetorics in Public Debate," *Social Research* 59, no. 2 (Summer 1992): 315–344.

The same logic is at work with loyalist parades. If parades are political, they are open to normal democratic politics and processes. Compromise becomes a necessary part of doing business. Accepting restraints and restrictions on parades becomes inevitable. And, possibly worst of all, to be political is to acknowledge the legitimacy of Catholic opposition. It means taking their objections seriously, which in turn requires a hard look in the mirror and the possibility of seeing something unexpected and undesirable. The distinction between "good, cultural us" and "bad, political them" disappears, and the moral landscape is suddenly level. This, then, is the power provided by the anti-politics of culture and tradition. It tries to protect parades from the distasteful compromises inherent in democratic politics; and it helps protect participants' moral vision of the world and their place in it.

CONCLUSION

"When," ask Verta Taylor, Leila Rupp, and Joshua Gamson, "is cultural performance a form of protest?" Their answer is that three factors "distinguish between events staged purely for entertainment and those staged for political ends": contestation, intentionality, and collective identity.[94] That is, the event must contest the dominant order, the actors must intend this contestation, and the actors must hold a collective identity. This model is a useful corrective that helps us to expand the boundaries of what we consider political action. It shows that events that look "merely cultural" from the outside can be understood as political activism on the inside. But this chapter has shown that in loyalist parades, the opposite is true. From the outside, parades look deeply political, but on the inside, participants see them as entirely and exclusively cultural. Paraders lack intentional political contestation.

Political rituals, Steven Pfaff and Guobin Yang argue, are double-edged because they can be used to support the regime *and* the opposition.[95] This has long been true of loyalist parades, but this chapter highlights a second

94. Verta Taylor, Leila J. Rupp, and Joshua Gamson, "Performing Protest: Drag Shows as Tactical Repertoires of the Gay and Lesbian Movement," *Research in Social Movements, Conflicts, and Change* 25 (2004): 107, 108. See also Leila J. Rupp and Verta Taylor, *Drag Queens at the 801 Cabaret* (Chicago: University of Chicago Press, 2003); Verta Taylor and Nella Van Dyke, " 'Get Up, Stand Up': Tactical Repertoires of Social Movements," in *The Blackwell Companion to Social Movements*, ed. David A. Snow, Sarah A. Soule, and Hanspeter Kriesi (Malden, MA: Blackwell, 2004), pp. 262–293; and Verta Taylor, Katrina Kimport, Nella Van Dyke, and Ellen Ann Andersen, "Culture and Mobilization: Tactical Repertoires, Same-Sex Weddings, and the Impact on Gay Activism," *American Sociological Review* 74, no. 6 (December 2009): 865–890.

95. Steven Pfaff and Guobin Yang, "Double-Edged Rituals and the Symbolic Resources of Collective Action: Political Commemorations and the Mobilization of Protest in 1989," *Theory and Society* 30, no. 4 (August 2001): 539–589.

way in which political rituals have a double-edged character. On the one hand, as Taylor and coauthors demonstrate, rituals and other cultural performances can make deliberate political claims. But on the other, as I showed, rituals and other cultural performances can *mask* political claims. The ritual character of parades allows participants to disavow their political claim-making and the political consequences of their efforts, or indeed disbelieve that they even occur. It allows them to make a political action apolitical, even anti-political. As rituals, parades provide participants with process-oriented reasons to act and symbolic ambiguity that muddles their meaning. This does not diminish the political quality of loyalist parades. Events can be unintentionally political,[96] particularly when political opponents interpret them so—as is clearly the case here. But it does push us to clarify how culture is used as a political strategy. By suggesting that cultural performances can be useful for promoting political claims, Taylor and colleagues reveal one edge. By suggesting that cultural performances can be useful for hiding political claims, I uncover the other.

96. See Olivier Fillieule, "The Independent Psychological Effects of Participation in Demonstrations," *Mobilization* 17, no. 3 (September 2012): 236; and Rupp and Taylor, *Drag Queens at the 801 Cabaret*, p. 218.

Conclusion

At midnight on July 12, 2013, I stood with several friends and hundreds of strangers to watch a sprawling heap of wood pallets and assorted debris catch fire. Some of the bonfires erected in Protestant communities across Northern Ireland to mark the start of the Twelfth are enormous—true feats of amateur engineering—though ours was more hastily constructed, not that anyone seemed to mind. It was a rare beautiful night in Belfast: clear skies, warm air. The music was pulsing. Some people were dancing; many were drinking. Everyone looked to be having a great time. Even some African and Asian immigrants who lived in the neighborhood had come out for the party. It was a true community celebration. In many ways, it was the best of communal life.

But not quite. The bonfire, like most across Northern Ireland that night, was topped by the flag of Ireland. In our case, there were actually two of them fluttering atop the pile of scrap wood, old sofas, and other flammable detritus that local boys had gathered in the previous weeks. As the flames grew, people around me snapped photos on cameras and phones. Four young children, maybe ten or eleven years old, one gripping a small Union Flag, stood in front of me, watching, waiting.

When the first tricolor caught fire, a loud cheer erupted from the crowd. Even the four kids leaped up and, with fists pumping, shouted for joy. As the flags burned, revelry turned to rivalry, excitement to incitement, and I saw community transform into chauvinism.

Standing on the grassy bank, feeling the harsh heat of the pyre on my face and arms, I took in the contradictions splayed out before me. Even today, writing at a distance of thousands of miles and several years, I can't help being transfixed.

It is all too easy, at such a far remove, to tell only one side of this story. To write of their generous treatment of me and one another and write off their ungenerous acts toward their neighbors. Or to stress the truculence and thoughtlessness of it all while burying the spirit of solidarity that springs from sharing something profound with others. It would be easy, but it would be dishonest. We cannot walk away from the contradictions because both sides of the story are true. To ignore either perspective is to whitewash the messiness of social life after political violence. It is to make difficult problems look deceptively simple, and to dismiss the pains and pleasures of living in a bisected society in an unhealed land.

Contentious rituals in such a place carry the capacity to uplift and to demean. They mark, enforce, and glorify the boundaries of belonging, and in so doing they straddle the seam of pride and prejudice. Because they are both ritual *and* political, cultural *and* contentious, we can find within them the highs and lows of human community: acceptance and rejection, companionship and alienation, solidarity and separation. To insiders they beckon, "You are one of us. Let's celebrate together." To outsiders they sneer, "You are *not* one of us. We celebrate your exclusion." Contentious rituals, as a result, are nothing if not sites of simultaneous love and hate. It is this peculiar union that, I hope, this book has helped disentangle.

* * *

I began this book with a question: why do people choose to take part in cultural performances that fellow citizens find offensive and hateful? Particularly in fragile, deeply divided societies, why do people actively drive wedges between groups, fan the flames of suspicion and hostility, and occasionally spark violence? To seek an answer, I turned to Northern Ireland, asking why some Protestants participate in parades that to many Catholics and other outsiders appear so provocative, so disrespectful, so deliberately mean-spirited.

Dissatisfied with the prominent explanation that large-scale challenges to peace are the product of elite spoilers, I examined the choices made by ordinary people to participate or not in loyalist parades. The answer I found is that people choose to join loyalist parades in large part because they are a ritual. In talking to paraders and spending time with them, I discovered that they are most interested in the benefits intrinsic to participation in parades, rather than selective material gains or the chance to intimidate Catholics. As a result, people make decisions to participate in contentious parades without consideration of their actions' profoundly political consequences. The ritual nature of parades severs the expected connection between participation and the external, often negative, consequences, thus creating the environment for sustained conflict.

THE ARGUMENT AND FINDINGS IN BRIEF

Contentious rituals, such as loyalist parades, present several puzzles for scholars of contentious politics and ethnic conflict. First, since contentious rituals produce collective outcomes, they face the free-rider problem. Second, the outcomes that contentious rituals produce are often socially harmful, with participants among the most likely to suffer. And third, contentious rituals are characterized by distinctive aspects of ritual, such as repetition, that are often thought to be unappealing. Given these features, why would anyone decide to participate?

One answer is that power-hungry elites get the masses to take part in self-serving contentious rituals. The elite manipulation approach does well explaining why ethnic elites might support contentious rituals, but it never accounts for mass participation. While it assumes that ethnic elites are clever and calculating, the theory fails to give the same agency to ordinary people or understand their choices.

Perhaps participants hold extreme ethnic attitudes. They participate in contentious rituals because of strongly held beliefs about the superiority of their own group and the inferiority of rival groups. If true, participants should be notably chauvinistic. But my survey of randomly selected Belfast participants and comparable nonparticipants suggests that participants are not distinguished by their positive attachment toward other Protestants or their negative feelings toward Catholics. They may choose to behave differently, but participants and nonparticipants share many of the same ethnic attitudes.

Maybe participants are simply self-interested, rational actors. They choose to join in when the personal benefits of participation are higher than the personal costs. But again, the evidence does not confirm the theory. The survey and interviews showed that paraders do not receive material incentives; in fact, they pay to be able to take part. The evidence regarding social sanctions was more mixed. Some quantitative data suggested that participants are more likely to experience pressure to parade, but interview data suggested no such pressure. What is clear is that non-tangible, social factors play a more definite role than material ones. Structural conditions that can reduce the costs of participation, such as knowing other participants and being biographically available for a large time commitment, also do not correlate with the likelihood of taking part.

None of the prominent existing approaches provide compelling answers that can withstand empirical scrutiny. This is because these theories do not account for the ritual nature of contentious rituals. My argument, in contrast, rests on two fundamental insights from multidisciplinary research on rituals. I argued that rituals provide participants with process benefits intrinsic to the very act of participation and that rituals are multivocal and their meaning is ambiguous. Together, these claims explain why people participate in contentious rituals that produce collective and divisive outcomes.

To substantiate my argument, I provided interview, survey, and ethno-graphic evidence that showed that participants are primarily interested in the internal processes, not the external consequences, of participation. I identified four reasons for acting: collective identity expression, tradition, the pleasures of participation, and external communication. The first three reasons, which appeared more often and with more vigor, lean toward pro-cess-oriented reasoning. The latter was the only recurring outcome-oriented reason articulated by participants. The mix of reasons points to the futility of theoretical efforts to distill human behavior to a single motivation.

To explain how participants seem to ignore the serious external political consequences of their parades, I argued that they understand parades as anti-political. I showed that participants define culture against politics and place parades firmly in the culture category. Their beliefs are sustained by the ritual nature of parades, which provides participants with process-oriented reasons and symbolic ambiguity to maintain their own interpreta-tions. In sum, the evidence presented in this book supports the view that contentious rituals must be understood as rituals.

CONTENTIOUS RITUALS IN OTHER DIVIDED SOCIETIES

The importance of loyalist parades in perpetuating sectarian conflict and violence demonstrates the significant material effects that contentious ritu-als have on political life in Northern Ireland. But are contentious rituals a wider phenomenon? Does my argument travel? Throughout the book, I occasionally pointed to contentious rituals in other societies, but did not dwell on them for long. In the pages that remain, I turn my attention to two of the most similar outside cases, providing short accounts of divisive pro-cessions in Jerusalem and India and reflecting on the comparisons. In all three places, processions have long histories of fusing nationalism, religion, territory, power, and violence. They also all continue to polarize communi-ties and ignite conflict to this day.

Israeli Processions in Jerusalem

Home to three religions and two nations, Jerusalem is heavy with contested historical, spiritual, and political weight. In a city "that is both material metropolis and transcendent symbol," where even "the routines of life easily get caught up in cultural battles over the identity of Israel and Palestine, Judaism and Islam," the public rituals that embody and display these identities can become all the more contentious.[1] The most prominent disputed procession in contemporary Jerusalem takes place each year on Jerusalem Day (*Yom Yerushalayim*). On this day, Israeli Jews celebrate the capture of the Old City and the reunification of Jerusalem during the 1967 Six-Day War.[2] The victory for Israel, however, is understood as a defeat for the city's Palestinians, who mostly live as non-citizen permanent residents. In recent years, the holiday's celebrations include the *Rikud Degalim* ("Flag Dance"), a march by tens of thousands of primarily right-wing, nationalist-religious teenagers waving Israeli flags through the city.[3] Starting in 2011, the parade route has included Palestinian neighborhoods in East Jerusalem.[4] In years since, the parade has been marked by violence between Jews and Arabs as well as between right-wing and left-wing Israeli Jews.[5] Issawi Freij, an Israeli Arab Knesset Member, has called the Flag Dance "nothing but a euphemism for a parade of hatred and provocation on the part of thousands of radical right-wing activists in the midst of the Arab neighborhoods."[6] During the march, Palestinian shopkeepers are ordered by the police to close their shops to "prevent friction."[7] Parading past shuttered Arab shops

1. Roger Friedland and Richard Hecht, *To Rule Jerusalem* (Berkeley: University of California Press, 2000), pp. 14, 1.

2. The holiday is celebrated almost exclusively by nationalist-religious Jews. For most other Israelis, the day "has lost almost all meaning." Michael Feige, *Settling in the Hearts: Jewish Fundamentalism in the Occupied Territories* (Detroit: Wayne State University Press, 2009), p. 56.

3. See Tanya Sermer, "The Battle for the Soul of Jerusalem: Musical Language, Public Performance, and Competing Discourses of the Israeli Nation-State" (PhD diss., University of Rochester, 2015), pp. 344–349. Also Joel Greenberg, "Celebration or Provocation?: A Stroll Through the Old City on Jerusalem Day," *Haaretz*, May 21, 2012, http://www.haaretz.com/news/features/double-take-celebration-or-provocation-a-stroll-through-the-old-city-on-jerusalem-day-1.431791; and Mitch Ginsburg, "Jerusalem's Annual Liberation Party Degenerates, Again, From Sweet Fervor to Mini-Rioting," *Times of Israel*, May 21, 2012, http://www.timesofisrael.com/the-biggest-party-of-the-year-national-religious-teens-march-to-the-western-wall/, accessed March 28, 2015.

4. Rachel Busbridge, "Frontier Jerusalem: Blurred Separation and Uneasy Coexistence in a Divided City," *Thesis Eleven* 121, no. 1 (April 2014): 77.

5. Omri Efraim, "Violent Clashes Erupt During Jerusalem Day Parade," *Ynetnews.com*, June 1, 2011, http://www.ynetnews.com/articles/0,7340,L-4077124,00.html; Omri Efraim, "Jerusalem: 30,000 Take Part in 'Flag Dance' Parade," *Ynetnews.com*, May 20, 2012, http://www.ynetnews.com/articles/0,7340,L-4231760,00.html; Gavriel Fiske, "On Jerusalem Day, Clashes and Arrests in Old City," *Times of Israel*, May 8, 2013, http://www.timesofisrael.com/on-jerusalem-day-clashes-and-arrests-in-old-city/#ixzz3VQhmhXlD; and Jonathan Lis, "Left and Right Play Tug-of-War Over Jerusalem Day," *Haaretz*, May 28, 2014, http://www.haaretz.com/news/national/.premium-1.595780, accessed March 28, 2015.

6. Lis, "Left and Right Play Tug-of-War over Jerusalem Day."

7. Greenberg, "Celebration or Provocation?"

and homes, some celebrants have chanted "death to the Arabs," "let your village burn," and "death to all leftists."[8]

In addition to the Flag Dance on Jerusalem Day, other contentious rituals reverberate across the city. For instance, to mark the first day of each Hebrew month, hundreds of nationalist-religious Israelis circum-ambulate the Temple Mount/Haram al-Sharif in the *Sivuv She'arim* ("Circling the Gates") ceremonial procession. During the ritual, which necessitates the closing of streets in the Old City's Muslim Quarter, par-ticipants dance, sing, and pray for the rebuilding of the Temple.[9] There are also the many contested ritual performances in holy places claimed by multiple religious groups. Attempts at Jewish prayer atop the Temple Mount/Haram al-Sharif have the most consequential political ramifica-tions, but even disputes between Christian denominations over the loca-tion of rituals inside the Church of the Holy Sepulchre have erupted in brawls.[10]

Israeli Jews, too, have intra-communal conflicts over certain rituals. In recent years, two have been particularly controversial: Women of the Wall's monthly prayer sessions at the Western Wall, and the Jerusalem gay pride parade. Since 1988, the Jewish feminist organization Women of the Wall has held public, organized, woman-led prayer in the women's section of the Western Wall. Promoting gender equality, the women adopt ritual practices traditionally reserved for men, such as chanting aloud from a Torah scroll and donning prayer shawls. But the ultra-orthodox Jews who control the site view such actions as heretical, and have reacted on many occasions with verbal abuse, organized protests, and legal action, and sometimes even with violence.[11]

8. Noam Sheizaf, "Watch: Jerusalem Day's Racist March, Escorted by Police," +972, June 1, 2011, http://972mag.com/watch-jerusalem-days-racist-march-escorted-by-police/15554/; Nir Hasson, "Right-Wing March to Pass Through East Jerusalem, Despite Past Spats," *Haaretz*, May 15, 2012, http://www.haaretz.com/news/national/right-wing-march-to-pass-through-east-jerusalem-despite-past-spats-1.430568, accessed March 28, 2015.

9. Yizhar Be'er, *Dangerous Liaison: The Dynamics of the Rise of the Temple Movements and Their Implications* (Jerusalem: Keshev and Ir Amim, 2013), pp. 43–44; and Abigail Wood, "The Cantor and the Muezzin's Duet: Contested Soundscapes at Jerusalem's Western Wall," *Contemporary Jewry* 35, no. 1 (April 2015): 65–66.

10. Gershom Gorenberg, *The End of Days: Fundamentalism and the Struggle for the Temple Mount* (New York: Oxford University Press, 2002); Ron E. Hassner, *War on Sacred Grounds* (Ithaca: Cornell University Press, 2009), p. 76; and Michael Dumper, *Jerusalem Unbound: Geography, History, and the Future of the Holy City* (New York: Columbia University Press, 2014), p. 112.

11. Yitzhak Reiter, "Feminists in the Temple of Orthodoxy: The Struggle of the Women of the Wall to Change the Status Quo," *Shofar: An Interdisciplinary Journal of Jewish Studies* 34, no. 2 (Winter 2016): 79–107.

While the Women of the Wall take a long-standing local tradition and subvert one element, the Jerusalem gay pride parade is an entirely new collective ritual for the city. The annual parade, which has taken place since 2002, is far more subdued than the teeming and jubilant festivities seen in Tel Aviv. Yet even with "no decorated trucks or floats, no bare chests and bikinis, and very little kissing and dancing," the parade has been confronted by numerous legal challenges and violent opposition from some of Jerusalem's religious residents.[12] Paraders commonly face death threats and have stink bombs tossed at them. An ultra-Orthodox man even stabbed three people during the 2005 parade and, after being released from prison, murdered a teenage girl at the parade in 2015. The city's religious and political leadership has done little to discourage the violence: the parade has the rare distinction of being able to unite Jerusalem's Jewish, Muslim, and Christian clergy in opposition to it, and the ultra-Orthodox then-mayor called it a "desecration of the holy city," likening the parade to "going to the Temple Mount with a pig's head."[13]

Conflicts over public religious rituals in Jerusalem date to at least the early twentieth century, when significant numbers of Jews began to immigrate. Historian Bernard Wasserstein comments that the "calendar of communal violence in [Mandatory] Palestine was closely bound up with the calendar of religious festivity," though "secular anniversaries or commemorations" could also play the "red rag to the bull of communal riot."[14] It was always especially dangerous when multiple religions or nationalities celebrated holidays on the same day. On such occasions, the crowds gathered to perform the required holiday rituals often met in combat.[15] For instance, in 1920, Passover and Nebi Musa, a Muslim pilgrimage festival in honor of Moses, overlapped and an unknown spark set off three days of riots that left 9 dead and nearly 250 wounded. The Ottomans understood the potential for disorder and would increase the security presence during the massive Nebi Musa procession, but the British, newly in charge of Palestine, ignored

12. Lihi Ben Shirit, "Fighting Pinkwashing in Israel," Carnegie Endowment for International Peace, August 9, 2016, http://carnegieendowment.org/sada/64285, accessed April 28, 2018.

13. Madelaine Adelman, "Sex and the City: The Politics of Gay Pride in Jerusalem," in *Jerusalem: Conflict and Cooperation in a Contested City*, ed. Madelaine Adelman and Miriam Fendius Elman (Syracuse: Syracuse University Press, 2014), pp. 245, 235; and Gilly Hartal, "The Politics of Holding: Home and LGBT Visibility in Contested Jerusalem," *Gender, Place and Culture* 23, no. 8 (2016): 1198.

14. Bernard Wasserstein, "Patterns of Communal Conflict in Palestine," in *Jewish History: Essays in Honour of Chimen Abramsky*, ed. Ada Rapoport-Albert and Steven J. Zipperstein (London: Peter Halban, 1988), p. 611.

15. Ibid.

warning signs and failed to prevent the violence.[16] The "clash of dates" continues to cause problems in the city today.[17]

Hindu Processions in India

Of all countries, the role of ritual processions in producing conflict and violence is most pronounced in India. According to anthropologist Peter van der Veer, the "direct connection between ritual performances in public space and riots [in India] seems...obvious."[18] Episodes of violence erupting from religious processions can be found throughout the last three centuries,[19] but the connection between ritual and riot deepened in the 1980s. Starting then, Hindu nationalists promoted the use of *yatra* ("pilgrimage") processions for political mobilization and to unify the Hindu nation.[20] In the years that followed, according to the leading scholar of Hindu processions, Christophe Jaffrelot, "the religious element almost disappeared from them; they were converted into demonstrations of strength, pure and simple."[21] Since processions build Hindu solidarity by (momentarily) erasing internal caste boundaries, claim space on behalf of the Hindu community, and clearly demarcate the Hindu in-group in contrast to the

16. Tom Segev, *One Palestine, Complete: Jews and Arabs Under the British Mandate*, trans. Haim Watzman (New York: Henry Holt, 2000), pp. 127–138.

17. Dumper, *Jerusalem Unbound*, p. 231. In 2016, for instance, the Flag Dance took place on the first night of Ramadan. The High Court of Israel ruled that the parade must take place slightly earlier than usual "in order," as a police spokesperson put it, "to reduce the chance that Jewish marchers and Muslim worshipers will clash with one another." Ben Hartman, "Police, Organizers Agree to Alter Jerusalem Day March in Old City Due to Ramadan," *Jerusalem Post*, June 1, 2016, http://www.jpost.com/Israel-News/Police-organizers-agree-to-alter-Jerusalem-Day-march-in-Old-City-due-to-Ramadan-455657, accessed July 11, 2016.

18. Peter van der Veer, "Riots and Rituals: The Construction of Violence and Public Space in Hindu Nationalism," in *Riots and Pogroms*, ed. Paul R. Brass (New York: New York University Press, 1996), p. 155.

19. C. A. Bayly, "The Pre-History of 'Communalism'?: Religious Conflict in India, 1700–1860," *Modern Asian Studies* 19, no. 2 (1985): 177–203; and Anand A. Yang, "Sacred Symbol and Sacred Space in Rural India: Community Mobilization in the 'Anti-Cow Killing' Riot of 1893," *Comparative Studies in Society and History* 22, no. 4 (October 1980): 576–596.

20. Jackie Assayag, "Ritual Action or Political Reaction?: The Invention of Hindu Nationalist Processions in India During the 1980s," *South Asia Research* 18, no. 2 (September 1998): 125–146; and Arafaat A. Valiani, "Processions as Publics: Religious Ceremonials and Modes of Public Sphere Intervention in Western India," unpublished manuscript, Williams College, 2011, p. 5.

21. Christophe Jaffrelot, "The Politics of Processions and Hindu-Muslim Riots," in *Community Conflicts and the State in India*, ed. Amrita Basu and Atul Kohli (Delhi: Oxford University Press, 1998), p. 71.

Muslim out-group, they are "one of the institutions Hindu nationalists are most eager to exploit."[22]

Hindu processions are a common occurrence in India, but two are especially notable in the recent history of nationalist politics. The *Ekatmata Yatra* ("March for Unity") was invented in 1983 with the explicit goal of uniting India's Hindus behind "an undiluted version of Hindutva," or Hindu nationalism.[23] Massive processions left different parts of India heading toward the geographic center of the country, carrying water from the sacred Ganges River that they distributed along the way. The processions were at once displays of religious devotion drawing on elements of traditional Hindu rituals and demonstrations of the political strength of the nationalist movement.[24] But probably the most well-known case is the *Rath Yatra* ("Chariot Pilgrimage") undertaken in 1990 by L. K. Advani, president of the nationalist Bharatiya Janata Party (BJP), from Sommath, Gujarat, to Ayodhya, Uttar Pradesh, ten thousand kilometers away. The pilgrimage, which was timed to coincide with religious festivals and whose vehicles were adorned with Hindu symbols, was designed to gather support for the campaign to demolish the Babri Mosque in Ayodhya, which was believed to sit on the birthplace of the Hindu god Rama.[25] Advani's *Rath Yatra* triggered communal riots all along its path.[26]

Beyond these two famous one-time national processions, there are many local processions across India. This being India, however, local does not mean small. In the Gujarati city of Ahmedabad, for example, one annual procession alone has had upwards of two hundred thousand participants in recent years (the *Jagganath Rath Yatra* or "Chariot Pilgrimage of Lord

22. Christophe Jaffrelot, "The Hindu Nationalist Reinterpretation of Pilgrimage in India: The Limits of *Yatra* Politics," *Nations and Nationalism* 15, no. 1 (January 2009): 9. Also Steven I. Wilkinson, *Votes and Violence: Electoral Competition and Ethnic Riots in India* (New York: Cambridge University Press, 2004). On the political implications of the relative egalitarianism of religious rituals in India, see Pradeep K. Chhibber, *Religious Practice and Democracy in India* (New York: Cambridge University Press, 2014).

23. Jaffrelot, "The Hindu Nationalist Reinterpretation of Pilgrimage," p. 10.

24. Assayag, "Ritual Action or Political Reaction?" p. 135; Christophe Jaffrelot, *The Hindu Nationalist Movement in India* (New York: Columbia University Press, 1996), pp. 360–362; and Jaffrelot, "The Hindu Nationalist Reinterpretation of Pilgrimage," pp. 9–11.

25. Advani never reached Ayodhya; he was arrested along the way. But forty thousand activists continued without him and stormed the mosque. Thirty people died in ensuing violence. The ashes of the dead were then carried on processions that triggered more riots. Jaffrelot, "The Hindu Nationalist Reinterpretation of Pilgrimage," p. 13.

26. Jaffrelot, *The Hindu Nationalist Movement*, pp. 416–419; Assayag, "Ritual Action or Political Reaction?" pp. 137–138; Jaffrelot, "The Politics of Processions," pp. 81–84; Thomas Blom Hansen, *The Saffron Wave: Democracy and Hindu Nationalism in Modern India* (Princeton: Princeton University Press, 1999), pp. 164–165; and Jaffrelot, "The Hindu Nationalist Reinterpretation of Pilgrimage," pp. 11–13.

Jagganath").[27] Each year, the ritual passes through Muslim neighborhoods with heavy security and a curfew on residents.[28] According to ethnographic research by Arafaat Valiani, participants "seemed to take advantage of the thick police cover which surrounded them and taunted the Muslims with catcalls and slogans."[29] This pattern of unwelcome Hindu religious processions entering Muslim neighborhoods is a major trigger of ethnic riots in India.[30]

Reasons for Participation in Jerusalem and India

As in Northern Ireland, the reasons people parade in Jerusalem and India are more complicated than they appear at first glance. From the outside, they can look like deliberate incitement, pure and simple. The natural conclusion, then, is that people choose to take part in order to incite. I am sure many observers would share the view reached by Issawi Freij, the Israeli Arab Knesset Member: "It's not Jerusalem that celebrants are happy about; it's belligerence, arrogance and provocation."[31] Substitute "Northern Ireland," "India," or any other contested site for "Jerusalem" and the judgment would travel.

But our understanding of these events and other contentious rituals cannot be based solely on perceptions from outside of them. Scholars who have spent time studying the people who actually march in these processions often find that their views are rather different. In her research on the Jerusalem Day Flag Dance, ethnomusicologist Tanya Sermer finds that for paraders, participation is a mode of identity formation and re-formation. As she explains, "T-shirts, flags, and type of dance are not just signs of pride in an already-existing identity, they are tools through which these young men and women are constituted as bodies that belong to a certain yeshiva [religious boys' school], ulpana [religious girls' school], or youth movement, and which belong to the larger dati leumi [national religious] community

27. Valiani, "Processions as Publics," p. 29.
28. Ibid., pp. 50–52. At times, the procession has even defied requests by the police and army to avoid Muslim areas. Ornit Shani, *Communalism, Caste and Hindu Nationalism: The Violence in Gujarat* (Cambridge: Cambridge University Press, 2007), p. 100.
29. Valiani, "Processions as Publics," p. 56.
30. Jaffrelot, "The Politics of Processions"; Wilkinson, *Votes and Violence*; Paul R. Brass, *The Production of Hindu-Muslim Violence in Contemporary India* (Seattle: University of Washington Press, 2005), esp. pp. 364–365; and Steven I. Wilkinson, "Which Group Identities Lead to Most Violence?: Evidence from India," in *Order, Conflict, and Violence*, ed. Stathis N. Kalyvas, Ian Shapiro, and Tarek Masoud (New York: Cambridge University Press, 2008), pp. 271–300.
31. Lis, "Left and Right Play Tug-of-War over Jerusalem Day."

and a particular conception of Am Yisrael [the People of Israel]."[32] Beyond fashioning themselves as members of these communities, participants come to understand themselves as guardians of the city. Through her ethnography, Sermer finds that "singing, dancing, and praying are conceived of by performers as acts equivalent to guarding, defending, and liberating territory."[33] Marching through their sacred city, then, is about much more than asserting dominance or ethnic superiority.

In India, Jaffrelot shows that while some Hindu procession participants are motivated by their religious faith and nationalist beliefs, many take part for other reasons, such as "a taste for adventure," "a desire for social recognition," "to defy the authorities," or to "accomplish a sacred—and therefore prestigious—exploit."[34] Such "personal motivations," he finds, are particularly salient for women.[35] Hindu women are normally restricted from active participation in public life, but the religious nature of the processions delivers "a unique occasion to act in a public space to which Hindu women generally do not have access." Processions provide a "time they could legitimately take to the street ... [and] gain an unprecedented slice of freedom."[36] Describing a particular Hindu nationalist procession that took place in 1990, political scientist Amrita Basu similarly observes that "for women the occasion provided an opportunity to break dramatically with their traditional, housebound roles. What made their activism especially exhilarating was that it was directed against a powerful state, which was afraid to restrict their actions in part because they were women."[37] While religiosity may motivate many women to participate, Jaffrelot cautions that "one should not neglect the a-religious and nevertheless deep motivations of some of the women who took part in the *Rath Yatra*."[38]

Seen together, the conclusions reached by scholars such as Sermer, Jaffrelot, Basu, and myself suggest a common theme among participants in contentious rituals. In contrast to the externally and outcome-oriented reasons for participation often attributed to them, participants are often more interested in reasons that are internally and process-oriented. The reasons that resonate with them, we all find, are linked to the public expression of identity, the articulation of dignity through action, and the great pleasures of participation, not provocation nor intimidation. This reflects what

32. Sermer, "The Battle for the Soul of Jerusalem," pp. 347–348.
33. Ibid., p. 364.
34. Jaffrelot, "The Hindu Nationalist Reinterpretation of Pilgrimage," p. 14.
35. Ibid., p. 16.
36. Ibid., p. 15.
37. Amrita Basu, "Why Local Riots Are Not Simply Local: Collective Violence and the State in Bijnor, India 1988–1993," *Theory and Society* 24, no. 1 (February 1995): 45.
38. Jaffrelot, "The Hindu Nationalist Reinterpretation of Pilgrimage," pp. 14–15.

Jaffrelot calls "the limits of instrumentalisation." Even if ethnic elites use contentious rituals to polarize society for their own narrow benefit, "citizens do not always shift into action for the same reasons for which instigators seek to mobilise them."[39]

Yet the dissonance between what is strongly felt by the performers of a contentious ritual—as well as by those who share their worldview—and what observably transpires is unmissable. It would be easier to simply dismiss the insider view as false and accept the outsider position. In other words: contentious rituals are provocative, so participants intend to provoke. (This book certainly would have been shorter!) The more productive approach, as I hope I have demonstrated, is to understand and explain the contradiction. Future scholars should advance this research by gathering more data on the men and women who choose to play a role (or not) in contentious rituals around the world. Only with new data from new cases will we know if the insights from the study of ritual adopted here help explain participation globally.

FINAL THOUGHTS: CONTENTIOUS RITUALS, POWER, AND PLURALISM

A counterintuitive pattern emerges from the comparison of processions by Protestants in Northern Ireland, Israelis in Jerusalem, and Hindus in India. In all three cases, the contentious rituals are performed by members of the majority ethnic group—albeit majorities "with a minority complex."[40] We might assume that symbolic aggressions are weapons of the weak, something a group does when it lacks material power. But symbolic confrontations are not a substitute for strength; they require strength. As these cases reveal, the ability to carry out mass provocations in public space is a luxury of the powerful. This is because "ritual rights," like all rights, are not self-enforcing; they "ultimately depend on the authority and coercive capacities

39. Ibid., pp. 14, 17. Segev, *One Palestine, Complete*, p. 127, gives another illustration of this dynamic. "'The Nebi Musa festival in Jerusalem is political, not religious,' Sakakini [an Arab Christian Jerusalemite living under the British Mandate] wrote. At this time of year, Christians from all the countries of the world would flock to Jerusalem, he explained, and so Muslims had to mass in Jerusalem as well, to prevent the Christians from overwhelming the city.... The religious aspect of the holiday was designed only to draw the masses, otherwise they would not come. Food was handed out for the same reason, he wrote."

40. S. J. Tambiah, *Sri Lanka: Ethnic Fratricide and the Dismantling of Democracy* (Chicago: University of Chicago Press, 1986), p. 92. Though Protestants are no longer the majority in Northern Ireland, they remain the largest group for now, and parading developed when they were demographically and political dominant. For one possible explanation of the motivations of majority groups, see Arjun Appadurai, *Fear of Small Numbers: An Essay on the Geography of Anger* (Durham, NC: Duke University Press, 2006).

of the state," as Roger Friedland and Richard Hecht argue.[41] In particular, parading through a hostile area generally requires the permission and protection of the state.[42] In Jerusalem and India, that includes imposing curfews on minority residents; in all three cases it requires significant policing operations.

Thus one of the ways that provocative processions project dominance is by embodying dominance. They are performed with the state's sanction and with state-provided security.[43] Subordinate groups seeking to provoke the majority are often granted neither permission nor protection.[44] As a Palestinian journalist writes: "Imagine for a moment that Palestinians decide to celebrate their heritage in [predominantly Jewish] West Jerusalem and march through Jaffa and Ben Yehuda streets! Would they be given full police protection? Would the police dare to ask shops in West Jerusalem to close their doors to reduce tension?"[45]

This is not to say that minorities in divided societies do not engage in symbolic provocations. They do, but they tend to antagonize using a different repertoire of contention than groups in power because the types of public contentious rituals described in this book may not always be available to them. Prevented from large-scale, mass provocations, minorities can use smaller-scale, but no less inflammatory, symbolic acts.[46] For example, in the early days of Protestantism in France, when Protestants were few in numbers, they could successfully provoke Catholics with a only a few believers

41. Roger Friedland and Richard Hecht, "The Bodies of Nations: A Comparative Study of Religious Violence in Jerusalem and Ayodhya," *History of Religions* 38, no. 2 (November 1998): 112.

42. Gideon Aran and Ron E. Hassner, "Religious Violence in Judaism: Past and Present," *Terrorism and Political Violence* 25, no. 3 (July 2013): 393, provide an intriguing alternative conclusion. In explaining why religious violence by Jews occurs almost entirely in Israel, they write, "Jews seem to act out violent drives under the auspices of Jewish rule and as members of an absolutely dominant Jewish majority that they would not otherwise engage in. This is not just a matter of tolerance by the state. Territorial autonomy and political sovereignty make violence possible and for some even religiously mandatory."

43. Dominic Bryan, *Orange Parades: The Politics of Ritual, Tradition, and Control* (London: Pluto, 2000), p. 95, argues that during the Troubles, opposition to parades mounted not only because of what parades represented to Catholics, but because their performance meant the presence of the reviled police forces.

44. Recall that Stormont used draconian public order laws to suppress Catholic parades in Northern Ireland.

45. Aziz Abu Sarah, "Palestinians Asked to Close Their Shops for Jerusalem Day," +972, May 20, 2012, http://972mag.com/palestinians-asked-to-close-their-shops-for-jerusalem-day/46355/, accessed March 28, 2015.

46. Such actions are still more directly confrontational than Scott's account of how "the poor *symbolically undermine* the self-awarded status of the rich by inventing nicknames, by malicious gossip, by boycotting their feasts, by blaming their greed and stinginess for the current state of affairs" (my emphasis). James C. Scott, *Weapons of the Weak: Everyday Forms of Peasant Resistance* (New Haven: Yale University Press, 1985), p. 240.

sneaking into a church at night to desecrate Catholic religious objects.[47] Similarly, in 1982, Sikh militants placed two severed cow heads outside a Hindu temple in Amritsar, India. The act, performed before dawn, likely involved no more than a few people acting under the cover of darkness. But it worked as intended: the violation triggered a violent reaction.[48]

Another tentative conclusion we can draw from the comparisons is that successful symbolic provocation is the product of "intimate enmity."[49] Effectively antagonizing the other group requires knowing them well: what is held dear, what is taboo, where is sacred, when they are particularly sensitive to insults. Without this intimate knowledge, attempts to enrage can fall flat—desecrating a profane place will prompt little more than a shrug.[50] But with the right knowledge—gained from the continuous interaction that comes from living in close proximity—"symbolic challenges...can rapidly spawn a spiraling tornado of violence."[51] So in addition to rioting after discovering the cow heads in front of their temple, Hindus flung cigarettes into Sikh holy places, knowing that tobacco is taboo for Sikhs.[52] Like an unhappily married couple, groups in divided societies know how to push each others' buttons like no one else.[53]

While these actions are characterized by intimacy, they plainly lack empathy. Despite, or perhaps because of, the proximity of the ethnic communities in divided societies, many people seem unable or unwilling to empathize across the ethnic boundary. There is an unwillingness to recognize that a ritual that is so wonderful for you may be so terrible for someone

47. Natalie Zemon Davis, "Rites of Violence: Religious Riot in Sixteenth-Century France," *Past and Present* 59 (May 1973): 72.

48. Stanley Tambiah, *Leveling Crowds: Ethnonationalist Conflicts and Collective Violence in South Asia* (Berkeley: University of California Press, 1996), p. 236.

49. Meron Benvenisti, *Intimate Enemies: Jews and Arabs in a Shared Land* (Berkeley: University of California Press, 1995), p. 82; and Naveeda Khan, "The Acoustics of Muslim Striving: Loudspeaker Use in Ritual Practice in Pakistan," *Comparative Studies in Society and History* 53, no. 3 (July 2011): 579. Without using the term, Marc Gaborieau, "From Al-Beruni to Jinnah: Idiom, Ritual and Ideology of the Hindu-Muslim Confrontation in South Asia," *Anthropology Today* 1, no. 3 (June 1985): 9–10, describes the concept in great detail.

50. Rogers Brubaker, Margit Feischmidt, Jon Fox, and Liana Grancea, *Nationalist Politics and Everyday Ethnicity in a Transylvanian Town* (Princeton: Princeton University Press, 2006), pp. 1–4, describes an episode of a failed symbolic provocation involving the removal of a Hungarian flag from the Hungarian Consulate by Romanian nationalists in Cluj, Romania.

51. Tambiah, *Leveling Crowds*, p. 236.

52. Ibid.. For an earlier case of intimate retaliation involving slaughtered cows left in a Hindu temple (this time the cow was revenge for a dead pig that was tossed into a mosque), see Shabnum Tejani, "Music, Mosques and Custom: Local Conflict and 'Communalism' in a Maharashtrian Weaving Town, 1893–1894," *South Asia* 30, no. 2 (August 2007): 223.

53. As historian A. T. Q. Stewart remarks: Catholics and Protestants do not "need to get to know each other better. They know each other only too well, having lived alongside each other for four centuries." A. T. Q. Stewart, *The Shape of Irish History* (Belfast: Blackstaff, 2001), p. 185.

else. Returning to where we began, to the streets of Belfast, neither Protestant paraders nor Catholic protesters seem prepared to imagine the significant pain they impose on the other. Most paraders are unprepared to accept that marching by Catholic homes and churches causes real hurt for many Catholics, for whom parades are degrading symbols of hate. Most protesters are unprepared to accept that stopping parades causes real hurt for many Protestants, for whom parades are a deeply meaningful ritual inseparable from personal and collective identities, as well as cherished moments in life. A degree of empathy might break the cycle of mutual antagonizing and create the conditions for true and lasting peace.[54]

54. For evidence from psychology, see Walter G. Stephan and Krystina Finlay, "The Role of Empathy in Improving Intergroup Relations," *Journal of Social Issues* 55, no. 4 (Winter 1999): 729–743; Krystina A. Finlay and Walter G. Stephan, "Improving Intergroup Relations: The Effects of Empathy on Racial Attitudes," *Journal of Applied Social Psychology* 30, no. 8 (August 2000): 1720–1737; James D. Johnson, Carolyn H. Simmons, Amanda Jordan, Leslie MacLean, Jeffrey Taddei, Duane Thomas, John F. Dovidio, and William Reed, "Rodney King and O. J. Revisited: The Impact of Race and Defendant Empathy Induction on Judicial Decisions," *Journal of Applied Social Psychology* 32, no. 6 (June 2002): 1208–1223; C. Daniel Batson, Johee Chang, Ryan Orr, and Jennifer Rowland, "Empathy, Attitudes, and Action: Can Feeling for a Member of a Stigmatized Group Motivate One to Help the Group?" *Personality and Social Psychology Bulletin* 28, no. 12 (December 2002): 1656–1666; and C. Daniel Batson and Nadia Y. Ahmad, "Using Empathy to Improve Intergroup Attitudes and Relations," *Social Issues and Policy Review* 3, no. 1 (December 2009): 141–177.

APPENDIX A

Study Methodology

My research strategy centered on gathering accounts of the experiences, beliefs, and emotions from parade participants and nonparticipants. To do so, I employed three techniques over the course of eight months of field-work in Northern Ireland (in July–August 2012, November–December 2012, April–August 2013, and June 2014): interviews, a randomized household survey, and ethnographic observations.[1] This appendix provides a brief discussion of how I conducted the research, why I made certain research decisions, and the strengths and limitations of my approach, so that the reader can better assess my interpretations and the conclusions I draw.

SEMI-STRUCTURED INTERVIEWS

My primary source of data through most of the book are formal interviews I conducted with eighty-one people in Northern Ireland. I interviewed members of all the loyal orders (Orange Order, Royal Arch Purple, Royal Black Institution, Apprentice Boys of Derry, and Independent Orange Order) and members of blood and thunder marching bands and melody bands. I also interviewed people from a Protestant background who are not members of a parading organization, some of whom used to be paraders, but have since left; others of whom have never been paraders. Some of the nonparticipants attend all of parades that they can, others only go on the Twelfth of July, and still others stay as far away from parades as possible.

---

1. All research was approved by Columbia University's Institutional Review Board.

In addition, I interviewed current or former leaders from each of the loyal orders; members of the Northern Ireland Assembly; local councillors; ministers from the Presbyterian Church, Church of Ireland, Methodist Church, and Free Presbyterian Church; Ulster Defence Association and Ulster Volunteer Force ex-prisoners; and leaders of community organizations. In total, I spoke with forty-five current participants and thirty-seven current nonparticipants.[2]

I selected some interview subjects purposely (mainly people in leadership positions in parading organizations), but I found most interviewees using snowball sampling. Several others I met through my ethnographic work or they contacted me after completing a survey and wished to speak more (and one, as described in the opening to chapter 2, heard of my work from someone and reached out to me). To generate the snowball sample, I ended each interview by asking for one parader and one non-parader that I could contact (though people often had an easier time thinking of a parader). My starting points for these chains included local academics, loyal order leadership, and ex-paramilitaries. Most interviewees lived in greater Belfast, though I also sought the views of some people from the rest of the province. Reflecting the gender of paraders, the majority of my interviewees were male.

Interviews took place in a range of locations chosen by the respondent, including homes, workplaces, band halls, pubs, cafes, and restaurants. Interviewees seemed as open with me in public spaces as they were in private spaces, and I did not notice a concern for privacy when in public places. We would try to sit at a quiet table, but interviewees never expressed concern or took precautions when meeting me in public. I conducted all interviews myself. Almost all were one-on-one, except for four interviews when multiple people showed up expecting to take part in the interview, which I was happy to oblige. Interviews averaged one hour and twenty minutes, with the longest ones reaching about three and one-half hours. Nearly all interviews were digitally recorded and transcribed in full; all were analyzed using NVivo, a qualitative data analysis software.[3]

The interviews were open-ended and semi-structured, meaning that I had a rough questionnaire but encouraged the conversation to flow in unexpected directions. This method—what Michèle Lamont and Ann Swidler call an "open-ended and pragmatic approach to interviewing"— ensured I remained focused and covered all the necessary topics, but gave

---

2. One person is counted in both categories (and so they sum to eighty-two) because I interviewed him as a parader and then re-interviewed him months later after he had quit parading.

3. Two people asked that I not record the interview (each thought the recorder would make them too self-conscious), so I took notes instead.

me and the interviewee the freedom to explore issues, ideas, and experiences sufficiently.[4] The flexible style meant that I could probe responses, ask for clarifications and examples, pose counterfactuals, and even at times challenge interviewees. It also allowed respondents to help direct the course of the interview toward the topics they found important and meaningful. Interviewees went off on tangents, many productive, even illuminating, others much less so. As a result, I often deviated from my prepared questions or asked them in different orders. Overall, I tried as best I could to turn what could be an awkward, stilted "Interview" into something approaching a conversation. Yet it remained a structured conversation with a certain sense of the out-of-the-ordinary: I had certain topics to cover, I scribbled in an open notebook, and there was a definite beginning and end, marked by turning on and off the recording function of an iPhone that sat between us.

After interviewing a distinguished clergyman, who had been interviewed by academics and journalists many times before, I half-jokingly asked how I had done. He said he really appreciated how I often paused to think before asking a question. So many other researchers sat down, asked their pre-written questions, and left that he valued the thought I put into really engaging with him. My silences—some rather long—were not dead time, they reflected how seriously I took him, his opinions, and our time together.[5] Our published interview data are usually so clean and deliberate that we often forget how messy the collection can be: pauses; false starts; stuttered, incoherent questions that get met with a blank stare. But open-ended, semistructured (and unstructured) interviews are untidy and unpredictable, which is what makes them interesting and exciting.

Behind what I'm sure appeared as the opposite of clinical and scientific was a specific goal: collecting data. Probing respondents' ideas, pushing back on certain points, and letting them steer the conversation along with me were purposeful techniques. Messy does not mean sloppy. I wanted participants and nonparticipants to speak for themselves to help me understand "mobilization from the perspective of movement actors or audiences."[6] This bottom-up, personal perspective may leave out "causal mechanisms such as structural and demographic factors," but is vital nonetheless. In her

4. Michèle Lamont and Ann Swidler, "Methodological Pluralism and the Possibilities and Limits of Interviewing," *Qualitative Sociology* 37, no. 2 (June 2014): 157.

5. A short excerpt from the transcript of this interview that includes every "um," "err," pause, and a sneeze is printed in Lee Ann Fujii, *Interviewing in Social Science Research: A Relational Approach* (New York: Routledge, 2018), pp. 97–99.

6. Kathleen M. Blee and Verta Taylor, "Semi-Structured Interviewing in Social Movement Research," in *Methods of Social Movement Research*, ed. Bert Klandermans and Suzanne Staggenborg (Minneapolis: University of Minnesota Press, 2002), p. 92.

thoughtful discussion of the ethics and practicalities of conducting "research in the shadow of civil war" in El Salvador, Elisabeth Wood argues: "the choice to participate in a movement or not to do so rests on perceptions and interpretations of structures and processes by individuals (shaped, to be sure, by their participation in organizations). Scholarly analysis of such perceptions and interpretations necessarily relies in part on the reports of potential participants in interviews, memoirs, and similar sources."[7] These first-person accounts are indispensable to study the processes of individual mobilization and the decisions people make along the way. Furthermore, as Lamont and Swidler put it, the goal in such interviews is "to collect data not only, or primarily, about behavior, but also about representations, classification systems, boundary work, identity, imagined realities and cultural ideals, as well as emotional states."[8] While data on behavior can be collected numerous ways—and self-reported data are not always the best—data on these other variables of interest must come from the people we study in their own words.

The drawback of semi-structured interviews—particularly the emphasis-on-the-"semi-" variety that I practice and advocate—is the "reduced ability to make systematic comparisons between interview responses."[9] But analyzing my interviews alongside my other two data sources helps ameliorate the problem.

QUANTITATIVE HOUSEHOLD SURVEY

The second form of data I analyze comes from a randomized household survey in Belfast. Local interviewers conducted 228 valid face-to-face surveys in nine neighborhoods from late May to mid-August 2013. Since the purpose of the survey was to determine who participates in parades and who does not, I sought a sample that included participants and comparable nonparticipants. The way I did this was to conduct the survey in neighborhoods that are (a) Protestant and (b) home to a large number of paraders.[10] Sectarian housing segregation means that finding predominantly Protestant neighborhoods is easy. I determined which areas had high concentrations

7. Elisabeth Jean Wood, *Insurgent Collective Action and Civil War in El Salvador* (New York: Cambridge University Press, 2003), pp. 39–40.

8. Lamont and Swidler, "Methodological Pluralism," p. 157.

9. Blee and Taylor, "Semi-Structured Interviewing in Social Movement Research," pp. 92–93.

10. A nationally representative sample would not have been efficient or cost-effective, since it would have included many Catholics, who are not potential participants (and so they are not a comparable group of nonparticipants).

of paraders based on conversations with academic experts and leaders of parading organizations, as well as my own observations. Given the working-class dominance of contemporary parading, the survey mainly took place in the Victorian- and Edwardian-era red-brick terrace houses and the mid-twentieth-century public housing estates. But to gain a more representative sample, I also included two middle-class Protestant neighborhoods, neither of which was known to be a hotbed of parading.

Life in Belfast's working-class communities is such that I could not simply pick areas that matched the criteria I was looking for and begin interviewing. The many legacies of violence and the continued active presence of paramilitaries meant two things for fielding my survey. First, I generally had to gain the consent of local ex-paramilitary "gatekeepers" to work in "their" areas.[11] This posed ethical and methodological dilemmas for me. Ethically, I was concerned that my research teams could be viewed as coercive. I could not accept that my interviewers' knock on a door might carry an implicit "respond or else." Methodologically, I worried that respondents might feel the need to give answers they think the paramilitaries want to hear. For both these reasons I worked hard to ensure that I employed interviewers who were not seen as affiliated with a paramilitary. A result of this decision was that a majority of interviewers were female.

Second, I had to find interviewers who could work effectively and safely in each neighborhood. The neighborhoods I wanted to study tend to be highly insular. Belfast, I was often told, is really a collection of villages. Within each village-like neighborhood, everyone knows one another and their business, and is suspicious of outsiders. This limited my choice of interviewers. I consulted with many local academics, community activists, and residents, and they told me almost uniformly that I needed to use interviewers familiar to the residents of a particular neighborhood. Sending outsiders door to door, I was warned, would reduce the likelihood that selected respondents would take part, and it could put the interviewers at risk. Not everyone agreed with this latter assessment, but enough people I trusted thought it was a concern that I decided I could not hire a single team to use everywhere. Instead, I hired and trained people to conduct the survey in the neighborhood in which they lived or worked.

---

11. On paramilitary gatekeepers in Northern Ireland, see James W. McAuley, Jonathan Tonge, and Peter Shirlow, "Conflict, Transformation, and Former Loyalist Paramilitary Prisoners in Northern Ireland," *Terrorism and Political Violence* 22, no. 1 (2009): 37n8. Note that formally, they are "former" commanders, since the military structures were decommissioned. I heard rumors that some of them are less "former" than others, but I did not ask about it.

In order to work in a neighborhood, therefore, I needed to find a team of interviewers who could conduct the survey there. Of course, this plan involved a trade-off. While using local interviewers meant that respondents were more likely to take the survey, they also might not divulge certain things about themselves to people they see on a regular basis. Ultimately, I decided that it was a compromise I had to make; given the possible risk to outside interviewers, I could not employ them in good conscience.

The issue then became finding suitable interviewers in neighborhoods that fit my criteria (mainly Protestant with a strong parading scene). To do this I used every connection I had, made cold calls, and followed every lead. I established five teams (four with three members, one with four members) through a local housing association, a conflict resolution organization, a women's center, a youth club, and a personal connection. I trained each team and then monitored their work as they conducted the survey. Thankfully, no safety problems ever emerged.

In the end, the neighborhoods in which the survey was conducted— three in West Belfast, three in South Belfast, and three in East Belfast— were in part chosen by me based on demographic characteristics, but also chosen for me based on where I was able to assemble a team and get local permission to work. (Table A.1 provides demographic information from the 2011 Census on the nine neighborhoods included in the survey.) The enumerated areas are therefore not representative of any larger population. However, I have no reason to suspect that any additional bias was created based on where I was able to work and where I was not. Neighborhoods that fell through did so because contacts did not return phone calls, particular individuals were not interested, and so on, not factors about the neighborhood that would likely matter to the results of the survey. In other words, I have no reason to suspect that the neighborhoods where the survey did take place are meaningfully different from *similar* neighborhoods where it did not take place. That said, since the areas were selected purposefully, rather than randomly, the respondents in the survey are not representative of the Protestant population of Belfast or Northern Ireland.

Within each neighborhood, however, I did select respondents randomly. I began by using detailed maps created by the Land and Property Services to generate a list of each address in a Small Area, the smallest geographic unit in the census.[12] Each Small Area generally contains one hundred to two hundred households and two hundred to four hundred people. Since

12. Detailed maps that show each address are available at https://www.spatialni.gov.uk/geoportal/viewer/index.jsp?title=&resource, accessed October 7, 2013. Maps of each Small Area are available at http://www.ninis2.nisra.gov.uk/public/StaticMapsAddress.aspx, accessed October 7, 2013.

Table A.1. INFORMATION ON THE NEIGHBORHOODS INCLUDED IN
THE SURVEY

	Census information			Comparing: % British		Comparing: % Employed full-time	
	House-holds	% Protestant	Sample (Source: Survey)	Survey	Census	Survey	Census
East Belfast 1	652	82.1%	39	65.8%	75.9%	53.9%	48.9%
East Belfast 2	625	87.1%	34	67.7%	80.8%	44.1%	55.2%
East Belfast 3	655	67.5%	13	61.5%	65.5%	16.7%	38.0%
South Belfast 1	485	70.4%	13	77.8%	70.1%	16.7%	33.6%
South Belfast 2	1,770	62.0%	34	93.9%	60.0%	29.4%	40.9%
South Belfast 3	394	78.9%	50	89.8%	73.8%	44.0%	37.6%
West Belfast 1	1,126	85.0%	26	96.2%	80.9%	34.8%	40.0%
West Belfast 2	594	89.7%	10	90.0%	85.0%	11.1%	26.7%
West Belfast 3	244	87.3%	9	100.0%	77.1%	33.3%	33.9%

Note: The census data are the sums of the Small Areas that I sampled in a neighborhood, and not necessarily the entire geographic area which locals consider their neighborhood. Also note that the percentages of British and full-time employment from the census are for the entire population of the area, while my survey only sampled Protestants. We would expect, therefore, that the percent identifying as British should be higher in the survey than in the census, which it is in six of the nine areas.

Sources: 2011 Northern Ireland Census. Households: Households (Statistical Geographies); % Protestant: Religion or Religion Brought Up In: KS212NI (statistical geographies); % British: National Identity (Classification 2): KS203NI (statistical geographies); % full-time: Economic Activity—Males: KS602NI (statistical geographies).

neighborhoods are made up of a number of Small Areas whose boundaries do not always align with local definitions, I used Small Areas entirely within the local understanding of the neighborhood. Then, I used a random number generator to select houses in each Small Area for an interview.

Lists of selected addresses in hand, interviewers went to each house to find target subjects to interview. At each address they explained that they were conducting a survey about "parades and culture in Northern Ireland" for an American university and asked if there were any eligible respondents—males, eighteen years old or older and from a Protestant background—who usually live there. Since the vast majority of parade participants are male, including females in the sample would have reduced the number of participants surveyed. This trade-off reduced costs at the expense of the richness of the data. If the house had more than one eligible subject, to keep the process random, the one with the most recent birthday in the calendar was selected for the sample. If the household did not have an eligible subject (single mothers with children and elderly widows were common in the surveyed areas), the address was replaced using the original randomization. I did the same if the respondent refused to participate. If the respondent was not home, enumerators were to try to make an appointment, or, if that was not possible, to return to the house until he was home (up to four times).

Once the enumerator identified and reached the selected respondent, they conducted the interview in person, recording the responses on paper.[13] This process yielded 228 responses. The last four columns of table A.1 compare the census figures to the survey figures on two measures, the percent identifying as British and the percent of men with full-time jobs. As we can see, the survey did a fairly good job matching the general characteristics of each neighborhood.

ETHNOGRAPHIC OBSERVATION

The third form of data are my field notes from the observation of many parades, protests, bonfires, public meetings, marching band practices, and other related events. The style of ethnography I practiced emphasized observation over participation. I read local newspapers, followed local blogs, and had many, many informal conversations about parades, but I did not aspire to "immersion in the place and lives of people under study."[14] Rather, I observed discrete parade-related events as unobtrusively as possible. At marching band practices, meetings, and other indoor events—which I was always invited to attend—I sat in the back or off to the side, watched what happened, and happily chatted with anyone who approached me. My presence was obvious—I was not the mythical fly on the wall. But neither did I ever pick up a musical instrument or take an active role parading in the way that some participant-observers have done.[15]

At parades and other outdoor events, I stood in the crowd or walked around. For smaller parades, I followed the route on foot (or occasionally on bike). I was not a participant in the sense of putting on a uniform and marching, though being an audience member is a form of participation in public performances.[16] Even at large, public events, I was not unnoticed.

13. In one neighborhood, interviewers had trouble gaining cooperation for face-to-face interviews and therefore left the questionnaire to be filled out by the selected respondent. Wherever possible, they sat with the respondent as they filled it out.

14. Lisa Wedeen, "Reflections on Ethnographic Work in Political Science," *Annual Review of Political Science* 13 (2010): 257.

15. Gordon Ramsey, for instance, conducted years of participant observation by actually playing a flute as a member of several marching bands. Gordon Ramsey, *Music, Emotion and Identity in Ulster Marching Bands: Flutes, Drums and Loyal Sons* (Bern: Peter Lang, 2011).

16. See Olivier Fillieule, "The Independent Psychological Effects of Participation in Demonstrations," *Mobilization* 17, no. 3 (September 2012): 236; Olivier Fillieule and Danielle

For instance, very early on in my fieldwork, I was standing in a crowd of parade supporters at Twaddell Roundabout, in North Belfast, as we waited for the parade to pass by protesters and reach us. I overheard an interesting remark—"Where's our shared space? Where's our shared space?"—and took out my notebook to write it down. A few minutes later, a woman approached me and bluntly asked who I was. People wanted to know, she told me, since some were getting nervous that a man they did not recognize was standing among them taking notes. For all they knew, I was a spy for Sinn Féin or dissident republicans. In tight-knit communities, an outsider such as myself could not always blend in.

Chastened by this encounter, I generally stopped taking notes openly when in a crowd, especially at contested parades. I wrote field notes as soon after the event as possible from memory with the aid of written jottings (at times I felt this was fine to do), voice recordings, and photographs made during the event.[17] My notes were primarily descriptions of the events (who, what, where, when, etc.), but also included particular details that stood out, things that happened to me, and first takes of my analysis.

ANALYSIS

I analyzed the three data sources together and I am more confident in my conclusions because, in general, all the evidence points in the same direction. When they do not (for example, in the discussion of the impact of social pressure on participation in chapter 2), I present the results of all the relevant data, my interpretations of them, and the reasoning behind my conclusions.

I approached the interview data with particular care. While collecting the data and analyzing them, I was cognizant that loyalist parades are a highly politicized topic in Northern Ireland and that participants and supporters have good reason to present and defend their position. I thus conducted the interviews and analyzed the transcripts with skepticism, so that statements that are outside the dominant Protestant narrative are given special value. That said, in my analysis, I take seriously what people said

Tartakowsky, *Demonstrations*, trans. Phyllis Aronoff and Howard Scott (Halifax: Fernwood, 2013), pp. 16–17; Mabel Berezin, *Making the Fascist Self: The Political Culture of Interwar Italy* (Ithaca: Cornell University Press, 1997), p. 250; Robert Bocock, *Ritual in Industrial Society: A Sociological Analysis of Ritualism in Modern England* (London: George Allen & Unwin, 1974), p. 59; and Clifford Geertz, "Religion as a Cultural System," in *The Interpretation of Cultures* (New York: Basic Books, 1973), pp. 114–118.

17. See Robert M. Emerson, Rachel I. Fretz, and Linda L. Shaw, *Writing Ethnographic Fieldnotes* (Chicago: University of Chicago Press, 1995).

about how they view the world, their own actions, and their own motivations. There are problems with this stance for reasons such as imperfect memory and social desirability bias (discussed in chapter 3), but I believe that when analyzed carefully these data can provide essential information about the thoughts, emotions, and mental categories of interviewees.

APPENDIX B

Patterns of Participation

Although in most of my analysis I treat all parade participants as alike, in fact they were members of diverse organizations and followed differing trajectories of participation. Of the seventy respondents who have marched as adults, 47 percent were members of a loyal order at some point in their lives and 59 percent were members of a marching band. Among loyal order members, 88 percent were in the Orange Order, 27 percent were in the Apprentice Boys of Derry, and 18 percent were in the Royal Black Institution. Among band members, 68 percent have been in blood and thunder bands and 24 percent have been in other types of marching bands.[1] There is also some cross-membership, with 9 percent of participants having been in both a band and a loyal order (though not necessarily at the same time). Figure B.1 displays these graphically, with the general categories in dark gray and the specific organizations or subcategories in light gray.

The trend of switching membership between or among bands and loyal orders is common among participants. This reflects the simple fact that people often move in and out of organizations. Catherine Corrigal-Brown analyzed this pattern in her study of American social movements.[2] She identifies three ideal-type trajectories of participation: persistence, where an individual maintains his or her activism over time; disengagement, where an individual quits his or her activism and never again gets involved; and individual abeyance, where an individual stops participating but rejoins later in life. The same patterns exist among paraders. Twenty-one percent of

1. These figures do not add to 100 percent due to missing data on the type of band several respondents were in.
2. Catherine Corrigal-Brown, *Patterns of Protest: Trajectories of Participation in Social Movements* (Stanford: Stanford University Press, 2011).

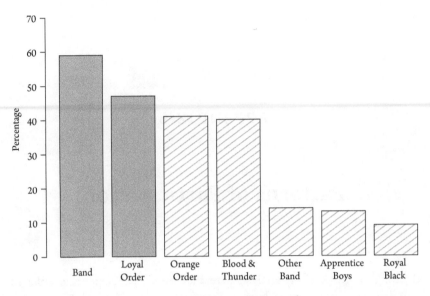

Figure B.1: Percentage of Participants in Each Organization (N = 70)

participants are persistent, meaning they joined one organization and have remained a member ever since. Fifty-nine percent of participants have disengaged, meaning they left their parading organization and have not paraded since. And 19 percent of participants have undergone some form of individual abeyance, meaning they are currently active paraders, but have also left a previous organization.[3]

---

3. Due to the survey questionnaire, I cannot measure abeyance precisely. So the 19 percent that underwent abeyance could have followed one of several time lines: joining Group A, quitting, then rejoining; joining both Groups A and B and then quitting A but continuing membership in B; or joining Group A, quitting, and then not parading for several years before joining Group B.

APPENDIX C

Definitions and Robustness Checks

DEFINITIONS AND EXPANDED RESULTS FOR TABLE 3.1

Table C.1 provides definitions and expanded results for Table 3.1, which shows that parade participants are more likely to attribute intrinsic purposes than instrumental purposes to their actions.

Table C.1. PURPOSES OF LOYALIST PARADES REPORTED BY PARTICIPANTS: INTRINSIC VS. INSTRUMENTAL (%), DEFINED AND EXPANDED FROM TABLE 3.1

	Definition	Current Participants	Ever Participated
Intrinsic Purposes		92%	88%
Tradition	It is a tradition to parade; to continue that tradition.	46%	47%
Culture	It is part of our culture to parade; or, parading maintains our culture.	38%	34%
Celebration	To celebrate Protestant culture and people.	29%	25%
Commemoration	To commemorate, celebrate, or mark the Protestant past.	17%	16%
Social	To bring people together to enjoy one another's company.	4%	8%
Fun/Carnival	To create a fun environment for people to enjoy; also to compete musically.	4%	3%

(*Continued*)

Table C.1. *(Continued)*

	Definition	Current Participants	Ever Participated
Instrumental Purposes		13%	14%
To Promote	To promote a particular agenda, such as Protestantism or Protestant unity.	8%	6%
Display Loyalty	To display loyalty to the Protestant group, Northern Ireland, or the UK.	4%	2%
Take a Stand	To show others what one believes in (culture, politics, etc.).	0%	3%
Negative	To cause trouble, be provocative, or send a message of triumphalism.	0%	2%
Intrinsic-Instrumental Difference		79%	73%
P-Value (Two-Tailed)		.00***	.00***
Observations (N)		24	64

Each response could take multiple codes, so columns do not sum to 100%.
* $p<.05$, ** $p<.01$, *** $p<.001$

ROBUSTNESS CHECKS
Original Dataset

In table 2.1 in chapter 2, I present the results of the analyses using multiply-imputed datasets to account of the loss of observations due to missing data.[1] The analysis of the original dataset in table C.2 produces similar results to what is presented with the multiple-imputation data in chapter 2. Income is not included due to high rates of non-response.

Rare Events Logit

When the proportion of "positive cases" or "events" in a binary dependent variable is low, logistic regressions can underestimate its likelihood. Though the percentage of current parades in the sample (12.4 percent) is above the

---

1. James Honaker and Gary King, "What to Do About Missing Values in Time-Series Cross-Section Data," *American Journal of Political Science* 54, no. 3 (April 2010): 561–581; and James Honaker, Gary King, and Matthew Blackwell, "AMELIA II: A Program for Missing Data," Harvard University, 2012.

Table C.2. DETERMINANTS OF CURRENT PARADE PARTICIPATION, LOGIT MODELS (ORIGINAL, NON-IMPUTED DATA)

	Model 1 (Limited model)	Model 2 (Main model)	Model 3 (Disaggregate social pressure)
Idealist Approach			
Protestant Identification	.04 [.11]	−.07 [.13]	−.07 [.13]
Anti-Catholicism	1.88 [1.26]	2.56 [1.92]	3.07 [1.87]
Rationalist Approach			
Social Pressure	.68 [.15]***	.79 [.17]***	
Family Expected Participation			.56 [.32]*
Community Thinks Less of Nonparticipants			1.12 [.39]***
Structural Approach			
Family Marched	−.04 [.83]	−.11 [.80]	−.04 [.83]
Close Friends at Age 16	.31 [.30]	.31 [.38]	.29 [.38]
Been Asked to March	.43 [.53]	.22 [.92]	.30 [.90]
Children Under 18		−1.48 [.74]**	−1.51 [.71]**
Full-Time Job		2.59 [.83]***	2.56 [.80]***
Age		−.05 [.03]	−.05 [.03]
Marched as Youth		.93 [.47]**	.96 [.49]**
Control Variables			
Education		−1.14 [.94]	−1.12 [.91]
Church Attendance		.35 [.15]**	.35 [.16]**
Constant	−4.93 [.90]***	−4.50 [2.14]**	−4.99 [2.45]**
Number of observations	174	160	160
Correctly predicted	90.80%	90.6%	91.25%
Reduction in error	23.81%	16.67%	22.22%

Standard errors clustered at neighborhood level in brackets. Enumerator fixed effects are not reported.
* *p<.10,* ** *p<.05,* *** *p<.01*

recommended cutoff for "rare events" (5 percent), given the small number of observations, it is worthwhile comparing the original results to results that correct for rarity.[2] The results are robust to the correction: there are no significant differences between the original results in table 2.1 and the results in table C.3.

2. Gary King and Langche Zeng, "Logistic Regression in Rare Events Data," *Political Analysis* 9, no. 2 (Spring 2001): 137–163.

Table C.3. ROBUSTNESS CHECK: RARE EVENTS LOGIT

	Model 1 (Limited model)	Model 2 (Main model)	Model 3 (Disaggregate social pressure)
Idealist Approach			
Protestant Identification	.02 [.10]	−.09 [.12]	−.09 [.12]
Anti-Catholicism	1.64 [1.20]	1.80 [1.76]	2.07 [1.71]
Rationalist Approach			
Social Pressure	.61 [.15]***	.58 [.16]***	
Family Expected Participation			.44 [.29]
Community Thinks Less of Nonparticipant			.76 [.36]**
Structural Approach			
Family Marched	.24 [.88]	−.07 [.74]	−.01 [.76]
Close Friends at Age 16	.29 [.29]	.22 [.35]	.19 [.35]
Been Asked to March	.42 [.51]	.18 [.85]	.25 [.82]
Children Under 18		−1.06 [.68]	−1.05 [.65]
Full-Time Job		1.84 [.76]**	1.75 [.73]**
Age		−.04 [.03]	−.03 [.03]
Marched as Youth		.73 [.43]*	.71 [.45]
Control Variables			
Education		−.84 [.86]	−.80 [.83]
Church Attendance		.28 [.14]**	.26 [.14]*
Constant	−4.34 [.86]***	−3.09 [1.97]	−3.34 [2.24]
Number of Observations	174	160	160

Standard errors clustered at neighborhood level in brackets. Enumerator fixed effects are not reported.
* p<.10, ** p<.05, *** p<.01

Alternative Measures of Key Variables

Table C.4 disaggregates the measure of Protestant identification and provides alternative measures for the variable. Table C.5 likewise disaggregates the measure of anti-Catholicism and provides alternative measures for the variable. It also disaggregates the measure of family parade participation. In both table C.4 and table C.5, the first column of results displays the main model from table C.2 for reference.

Generalized Ordered Logit

Throughout the book I have modeled parades as presenting just two options (participation and non-participation), but there are actually at least three

Table C.4. ROBUSTNESS CHECK: ALTERNATIVE MEASURES OF PROTESTANT IDENTIFICATION

	Main Model (Table C.2, Model 2)	Model 1 (Disaggregate Protestant ID)	Model 2 (British)	Model 3 (Unionist)
Idealist Approach				
Protestant Identification	−.07 [.13]			
Strong Ties to Other Protestants		−.02 [.56]		
Feels Like Other Protestants		.25 [.29]		
Proud to Be Called Protestant		−.21 [.32]		
British			−.82 [1.20]	
Unionist				1.39 [1.31]
Anti-Catholicism	2.56 [1.92]	2.26 [1.95]	1.95 [1.59]	2.14 [1.58]
Rationalist Approach				
Social Pressure	.79 [.17]***	.78 [.16]***	.72 [.24]***	.83 [.24]***
Structural Approach				
Family Marched	−.11 [.80]	−.15 [.83]	−.11 [.89]	−.17 [.86]
Close Friends at Age 16	.31 [.38]	.22 [.29]	.68 [.45]	.45 [.38]
Been Asked to March	.22 [.92]	.25 [.89]	.61 [.73]	.00 [.90]
Children Under 18	−1.48 [.74]**	−1.42 [.73]*	−1.52 [.91]*	−1.23 [.84]
Full-Time Job	2.59 [.83]***	2.50 [.82]***	2.30 [.78]***	2.16 [.70]***
Age	−.05 [.03]	−.05 [.03]	−.05 [.04]	−.06 [.04]*
Marched as Youth	.93 [.47]**	.96 [.47]**	.53 [.38]	.84 [.54]
Control Variables				
Education	-1.14 [.94]	-1.09 [.90]	−.72 [1.01]	−.83 [.81]
Church Attendance	.35 [.15]**	.37 [.14]***	.33 [.13]**	.32 [.12]***
Constant	-4.50 [2.14]**	-4.21 [2.26]*	-3.91 [2.48]	-5.32 [2.25]**
Number of Observations	160	160	160	164

Standard errors clustered at neighborhood level in brackets. Enumerator fixed effects are not reported.
* *p<.10,* ** *p<.05,* *** *p<.01*

Table C.5. ROBUSTNESS CHECK: ALTERNATIVE MEASURES OF ANTI-CATHOLICISM AND FAMILY TIES

	Main Model (Table C.2, Model 2)	Model 1 (Disaggregate Anti-Catholicism)	Model 2 (Anti-Cath. w/o Econ Deserve)	Model 3 (Disaggregate Family Marched)
Idealist Approach				
Protestant Identification	−.07 [.13]	−.05 [.17]	−.05 [.14]	−.08 [.13]
Anti-Catholicism	2.56 [1.92]			2.58 [1.95]
Caths. Cause Sectarian Tension		.27 [.64]		
Oppose Family Marrying Cath.		.41 [.45]		
Caths. Gained More Econ		1.48 [.61]**		
Caths. Need Reminder Live in UK		−.91 [.78]		
Alternative Anti-Catholicism			1.66 [1.89]	
Rationalist Approach				
Social Pressure	.79 [.17]***	.79 [.24]***	.82 [.17]***	.82 [.17]***
Structural Approach				
Family Marched	−.11 [.80]	−.35 [.79]	−.09 [.72]	
Father Marched				−.35 [1.43]
Other Family Marched				.12 [.59]
Close Friends at Age 16	.31 [.38]	.22 [.50]	.36 [.39]	.31 [.40]
Been Asked to March	.22 [.92]	−.16 [.83]	.30 [.92]	.27 [.85]
Children Under 18	-1.48 [.74]**	-2.06 [1.16]*	-1.53 [.70]**	-1.56 [.75]**
Full-Time Job	2.59 [.83]***	3.06 [1.13]***	2.49 [.88]***	2.63 [.90]***
Age	−.05 [.03]	−.07 [.04]*	−.06 [.03]*	−.05 [.03]
Marched as Youth	.93 [.47]**	.86 [.52]*	.94 [.47]**	.94 [.48]*
Control Variables				
Education	-1.14 [.94]	-1.79 [1.27]	-1.23 [1.00]	-1.08 [.90]
Church Attendance	.35 [.15]**	.47 [.20]**	.35 [.16]**	.34 [.14]**
Constant	-4.50 [2.14]**	-3.38 [1.87]*	-3.94 [2.33]*	-4.77 [2.23]**
Number of Observations	160	160	169	160

Standard errors clustered at neighborhood level in brackets. Enumerator fixed effects are not reported.
* *p<.10,* ** *p<.05,* *** *p<.01*

major options for Protestants: parading, attending parades as a spectator, and staying away altogether.[3] Table C.6 assess the determinants of this wider range of behavior. The important finding is that parade attenders and participants do not have significantly different levels of in-group identification, but Protestants who do not attend parades do express it at significantly lower levels (Model 1). This suggests that Protestants with little feeling of attachment to their ethnic in-group avoid parades, while spectators and paraders have similar feelings about the Protestant community.

The dependent variable in this analysis has three ordered categories: non-attendance ($= 0$), attendance ($= 1$), and parading ($= 2$). As a result, I employ generalized ordered logit with clustered standard errors in the following regressions. The generalized ordered logit model relaxes the assumption of the standard ordered logit that each independent variable has the same effect on each category of the dependent variable. This means that the effects of the independent variables can vary across the three outcomes: non-attendance, parade attendance, and parading. I made this modeling choice based on the theoretical expectation that switching between each category is a qualitatively different move. That is, going from non-attendance to attendance could be a one-time decision with no costs ("I'll go to one parade for a few hours this year, despite not attending in prior years"), whereas moving from attendance to parading is a large commitment in terms of time, energy, and even money. However, I also ran standard ordered logit regressions using the same variables since the statistical diagnostic tests on both models show that the proportional odds assumption has not been violated.[4] The generalized ordered logit regression generates a coefficient for each independent variable's effect on each category of the dependent variable (except the highest category). So Models 1 and 2 in table C.6 display the estimates for not attending parades in the left column and for attending parades in the right column. To interpret these results, note that "positive coefficients indicate that higher values on the explanatory

3. A number of scholars advocate moving beyond the binary activist/non-activist conception of participation common to studies of collective action. See Doug McAdam, "Recruitment to High-Risk Activism: The Case of Freedom Summer," *American Journal of Sociology* 92, no. 1 (July 1986): 64–90; Gregory L. Wiltfang and Doug McAdam, "The Costs and Risks of Social Activism: A Study of Sanctuary Movement Activism," *Social Forces* 69, no. 4 (June 1991): 987–1010; Sharon Erickson Nepstad and Christian Smith, "Rethinking Recruitment to High-Risk/High-Cost Activism: The Case of the Nicaragua Exchange," *Mobilization* 4, no. 1 (April 1999): 25–40; and Elisabeth Jean Wood, *Insurgent Collective Action and Civil War in El Salvador* (New York: Cambridge University Press, 2003).

4. In both cases the Brant Test yields p > chi-squared just over .05 (.063 and .059, respectively). If the test was statistically significant, it would indicate a violation of the proportional odds assumption. The closeness of these tests to conventional significance further suggests that the generalized model is preferable.

Table C.6. GENERALIZED ORDERED LOGIT AND ORDERED LOGIT RESULTS

| | Generalized Ordered Logit | | | | Ordered Logit | |
| | Model 1 | | Model 2 | | Model 3 | Model 4 |
	Non-Attendance	Attendance	Non-Attendance	Attendance	Participation	Participation
Idealist Approach						
Protestant Identification	.40***	-.16	.40***	.15*	.32***	.32***
	[.10]	[.13]	[.08]	[.06]	[.06]	[.05]
Anti-Catholicism	1.49	2.05	.95	1.38	1.45	1.29
	[1.93]	[1.70]	[1.42]	[1.10]	[1.28]	[.92]
Rationalist Approach						
Social Pressure	.18	.94***	.40**	.71***	.42***	.56***
	[.21]	[.18]	[.15]	[.16]	[.12]	[.15]
Structural Approach						
Family Marched	-.30	-.45	-.19	.18	-.15	-.05
	[.34]	[.95]	[.35]	[.84]	[.31]	[.31]
Close Friends at Age 16	.47	.38	.67	.22	.25	.46
	[.31]	[.38]	[.36]	[.30]	[.23]	[.25]
Been Asked to March	1.32*	.31	1.32**	.44	.89	.90*
	[.58]	[.90]	[.50]	[.55]	[.54]	[.43]
Children Under 18	.80	-1.73**			-.05	
	[.51]	[.64]			[.40]	

(*Continued*)

| | Generalized Ordered Logit | | | | Ordered Logit | |
| | Model 1 | | Model 2 | | Model 3 | Model 4 |
	Non-Attendance	Attendance	Non-Attendance	Attendance	Participation	Participation
Full-Time Job	-.11	2.71***			.50	
	[.64]	[.66]			[.63]	
Age	-.02	-.05			-.02	
	[.01]	[.03]			[.01]	
Marched as Youth	.55	1.01			.50	
	[.40]	[.54]			[.29]	
Control Variables						
Education	-.66*	-.95			-.71***	
	[.26]	[.67]			[.20]	
Church Attendance	.06	.35*			.08	
	[.13]	[.14]			[.07]	
Constant	-1.99	-3.77*	-3.17***	-4.99***		
	[1.24]	[1.88]	[.66]	[.90]		
Cut 1					1.05	2.57***
					[1.01]	[.74]
Cut 2					5.76***	6.87***
					[.78]	[.75]
Number of Observations	161		175		161	175

variable make it more likely that the respondent will be in a higher category of Y than the current one, whereas negative coefficients indicate that higher values on the explanatory variable increase the likelihood of being in the current or a lower category."[5] So a positive coefficient in the attendance column means that an increase in the independent variable increases the likelihood of the respondent marching in parades, while a negative coefficient in the same column means that an increase in the independent variable increases the likelihood of the respondent staying as an attender or being a non-attender.

5. Richard Williams, "Generalized Ordered Logit/Partial Proportional Odds Models for Ordinal Dependent Variables," *The Stata Journal* 6, no. 1 (2006): 63.

INDEX